Beyond Parliament

Nijhoff Law Specials

VOLUME 88

The titles published in this series are listed at *brill.com/nlsp*

Beyond Parliament

Human Rights and the Politics of Social Change in the Global South

By

Horman Chitonge

BRILL
NIJHOFF

LEIDEN | BOSTON

Cover illustration: Vulamasango Singene march down Oxford Street in East London, South Africa. The photograph was taken by Gerhard Kienast in 2010.

Library of Congress Cataloging-in-Publication Data

Chitonge, Horman, author.
Beyond parliament : human rights and the politics of social change in the global south / by Horman Chitonge.
pages cm. -- (Nijhoff law specials ; volume 88)
Includes bibliographical references and index.
ISBN 978-90-04-22620-3 (pbk. : alk. paper) -- ISBN 978-90-04-29955-9 (e-book) 1. Right to food--Developing countries. 2. Right to water--Developing countries. 3. Basic needs--Law and legislation--Developing countries. 4. Human rights--Social aspects--Developing countries. I. Title.

K3260.C485 2015
323.09172'4--dc23

2015025378

This publication has been typeset in the multilingual "Brill" typeface. With over 5,100 characters covering Latin, IPA, Greek, and Cyrillic, this typeface is especially suitable for use in the humanities.
For more information, please see www.brill.com/brill-typeface.

ISSN 0924-4549
ISBN 978-90-04-22620-3 (paperback)
ISBN 978-90-04-29955-9 (e-book)

I would like to dedicate this book to my mother, Susan Mulubwa Chitonge, my two children Chilufya and Alinda, and my wife Millicent Atujuna Chitonge

Contents

Preface IX
Acknowledgements XIII
List of Illustrations XIV
Abbreviations XV

1 The Politics of Drinking and Eating 1

2 The Human Rights Discourse
An Overview 31

3 Human Rights and Development
Building Bridges 58

4 Human Rights in Democratic Politics 84

5 The Right to Water
Foundation, Content and Scope 100

6 The Right to Food
Origin, Content and Scope 141

7 The Rights to Water and Food in International Politics 181

8 The Rights to Water and Food
Strategies and Lessons from Global South 208

Bibliography 243
Index 262

Preface

This book has been inspired by several ideas, but it is the second paragraph of the American Declaration of Independence which captured my attention: It says:

> We hold these truths to be self-evident, that all men are created equal, that they are endowed by their Creator with certain unalienable Rights, that among these are Life, Liberty and the pursuit of Happiness (Declaration of Independence, July 4, 1776).

Although this ideal is far from being realised anywhere in the world, the idea that each human being (each member of the species *homo sapiens*), regardless of his or her social status, physical appearance, colour of the skin, income, wealth, origin, gender, sexual orientation etc., is a repository of invaluable worth, is an attractive political concept. Though attractive as a concept, it is perhaps the most difficult formulation to implement in reality at the global, national, local government or even household level. The real world, where people are expected to eat, drink and compete with each other is made up of individuals very unequal in many respects including, appearance, intellectual capacity, height, physical and mental capabilities, talents, wealth, power, influence and status; and they are treated differently according to these differences.

In view of this, the practical question which arises here is this: is the idea that all human beings are endowed with incontrovertible worth and dignity, be they poor, uneducated, impoverished, weak etc., mere political rhetoric? Is this a kind of statement which moves mass crowds at political or activist rallies, yet it has no practical expression in real life where people treat each other as if all human being were created unequal – some with more dignity and worth than others? Of course there are people who believe that not all human beings have equal dignity and worth. Such people act according to this belief and many are unapologetic about their convictions and actions.

But at the collective level, where humans interrelate with each other to form communities nationally and globally, few have openly protested against the idea of human beings being endowed with unalienable dignity and worth, if not for the sake of the soundness of the idea itself, may be for the instrumental role this idea play in bringing about social order, justice, peace and security. Both the *United Nations Charter* (*UN Charter*, 1945) and the Universal *Declaration of Human Rights*(UDHR, 1948), recognise the social and political instrumentality of this idea as the foundation on which freedom, peace and justice in the world can be genuinely built (see the Preambles of both documents). Thus, the force of the idea that all human beings are endowed with unalienable rights (fundamental human rights) lies at the centre of public politics where it serves a very fundamental function. This is the idea that this book explores using the practical examples of the rights to water and food. The two rights are crucial to preserving human dignity and worth, and therefore should be seen as an important component of politics in any society.

It is particularly the purpose of this book to demonstrate that fundamental human rights, such as the right to food and water, are at the centre of politics at any level, to the extent that affirming and granting equal worth and dignity to all human beings charms many polities, some more explicitly while other tacitly. The book illustrates this by focusing on experiences from global south using the two most fundamental human rights: the right to water and the right to food. The starting point is that if all human beings are endowed with equal worth and dignity, then through the political appeal of this idea, all things that contribute to upholding this basic human dignity ought to be protected by the public whose existence relies on the fulfilment of this basic idea. This does not mean that all humans be treated equally in all things, but simply that the basic human dignity be protected by the public or community. The politics of this is that if a community affirms the values contained in the idea and inherent human dignity, then it can be argued that it gives itself the responsibility to ensure that this idea is achieved. Realising this is a challenge everywhere, but if a community is committed to the idea, it would ensure that this is realised. In other words, the public (local community, district, national or global) has a responsibility to protect the dignity of all its members, and to realise this requires engaging in radical politics resolutely against any affront to human dignity.

In the case of the right to water and the right to food, it is the basic duty of the community at various levels to ensure that basic levels of food and water, essential for preserving human dignity and worth, are secured for all people regardless of race, gender, income, social status, origin or religious beliefs. Consequently, those who are at risk of not achieving the basic levels of food and water required to preserve the fundamental dignity of the human person have a justifiable claim on the public to secure these basic needs, and on the other hand, the public, particularly the state, has the fundamental duty to ensure that such people are provided for to meet their basic human rights.

Clearly, this is very easy to state than to translate into reality. We know, as shown in this book, that there are more than 1 billion people who experience hunger and deprivation every day, and in most cases, the same people lack access to basic water services. This is not because the world, or some countries where most of these people live, has no enough food or water; the world produces enough food and has enough water to carter for the basic needs required to preserve the basic human dignity and worth of all the 7.2 billion people on the this planet. In the case of food, there is more food wasted than what is needed to prevent hunger among the 1 billion people (mostly in the global south), who go to bed hungry every day (see chapter 6). One billion people go to bed hungry because the political, social and economic structures which mediated access to water and food are constructed in such as a way that some human beings are treated as though they have less dignity and worth. Hundreds of millions of human beings go to bed hungry every day because those who have enough food and water have shied away from the radical politics which would necessitate the change in the way production, distribution, access and consumption of water and food are organised locally, nationally and globally.

To make this politically powerful idea that all human beings are endowed with unalienable dignity and worth, and that each of them should be a locus of public attention, especially in cases where this dignity is in danger, requires commitment to changing the way basic essentials are accessed, distributed, shared and consumed – hence the radical politics. Somehow, as Amartya Sen (2003) argues our world has grown used to a kind of defeatism, which accepts as given the way we share water and food locally, nationally and globally – we have taken this as "hard headed realism." In other words, giving effect to the idea of treating all human beings as repositories of unalienable worth, will only happen through radical politics for the reason that this idea acquires much force at the collective level, and it is through political action that changes to the current arrangements around the way water and food are accessed, produced, shared, distributed and consumed, can be brought about. Without this fundamental change to the structure through which water and food are delivered, the world will continue to produce an increasing amount of food while at the same time the number of people experiencing hunger every day will increase.

This book asserts that it is not that there are no human rights instruments which pronounce on these rights; there are several instruments which recognise fundamental human rights nationally, but more prominently, internationally. However, the main challenge lies beyond the pronouncements of human rights instruments and laws. In this sense, giving effect to the recognised rights, such as the rights to water and food, requires going beyond parliament to engage in the radical politics of changing public perceptions, power relations and institutional structures surrounding access to water and food. Following on this, this book argues that changing these institutional structures and power relations is not going to happen without continuous struggle for change. It is through a sustained struggle that the spaces where the rights to water and food can be given effect will be created. In this context, it is important to remember that human rights "historically are products of concrete social struggles, not simply textual or legal discourse" (Zeleza, 2006), and as such, human rights provide the tools for engaging in radical politics.

To illustrate that changing the current structures around water and food is possible, the book profiles some of the current and past struggles as examples of the channels through which social change, with regard to access to water and food, are being constituted by social forces, particularly local social movements in the global south. There are many other struggles for social change which employ a human rights approach which the book has not mentioned, but the few referenced in this book are meant to indicate that human rights discourse and strategies can be used as tools for social change. The argument that runs throughout the book is that human rights can only be an effective device for social change if human rights strategies are deployed within radical democratic politics. It is in this sense that human rights as tools for social changes require going beyond parliament – beyond mere pronouncements of rights and laws.

Acknowledgements

I would like first of all to thank my family; my very good friend and partner Millicent Atujuna Chitonge, and my two children, Chilufya and Alinda for being patient with me during the long time it took to put this book together. I would also like to thank my colleagues at the Centre for African Studies, University of Cape Town, Professor Lungisile Ntsebeza, Dr. Frank Matose, Associate Professor Harry Garuba, Associate Professor Nick Shepherd, Mr. Nkululeko Mabandla, and Ms Noma-Afrika for their encouragement and support.

My sincere thanks go to Sufian Bhukurura and Patrick Bond for their assistance and guidance during the time I was working on my PHD from which this book draws inspiration. I would also like to acknowledge the encouragement and advice I received from Professor Evance Kalula who for the past 8 years has been encouraging me to work on this book. My sincere thanks also go to Lindy Melman, Bea Timmer and the entire team at Brill-Nijhoff Publishers for taking interest in the manuscript and for the dedicated work from the beginning to the end of the publication process. I would also like to express my sincere thanks to Peter Kenyon for the dedicated work during the copy-editing of the manuscript and the anonymous reviewers for constructive comments and suggestions.

List of Illustrations

Figures

5.1 Global Water Availability Per Capita (1950–2000) 103
5.2 Global Per Capita Water Withdrawal (Domestic 1995/2020) 103

Tables

2.1 Hohfeldian Scheme of Jural Relations 38
2.2 Two Theories of Rights 46
4.1 Types and Dimensions of Power 93
5.1 Water Consumption by Sector (%) 105
5.2 Water Resources and Use Profile for Selected African Countries 107
5.3 Access to Improved Drinking Water for Selected African Countries (1990–2009, %) 110
5.4 International Water Conferences (1972–2012) 114
5.5 Normative Content of the Right to Water 132
6.1 Trends in Global Levels of Undernourishment (1969–2010) 143
6.2 Global Food Production and Consumption Profile (2008–13) 144
6.3 Percentage of Food Losses by Region and Food Type (2010) 145
6.4 Global Cereal Production and Consumption 2010–13 (millions of tons) 148
6.5 Undernourishment Prevalence in Selected African Countries (1990–2012) 150
6.6 Major International Conferences Affirming the Right to Food 154
6.7 Major International Human Rights Instruments Related to Food Security 162
6.8 The Normative Content of the Right to Food 167

Abbreviations

AAA	American Anthropological Association
ABRANDH (Portuguese)	Action for Nutrition and Human Rights
ACHPR	African Charter for Human and People's Rights
ACRWC	African Charter on the Rights and Welfare of the Child
AEFJN	Africa and Europe Faith and Justice Network
ANEW	African Civil Society Network on Water and Sanitation
ANORF	African Network on the Right to Food
APC	Anti-Privatisation Campaign
BNA	Basic Needs Approach
CAT	Convention Against Torture
CEDAW	Convention on the Elimination of Discrimination Against Women
CESCR	Committee on Economic Social and Cultural Rights
CNDV (Portuguese)	National Commission in Defence of Water and Life
CONSEA (Portuguese)	National Food and Nutrition Security Council
CRC	Convention of the Right of the Child
CRFSS	Campaign on the Right to Food and Social Security
CSO	Civil Society Organisation
DAWASA	Dar es Salaam Water and Sanitation Authority
DESA	Department of Economic and Social Affairs
DfID	Department for International Development
DRC	Democratic Republic of the Congo
DRD	Declaration of the Right to Development
ECOSOC	Economic and Social Council
ESCRS	Economic, Social and Cultural Rights
FAO	Food and Agriculture Organisation
GDP	Gross Domestic Product
GIS	Geographical Information Systems
GNI	Gross National Income
HDI	Human Development Indicators
HDR	Human Development Report
HIPC	Highly Indebted Poor Countries
HRBA	Human Rights-Based Approach
ICCPR	International Covenant on Civil and Political Rights
ICESCR	International Covenant on Economic, Social and Cultural Rights
IDS	Institute of Development Studies

IFAD	International Fund for Agricultural Development
IMF	International Monetary Fund
JW	Johannesburg Water
LIFDCS	Low Income Food Deficit Countries
LPDS	Local Development Platforms
NEPAD	New Partnership for African Development
NGO	Non-Governmental Organisation
NIEO	New International Economic Order
NNPC	Nigerian National Petroleum Company
NPA	National Prosecuting Authority
NRFN	National Right to Food Network
ODI	Overseas Development Institute
OGA	Operation Gcin Amanzi
OHCHR	Office of the High *Commission* for Human Rights
PIL	Public Interest Litigation
PRA	Participatory Rural Appraisal
PRS	Poverty Reduction Strategies
PRSPS	Poverty Reduction Strategy Papers
PUCL	People's Union for Civil Liberties
RBA	Rights-Based Approach
RFC	Right to Food Campaign
RtD	Right to Development
SAHRC	South African Human Rights Commission
SAPS	Structural Adjustment Programmes
SDC	Swiss Agency for Development Cooperation
SERAC	Social and Economic Rights Action Centre
SPDC	Shell Petroleum Development Corporation
SPI	Serikat Petani Indonesia
SSA	Sub-Saharan Africa
TAC	Treatment Action Campaign
TAWASANET	Tanzania Civil Society Network on Water and Sanitation
TNCS	Trans-National Corporations
TRIPS	Trade-Related Intellectual Property
UDHR	Universal Declaration of Human Rights
UN	United Nations
UNCED	United Nations Conference on Environment and Development
UNDP	United Nations Development Programme
UNECA	United Nations Economic Commission for Africa
UNESCO	United Nations Education, Science and Cultural Organisation
UNFPA	United Nations Population Fund

UNICEF	United Nations Children Emergence Fund
WFP	World Food Programme
WHO	World Health Organisation
WTO	World Trade Organisation
WWII	World War Two
ZAWASA	Zambia Water and Sanitation Alliance

CHAPTER 1

The Politics of Drinking and Eating

Introduction

Being able to secure clean water and adequate food, on a regular basis, is indispensable to living a dignified life. Failure to secure clean water and adequate food, regularly, often results in a life deprived of human dignity, self-esteem, confidence and a sense of security; and can lead to diseases and, in many cases, the loss of human life. Currently, there are almost one billion people who are unable to secure clean water and adequate food, most of them in the Global South.[1] In most instances, it is the same people who are unable to secure clean water who also suffer from the pangs of hunger, undernourishment and starvation. Available evidence on food and water resources suggests that the failure to secure these two essential needs for almost a billion people is not because there is inadequate water or food on the planet (Lappe and Collins 1986; World Bank 1986); the earth has enough fresh water, and produces enough food, to meet the basic requirement of all the seven billion or so people on the planet (Webb and Iskandarani 1998; FAO 2011b). The main reason for the current situation, in which at least one in every seven people on the planet go to bed hungry and without access to clean water, is precisely because of the way these resources are shared – the distribution and access question. It is for this reason that access to water and food should be deeply embedded in the *realpolitik* of drinking and eating. Seen from this perspective, it becomes apparent that access to water and food is shaped by the way humans interact with each other, and with the environment. As we shall see later, access to water and food does not entirely depend on personal capabilities; it very much depends on the collective decisions and actions taken (and not taken) which affect some individuals' capability to access them. Thus, access to water and food is fundamentally a social justice matter.

Because water and food are both central to the preservation of human life – and to leading a dignified life – the fact that almost 20 per cent of the world's

1 This is a term often used to refer to developing and emerging countries, including India, Brazil and China. The term does not refer to the geographical south; it refers to the countries which are not part of the Global North or the developed world. Here the term is used to refer to all developing and emerging countries in Africa, Latin America, the Caribbean, East Asia, South Asia, South East Asia and the Middle East.

 | DOI 10.1163/9789004299559_002

population has no access to clean water, and (in most cases) the same 20 per cent does not have access to adequate food, calls for a deeper reflection on the politics of water and food; and not just in the Global South. A situation where almost one billion people are unable to secure clean water and adequate food in a world where there is enough of each, raises a fundamental question about global social justice. Unfortunately, at the global level, the imperative of access to water and food are reduced to the moral sentiment of aid and humanitarian support – both of which are far removed from the real politics of drinking and eating.

Surprisingly, there are only a small number of people in the world who see access to water and food as essentially as a matter of social justice. It does not bother the majority of people that almost one billion people in the Global South often fail to secure clean water and adequate food (an "adequate standard of living")[2] on a daily basis. For the majority of people in the world (most of whom have access to clean water and adequate food every day), the fact that hundreds of millions of people do not have access to them is not an immediate concern; this is the problem of the poor in Africa, Asia and Latin America. However, some have stopped to reflect on this challenge, and have raised questions about the structures and institutions which regulate and impact on the way people everywhere access water and food. Many of those concerned about the plight of people living in situations where it is difficult to access clean water and adequate food have blamed the world economic model and entrenched global attitudes towards water and food.

The failure of hundreds of millions of the people in the Global South to acquire these basic human needs is a manifestation of unequal power relations within and between countries, communities and families. This situation, in turn, influences control over resources – including access to clean water and adequate food. It is these relations that affect the way land, water employment and other opportunities in society are allocated or distributed. Over the years, several suggestions about how to transform these relations and structures – to create conditions where all people have access to basic clean water and adequate food – have been proposed. One such proposal is the use of the rights-based approach (RBA)[3] as a strategy for challenging and transforming the current structures, institutions and relations around access to water and food.

---

2 This is the basic minimum stipulated by the *Universal Declaration of Human Rights* (*UDHR*, para. 25 (1)) as well as the *International Covenant on Economic, Social and Cultural Rights* (*ICESCR*, para. 12).

3 In the literature this is also referred to as the Human Rights Based Approach to Development (HRBA), which, though defined differently by different organisations, has been broadly

This book examines the various aspects of this strategy – its origins, conceptualisation, experiences, challenges and opportunities – focusing on access to water and food. Different ways in which the RBA has been deployed are discussed, drawing from various experiences mainly from the Global South. The right to water and the right to food[4] are used as the entry point to highlight some of the challenges and opportunities of using the RBA. Various ways in which this strategy has been deployed in the struggle for access to clean water and adequate food are discussed, drawing from past and current experiences in the Global South. This book is not meant to provide general guidelines concerning the struggles surrounding access to clean water and adequate food in the Global South; rather, its main focus is to draw attention to the current challenges and opportunities around issues of access within the RBA framework.

The Context

This book focuses mainly on experiences from the Global South, particularly Africa, since these areas are widely acknowledged to be facing the greatest challenge in terms of access to clean water and adequate food. This does not mean, however, that no challenges exist in this regard in the Global North; it is simply that the magnitude of such challenges is much greater in the Global South. In terms of access to water, Sub-Saharan Africa (SSA) faces the greatest challenge when compared to other regions – with current estimates suggesting that more than a third of the population has no access to clean water, while more than two-thirds has no access to improved sanitation (WHO/UNICEF 2012). With regard to access to adequate food, it has been estimated that almost one in four people in SSA suffer from hunger and undernourishment[5] – compared to 16 per cent in the South Asia and Pacific region, 9 per cent in Latin America, and 7 per cent in North Africa and the Middle East (FAO/IFAD, 2014). In view of the RBA adopted in this work, it is only appropriate that more attention is directed to regions facing the greatest challenges – for the simple reason

defined as the use of human rights principles in development cooperation and programmes (UNFPA 2004: 70). Here the acronym RBA will be used.

4 The right to food has two elements: the right to adequate food, as well as the right to be free from hunger. Unless otherwise stated, the term "right to food" is used throughout this work to refer to both components of the right.

5 While Asia and the Pacific recorded the largest number of undernourished people in 2010 (578 million) – compared to Sub-Saharan Africa's (SSA) 239 million – the proportion of undernourished people in SSA was almost 30 per cent, compared to 16 per cent in the Asia and Pacific region (see WFP/FAO, 2010: 10–11).

that it is in such places where people's rights to water and food are most at risk. While there is no clear correlation between a lack of access to basic human needs such as water, sanitation and food, and the violation of other human rights, it can be argued that in situations where a higher proportion of people lack these basic needs the chances are high that a broad range of civil and political rights are also not realised.

Within the rights framework the failure to secure these basic needs raises serious concerns because in such situations it is difficult to realise other human rights that are also required for living a dignified life. With specific reference to the right to food, it has been observed that the "right to adequate food is indivisibly linked to the inherent dignity of the human person and is indispensable for the fulfilment of other human rights" (CESCR, 1999: para. 4). A similar observation has been made on the right to water: "The human right to water is indispensable for leading a life in human dignity. It is a prerequisite for the realization of other human rights" (CESCR, 2002: para. 1). Thus, it is highly likely that in situations where people are unable to have their basic water and food needs met, the chances are high that other human rights will also not be fulfilled. This is mainly because access to clean water and adequate food forms the bedrock upon which other rights rest. A person suffering from undernourishment, hunger, starvation, diarrhoea, or other water-related illness, often has other rights – such as the right to freedom of assembly, the right to freedom of movement, and indeed the basic right to life – curtailed. Hence, access to water and food is widely acknowledged as indispensable to leading a dignified life, and should therefore be at the centre of democratic politics.

Before discussing the challenges and opportunities involved in giving effect to the right to water and food in the context of the rights approach, it is essential first to discuss the key concepts in this approach: human rights and development. While I have so far been using the term "right to water and food" as if these are recognised by everyone as human rights, it is important to note that there has been an extended contestation about whether access to them are, in fact, "real" human rights at all. Chapter 2 discusses the concept of human rights in general and whether this concept can be extended to include access to water. Contentious questions concerning the universality, interdependence, and generation and application of human rights, are discussed in this chapter. A brief discussion about what is meant by development in the context of the RBA is presented, drawing mainly from those experiences where the rights approach to development has been implemented. Contentious questions about what it means to have a right to food, for instance, are raised to highlight some of the challenging aspects of the RBA. For a person who has no means of securing adequate food or water, what difference does it make to tell such as person that she/he has a right to them? And for people who find themselves in such situations, what recourse do they have? Views that are critical of human rights in general, and of the RBA in particular, are also discussed to highlight the fact that these issues are seriously contested at both theoretical and practical levels.

Chapter 3 discusses the RBA discourse, highlighting the fact that this is a relatively new strategy that emphasises the empowerment of the poor in an effort to improve human life and living conditions. The RBA is also seen as a strategic response to matters of social justice and unequal power relations, and its proponents have argued that it offers a unique opportunity to engage in real politics where access to water and food can be brought into the broader struggles (Chapman *et al.* 2005; Barth Eide and Kracht 2005). The issues relating to the origin and nature of this approach are discussed in the broader context of the development and human rights discourses. To locate the RBA in the broader context of social change and transformation of power relations, a brief background of the context in which the RBA emerged as an approach that seeks to integrate human rights and development efforts is provided. While the chapter identifies several features of the RBA which make it different from other approaches, the various weaknesses and challenges of implementing the RBA are also discussed.

Chapter 4 discusses the conceptual foundations of the RBA, in particular, and human rights in general. This chapter locates the human rights discourse in the broader context of power relations and the politics of social change. By espousing the principles of equality and non-discrimination, it can be submitted that human rights are diametrically opposed to inequality in opportunity and access to basic needs such as water and food. Since unequal power relations are a reality in many (if not all) societies, and because there is always an attempt by those exercising or benefiting from these unequal relations to maintain the status quo, realising human rights such as the rights to water and food cannot be achieved without contesting this status quo. Thus, giving effect to human rights can only be a product of serious engagement in *realpolitik*, beyond the legislative politics. As such, a depoliticised approach to human rights and development can only lead to superficial victories. Seen from this angle, genuine protection of human dignity and rights is not something that is given on a silver platter; it involves a continuous struggle to create spaces where human dignity and rights can be asserted, sufficiently contested for, claimed, and given effect. One important issue discussed in this chapter is the role of power relations in the struggle to give effect to human rights for millions of people throughout the world.

Chapter 5 examines, critically, the "right to water" – including its origins, foundations, content, scope and application, using concrete cases. The chapter also discusses the nature of obligations generated by the right to water under both international human rights law, as well as municipal law. Using current statistics on water availability, distribution and consumption, this chapter shows that there is currently sufficient water in the world to secure a basic minimum for the more than seven billion people on the planet. The chapter presents data on current levels of access to water in different regions of the world as the context underlying the debate about the right to water. The chapter also discusses both the international and domestic basis for asserting the right to water; and notes that – unlike the case for other economic, social and cultural rights (ESCRs) – the right to water is not widely or explicitly recognised in international human rights instruments, and much less in national constitutions and legal frameworks. Concrete examples from selected countries of situations that impinge on the right to water are presented to illustrate some of the challenges and opportunities of implementing the right to water.

Chapter 6 focuses on the right to food – including its legal basis in international and domestic legal systems, its content, scope, different methods of implementation, and available recourses available to those whose rights are not being fulfilled. As with the case of the right to water, this chapter also presents current statistics on global and regional food production, and distribution and consumption patterns, to illustrate that the world today produces more than enough food to feed everyone. Unfortunately, as is the case with access to water, close to one billion people suffer from hunger, undernourishment and starvation, and many more millions are not captured by the official statistics. It is further shown in Chapter 6 that although the right to food is more explicitly recognised in international human rights instruments than is the case for the right to water, and although there are more countries that include this right either in their national constitutions or framework laws, the right to food is far from being a reality for many people today. In view of this, the chapter discusses the question of whether framing access to food in the language of rights makes any difference to the lives of the millions who suffer hunger, malnutrition and starvation.

Chapter 7 looks at the practical implications of both the right to water and the right to food in democratic politics. This chapter discusses the challenges involved in making the rights to water and food a reality for the poor. The basic question that the chapter grapples with is this: if so many people are unable to meet their basic needs, should we be talking about the human *right* to food or water in the first place? The chapter argues that a more explicit recognition of these rights makes it possible for a robust public debate, which in turn creates the possibility of building alliances and collective action as means of engaging in the *realpolitik* of drinking and eating. In the context of the identified challenges around the practical application of the rights approach, the broader problems arising from the nature of international human rights instruments are identified and discussed.

Chapter 8 explores the experience and lessons from different strategies adopted by different countries aimed at giving effect to the rights to water and food. Examples of actual cases and situations where the rights to water and food have been claimed, litigated, violated, ignored, protected, fulfilled, etc., are discussed as a way of elaborating on the various implications of using the RBA. From these experiences, a number of challenges involved in deploying a rights strategy are identified. Particular attention in this chapter is paid to the various ways in which these rights are threatened, and the possible ways through which they are given meaning and effect. The chapter also highlights some of the basic conditions which must be fulfilled if the human rights discourse and tools are to make a difference to the lives of those many poor people who find it difficult to access clean water and adequate food.

The Rights to Water and Food

In the discussions about these two rights, a general observation that is often made is that they are relatively "young" rights that have only recently been recognised as basic human rights, and as such there are few lessons to learn from. Because of this it has been suggested that alternative ways of giving effect to these rights are in their infancy stages (Courtis 2007). Accessing water and food has traditionally been viewed as an individual's private affair, and there has been no serious public discussion about what happens when these individuals (and households) are unable to access such essentials via the market – particularly in countries which have no broad-based public welfare systems.

Why the Right to Food and the Right to Water?

As will become clearer in subsequent chapters, there are many human rights that one can discuss – and therefore the reason(s) for choosing to focus on some and not others needs to be clarified. In this case there are a number of related reasons taken into account in the decision to focus on the rights to water and food. First, choosing to focus on these two rights was influenced by the view that, other than air, water and food are the most basic of all human needs; without them human life itself is threatened, and human dignity is difficult to achieve. Arguably, if the field of human rights is primarily concerned with protecting the value of human life and human dignity, then access to clean water and adequate food should be among our primary elements for examination since the contribution these two basic needs make towards sustaining life and securing dignity is critical. It is pointless to talk about human life and dignity in situations where access to these two essential needs is inadequate and insecure. In other words, it would be difficult to give meaningful effect to other human rights in the absence of water and food; human life itself is under threat in a situation where basic needs are inaccessible. The "basicness" of water and food in the human rights framework has been highlighted most prominently by the United Nations Committee on Economic, Social and Cultural Rights (CESCR, henceforth, the Committee), which has been mandated with elaborating the content, scope, obligations and implications of these rights under the *International Covenant on Economic, Social and Cultural Rights* (*ICESCR*, henceforth, the Covenant). Elaborating on the right to water in *General Comment 15*, and the right to food in *General Comment 12*, the Committee identified these two rights as indispensable to human dignity; and also as constituting the precondition for giving effect to other human rights. With specific reference to the right to food, the Committee in *General Comment 12* argues that "the human right to adequate food is of crucial importance for the enjoyment of all rights" (CESCR, 1999: para. 1).

Second, choosing to discuss these two rights together can be justified on the grounds that they are practically inseparable – although conceptually they have been formulated separately. As the Special Rapporteur on the right to food has observed, "it is impossible to discuss nutrition and food security without including safe drinking water. Safe drinking water is essential to adequate nutrition" (Ziegler 2002: 12). It is because of the close connection between these two basic rights that, before *General Comment 15* was formulated, the right to water was generally inferred from the right to food – which is explicitly provided for in international law instruments including the *UDHR*, *ICESCR*, the *Covenant on the Right of the Child* (*CRC*), and the *Convention on the Elimination of All Forms of Discrimination Against Women* (*CEDAW*).[6]

6 Prior to 2002, when the right to water was directly and individually recognised, it was argued that the "interconnectedness between food and water...is the reason for including water as a component of the right to food" (Ziegler 2002: 11). In a number of situations where the rights are not explicitly recognised, courts have asserted the right to food or water from the right to life itself. For example, Indian judges have been very progressive in granting other non-justiciable rights through a broad interpretation of core rights such as the right to life and dignity (Ahluwalia 2004).

However, as noted earlier, there has been an extended debate about whether economic social and cultural rights (ESCRS) – such as the rights to water and food – should actually be recognised as human rights. As will be discussed later in this chapter, ESCR critics argue that these are actually aspirational goals for social policy and *not* genuine human rights. It suffices here to note that excluding ESCRS from the list of human rights poses a serious challenge to the concept of human rights itself.

The other reason why the rights to water and food are chosen here is because these are probably the most difficult basic human rights to realise; as such, they help bring out some of the challenges inherent in using human rights discourse and strategies to secure basic needs. Realising the right to adequate clean water and food for everyone is definitely more challenging than ensuring the rights to freedom of speech, freedom of assembly, and freedom of movement (the so-called negative rights). Because of this, a critical analysis of the rights to water and food is most likely to highlight some of the challenges related to the practicality of giving effect to ESCRS, and some of the cases and examples presented in subsequent chapters help to illustrate this.

Further, the rights to water and food are highlighted here because of their multifaceted nature – such that, talking about the rights to water and food leads to a discussion of a broad range of other rights, including: the right to health, life, freedom of movement, housing, association, adequate standard of living, and the right to property (particularly the right to access land and water). Due to their multidimensional nature, the rights to water and food provide a broader window into the intricate connections between human rights and the broad field of development and poverty reduction. A society's adherence to the principles of human dignity and development is more likely to be reflected in the way it addresses issues of access to water and food for its population. This view has been stated clearly by the South African Constitutional Court, which has argued that a "society must seek to ensure that the basic necessities of life are provided to all if it is to be a society based on human dignity, freedom and equality".[7] In this regard, it can be argued that water and food are *the* fundamental human necessities that are indispensable to the achievement of human dignity and well-being. For this reason, some analysts have suggested that the right to food is the most fundamental social and economic issue facing the modern world (Alston 1984).

In addition to the above reasons, the rights to water and food are well positioned to illustrate the principles of interdependence and indivisibility of

---

7 See *Government of the Republic of South Africa v. Grootboom*, 2000 (11) BCLR 1169 (CC) para. 44.

human rights adopted at the *Vienna Convention on Human Rights* in 1993.[8] Water and food provide suitable examples of these principles in that, while implementation of human rights can be prioritised, a divided approach can prove to be less successful (Courtis 2007). For instance, asserting the right to life, by itself, becomes futile if there are no measures in place to ensure that other life-sustaining necessities such as water and food are available. Similarly, it may be futile to assert and protect the right to vote or the right to freedom of expression in a context where other rights – such as the rights to food and water – are not given effect. This idea was earlier stated by the Commission on World Hunger, appointed by former US president Jimmy Carter in 1980, when it argued that "the protection of other human rights becomes a mockery for those who must spend all their energy merely to maintain life itself" (cited in Cohen and Brown 2009: 139). Very few people with an empty stomach, not knowing where their next meal is coming from, would bother to stand in a queue to cast their vote, assemble with others to protest, or even go to school. In a fundamental way, therefore, the right to food – together with the right to water – is intricately linked to other human rights, "namely the right to life, right to health, right to livelihood, freedom of association, expression and information, right to private property, and the right to education" (Ahluwalia 2004: 14).

The other reason that influenced the decision to focus on the rights to water and food in this work, is the fact that the right to food is explicitly recognised in major international human rights legal instruments including the *UNDHR*, *ICESCR*, *CRC*, *CEDAW*, etc., whereas the right to water is not explicitly recognised in any of these instruments apart from the *CEDAW*, see Article 14 (2 h); the *CRC*, see para. 24 (2), and a few national constitutions.[9] Given that one right is given explicit recognition in major international human rights instruments while the other is only implicitly recognised, the interest here is to find out if this explicit recognition does actually make any recognisable difference in the way these rights are given effect through various means including collective action, advocacy, public protest and social mobilisation, etc. The key question explored in this regard is this: does explicit recognition make a difference in the way a right is given effect?

Given this interconnectedness of human rights, and although the focus in the following chapters is on two specific rights which have very specific normative

---

8 See the *Vienna Declaration and Programme of Action* (para. 5).

9 African countries that have explicitly provided for the right to water include South Africa, Uganda, Kenya and Ethiopia. Interestingly, most of the constitutions in Africa enacted after 1994 have included socioeconomic rights in their respective Bill of Rights. Examples include the Zambian Draft Constitution (2012) and the Kenyan Constitution (2008).

content, scope and application, the general principles and procedures may apply to other human rights – especially ESCRs. In view of this, the discussions in the following chapters take a broader approach to provide more general discussions on human rights in general, and the RBA in particular. A related question that is discussed in this book is this: what contribution does the framing of access to water and food as human rights make towards improving access to these basic necessities for those who are either unable, or find it difficult, to access them? In other words, does the use of the language of rights make any difference; and if it does, what difference does it make? What empirical evidence can one provide to show that framing access to water and adequate food as human rights *actually* makes a difference for the poor on the ground? In the chapters that follow the discussion avoids a narrow and legalistic approach to human rights so as to provide room for establishing the link between human rights and development discourses and practice.

Key Turning Points in Human Rights History

Although there had been previous documents and declarations that recognised human rights prior to the *UDHR*,[10] it is commonly acknowledged that the end of the Second World War marked the beginning of a new era in the conceptualisation of human rights. Several analysts have observed that prior to the *UDHR*, protection of human life and dignity did not apply universally to all human beings of different races, social status, gender, sexual orientation, religious beliefs and cultural practices. In most cases, human rights applied only to a specific category of propertied adult male. Rights such as the right to vote, assembly, movement, expression, participation in the political life of the community, work, and social security, were all restricted to a very small group of people in most societies. Universal suffrage that allowed women to vote, for instance, was only implemented after the Second World War in most countries. In the aftermath of that great conflict the international community, shocked

10 There were different ways in which communities in Africa, for instance, protected the rights of individuals and collectives from various infringements and arbitrary decisions – although these were not codified into written documents (Zeleza 2006). Examples of codified instruments include the famous *Magna Carta* in England (1215), which recognised and protected the rights of "some" members of the human family. Provisions such as "No one shall take the horse or carts of any free man"; "To none will we sell, to none we will deny, to none we will delay, right or justice" are examples of what we now call human rights. Other examples include France's *Vindicae Contra Tyrannos* (1579), and the *Declaration of the Rights of Man and Citizen* (1776). (See Wronka 1998; Mbaye 1991).

by the atrocities and egregious abuse of power and the extensive human suffering and loss of life during the war itself, was forced to begin looking for ways to prevent a recurrence. Proclamation of the inherent dignity and fundamental equality of all human beings proved to be an attractive and justifiable foundation on which human rights – and the defence against future atrocities committed by fellow human beings – could be affirmed. Affirmation of universal human dignity and fundamental freedoms thus provided a defensible foundation for securing world peace, justice and security. This vision is powerfully articulated in the preamble to the United Nations Charter (1945) as foundation for world peace:

> We the peoples of the United Nations, to save succeeding generations from the scourge of war, which twice in our lifetime has brought untold sorrow to mankind, and to reaffirm faith in fundamental human rights, in the dignity and worth of the human person, in the equal rights of men and women and of nations large and small, and to establish conditions under which justice and respect for the obligations arising from treaties and other sources of international law can be maintained, and to promote social progress and better standards of life in larger freedom...have resolved to combine our efforts to accomplish these aims.

The *UDHR* reaffirmed this resolution more pointedly when it asserted that "recognition of the inherent dignity and the equality and inalienable rights of all members of the human family is the foundation of freedom, justice and peace in the world" (see *Preamble* to the *UDHR* 1948).

Hence, immediately after the end of the Second World War, the doctrine of universal human dignity and equality was adopted and enshrined in the United Nations Charter, and later elaborated on in the *UDHR* in 1948 and subsequent international treaties.

Another important feature associated with the post-Second World War period that prompted the adoption of universal human rights, is that human rights became enshrined in international law (Bedjaoui 1991b). Prior to the *UDHR*, in whatever form and geographical location that human rights existed they were not subject to international relations and law; they were conveniently caged within nation states (Howard and Donnelly 1986: 33). In fact, not only did traditional international law exclude the concept of human rights, it did not even have a language with which to deplore human rights abuses (Donnelly 1989: 2).

Over the years it has been observed that even though the *UDHR* was not intended to be a binding treaty, it has nevertheless become a "powerful platform to argue cases of concern and build an ethical code from which to launch the development of human rights instruments". Experience over the past decades confirms the fact that the *UDHR* has inspired and consolidated human rights discourse in all parts of the world (Hinz 2009: 5). It has also been observed that the African struggle for independence against colonialism and imperial occupation drew much inspiration and support from human rights discourse to expose the abuses and injustices of colonial rule (Gawanas 2009: 136). Paul Zeleza goes even further, arguing that the struggle against slavery, colonialism and post-colonial tyrannies – and more recently against structural adjustment programmes (SAPs) – are fundamentally struggles for human rights, with "Africans trying to reclaim their inherent integrity and dignity as human beings" (Zeleza 2006: 48). Thus, the concept and language of rights has gained wide recognition, acceptance and usage – to such an extent that they are appealed to even by those who do *not* believe in human rights to defend themselves in cases where their interests are under threat (Booth 1999).

Appealing, but Contentious

Although the concept of universal human rights is apparently an appealing tool for promoting respect for human life and dignity, solidarity, peace and security, the universality of human rights asserted in the *UDHR* and other international human rights instruments has been a topic of extended and heated debate, and has remained a highly contested topic. Even at the time of adopting the *UDHR* in 1948, the notion of universal human rights caused divisions among country representatives to the extent that some decided to abstain from the vote to adopt the draft *UDHR* document. It is recorded that of the 56 countries represented at the UN General Assembly on 10 December 1948, 48 members voted in favour of the draft, while eight (for different reasons) abstained[11] (Steiner and Alston 2000). But it was not just country representatives at the UN General Assembly who opposed the notion of universal human rights; professional associations – notably the American Anthropological Association (AAA) – rejected the idea that human rights, as asserted in the *UDHR*, were universal principles applicable to every society (see M. Brown 2008). One of the main points of contention has been that human rights contained in the *UDHR*, and subsequent international human rights instruments, are based on Western experience and the West's cultural notion of the primacy of the individual. One specific complaint against the *UDHR* was the idea that the declaration privileged individual rights over the sort of collective and

11 At the time there were only four African member countries of the UN: Egypt, Ethiopia, Liberia and South Africa. During the vote to adopt the *UDHR*, South Africa abstained – together with Saudi Arabia and the Soviet Union, although all for different reasons.

group rights favoured by many of the world's (non-Western) peoples (see Pollis and Schwab 2006). Similarly, there have been several critics who have argued that human rights contained in the international human rights instruments are rights based on western culture, moral aspirations, political practice and worldview which do not apply to other cultures and cosmologies (see Daniel Bell, cited in Zeleza 2006: 43). On the basis of this argument, during the deliberation leading to the adoption of the *UDHR*, Saudi Arabia, for instance, contended that "freedom to marry and to change ones' religion were Western ideas ill-suited for universal application" (cited in Brown 2008: 366).

In the human rights discourse, the position that the *UDHR* enshrines universal values is referred to as *universalism*; while the view that the *UDHR* contains the cultural practices and moral aspirations of a dominant culture is referred to as *cultural relativism*. Detailed discussions of these different positions are provided in later chapters; here it suffices to note that these views are very much alive in the human rights discourse today. However, there are many analysts who have argued that both radical cultural relativism and universalism are not viable in a "cosmopolitan moral community", and have advocated for the intercultural development and enrichment of human rights (Donnelly 2006).

For some analysts, the main difficulty with human rights is their apparent appropriation by the West, which imposes itself as their custodian; it is not that all that is said in the *UDHR* is Western, but rather that the West presents itself as if it were the only culture endowed with the concept and practice of human rights. Unfortunately, this

> Western appropriation of human rights does grave intellectual and political disservice to global human rights discourse and movement. Intellectually, it homogenises and oversimplifies human rights traditions of both the West and the Rest [the rest of the World] and undermines theoretical advances that can come from serious and sustained intra- and intercultural comparisons and conversations. Politically, it weakens the human rights movement globally in that the South human rights advocates waste a lot of energy trying to demonstrate that human rights are indigenous and relevant against charges from arrogant outsiders...
>
> ZELEZA 2006: 43

In this sense, the human rights discourse is extensive and complex, and as such, discussions of rights such as the rights to water and food have to be situated in these broader debates. While there are few people who deny that the rights to water and food address universal human needs, the way these rights are conceptualised, claimed and implemented is influenced by some of the broader debates on human rights. For example, whether the right to water or food is seen as primarily an individual or a group right, or both, influences the normative content and scope given to the right.

The Hard and Practical Questions

Apart from the conceptual debates about whether rights are universal or not, or whether there are really human rights at all, there have been extended debates about what, in practice, the legal implications of ESCRs such as the rights to water and food are. Since the 1950s, when the two international covenants were being discussed, the debates at the practical level have centred on the justiciability of ESCRs – with critics arguing that ESCRs such as the rights to water and food are aspirational statements which do not impose a legally binding obligation on the state, especially those that are not party to the Covenant (*ICESCR*). Some legal analysts have argued, for instance, that implementing such rights is problematic because most states do not have enough resources to give effect to them; and that a duty to meet obligations is only reasonable when it is matched by the reasonable means to fulfil them. Challengers of ESCRs have argued that most of the ESCRs do not have "a clear rule of adjudication"; that the right-holder and duty-bearers are not clearly identified for a legal process to be properly instituted (see Courtis 2007: 320); and that the contents of such rights are often vague, such that the clarification of entitlements and obligations can be a nightmare (see Dennis and Stewart 2004).

Although coming from a different angle, many activists argue that the emphasis placed on judicial recognition and procedures in the rights discourse can be counterproductive – because often the judicial process, while important, is insufficient to turn most rights into something tangible for the millions of poor people around the world (see Cohen and Brown 2008). Radical activists even argue that the whole issue of human rights can be a distraction from the real struggle for basic human entitlements – which are often given more meaning and effect through social and political mobilisation (Kennedy 2001). Some critics have observed that a more legalistic approach to human rights has often meant a narrow focus on what the law says, ignoring the political dynamics that shape both the law and the practice of human rights (Vaneklasen *et al.* 2004).

These debates raise the fundamental question of how to translate human rights such as the rights to food and water into real entitlements; into tangible effects on the ground. These hard and practical questions bring out the challenge of deploying the rights approach. For instance, can a person who is unable to acquire adequate food through his or her own means use these rights to secure access to these basic needs? Should that be the focus and priority of the human rights approach?

While many analysts have recognised the important role which the judicial process plays in giving effect to these rights, it has been observed that the legal route to realising human rights in general – and ESCRs in particular – should be seen as one among many possible ways. Human rights practitioners and activists identify several other ways in which rights can be given effect, including through social and political mobilisation around a particular issue. For example, the right to food or water, electricity, etc., can be given meaning through participation in public policy debates where service delivery policies and programmes are discussed and decided. Therefore, the question of whether a right is justiciable or not may only be relevant in cases where a strict legal strategy is pursued.

Given that there are several means of giving effect to human rights, a case for an integrated approach that combines different strategies in the struggle for basic entitlements, can be made. In this regard, constitutional provisions without a progressive judiciary and a vibrant civil society would make the realisation of such rights almost impossible. A clear constitutional provision and recognition of basic rights, and a strong and vibrant civil society,[12] together with a progressive judiciary that pays close attention to the core values recognised in the constitution, can create a situation where many rights – including those not listed in the Bill of Rights – can be given meaning in people's lives (Cohen and Brown 2008: 141). Examples and cases presented in subsequent chapters show that where these three aspects reinforce each other, more progress has been recorded in making human rights a reality in the lives of the poor. In contrast, in countries where there have been no synergies created between constitutional provisions, the judiciary and civil society, little progress is achieved in realising even the most basic rights. In all of this it is evident that the collective struggles of ordinary people as they assert their basic human needs and entitlements in society – whether through the courts or by taking to the streets – have been the most effective way of giving effect to human rights (Heyns 2006). In this regard, we are reminded that "apartheid was not ended either by a book or [a] court case [and] neither were colonialism nor slavery…" (Zeleza 2006: 42). Realisation of genuine human rights has always involved contestation of some sort, often by the masses who are subjected to unjust and oppressive structures, institutions and practices.

---

12 Civil society is here used in a broad sense that includes trade unions, church organisations, opposition parties, professional associations, social movements, the private media, etc.

The State as Contested Space

In this context, the idea that the state is a highly contested space becomes a helpful way of conceptualising and strategising on how to give effect to human rights. This view is clearly elaborated by Lefebvre (1994) in his book, *The Production of Space,* where he argues that *social space* (socio-political) is not a passive *surface* or *ether*, but rather an active product of contestation among the various groups of people who inhabit that space. Accordingly, social relations are seen as *producers* of *active space* in which human rights such as the rights to water and food are claimed, contested, ignored or given effect. In view of this, in order to understand the *state-space*, the analysis should not end at the right to water or food as a "thing" in the state-space, but should be extended to the "actual production of space" which shape how rights are contested, recognised or denied, realised or ignored. In other words, the social-political relations are crucial to understanding the dynamics that surround issues of access to water and food, and why so many people go without when there is sufficient.

Since the delivery of rights via the state-space is a product of constant contestation, human rights in general – and the rights to water and food in particular – are subject to these contestations (Veneklasen *et al.* 2004). And if one accepts the view that different human rights contest for attention with other rights or "interests" in the state-space, then it can be argued that rights are not a *given*, but can only be given effect through this process of contestation. It is in this sense that the state (municipal, local/provincial or federal) becomes an arena of contestation. Because of the critical role of the state in this contest, special attention throughout the book is given to the activities within this space, and how these activities promote or hinder the means by which the rights to water and food are given effect.

It is also illustrated in subsequent chapters that genuine realisation of human rights, in this framework, is intricately interrelated and interdependent. For example, the right to water or food can only be realised through the exercise of other rights such as the right to freedom of expression, movement, assembly and association; and the right to information, the right to participate in public processes, etc. When these civil rights are guaranteed and respected, it is possible to use them to protect other human rights such as the rights to water and food. Conversely, realisation of the rights to water, food, education and health, increases the chance of giving effect to other rights such as the right to freedom of expression, assembly, association and information. In this sense, civil and political rights, and ESCRs, reinforce each other such that situations where one set of rights is not respected, often leads to the non-fulfilment of another set (Cohen and Brown 2008).

The Human Rights Discourse

Often, human rights analysts begin from the assumption that the meaning of the two key terms – "human" and "rights" – have one settled meaning. However, while there may be no open contestation around what the term "human" refers to today, a review of the existing literature on the concept of "rights" shows that there are several meanings attached to this concept; and this has often been a source of controversy. Thus, it is essential here to briefly discuss the various meanings attached to the terms "human" and "rights" before discussing the composite term "human rights". The *Oxford English Dictionary* defines the term "human" as "of or belonging to species *homo sapiens*, having characteristics of humankind, as being weak, feeble, sympathetic, etc." Human rights are then defined as "those held to belong to all people", which in this case means all humans. The biological nuance in this definition of the term "human" is probably more helpful here because it sets limits to what should be included in the category, or species, *homo sapiens*. In biological terms, a "species" is a group of organisms with common characteristics, capable of mating to produce viable progeny. While today the definition of "human being" is almost taken for granted, in the past there have been convenient arguments about who should be counted and to what degree one should be accorded the status of *being human*. A lot of ink (and breath) has been expended defending views about the degree of "humanness" among peoples – implying that the concept of being human is graded. It is in this sense that the biological definition of "human" is probably more helpful in using a clear category of species, *homo sapiens*, to refer to humans. In this way, a human is not conceptualised in terms of grades, or degrees of humanness, but in categorical terms of belonging to a specific species, *homo sapiens*. This categorical approach – as opposed to a graded understanding – fits well with the composite term "human right", which ascribes equality and inherent dignity to anyone who is included in the category of humans. As such, human rights are taken to mean the entitlements that are accorded to every human being by virtue of being human, or by virtue of belonging to the category or species, *home sapiens*.

However, it must be noted here that the concept of "human right" is somehow mysterious and often not easy to define (Midgley 1999: 160). Like the term "human right", the term "right" is often tricky to define on its own. For instance, it has been argued that a formal definition of the term "right" may paralyse any attempt to understand the meaning of the term. "Here as elsewhere in philosophy this will have the effect of making the commonplace seem necessarily mysterious" (Feinburg 1973). While a formal definition of the term "right" is not attempted here, the different common meanings and usages of the term are discussed in the next chapter. Here it is important to note that in the common usage of the term "right", different connotations are attached to it – though the meaning given is often made clear by the context in which the term is used. In view of the different usages of the term "right", and because of the focus on the rights to food and water adopted here, the term "rights" will be given the meaning of entitlement or benefit, unless stated otherwise.

The rights to water and food fall within a group of rights called economic, social and cultural rights (ESCRS), or second generation rights. ESCRS are also widely associated with development and are often referred to as development rights. The term "development" is used here in a broad sense to refer to the improvement and changes in the well-being and living conditions of human beings. Improvements, in this sense, are not limited to the economic sphere, but include cultural, environmental, social, political and institutional progress. In the context of the rights to water and food, the development aspects focus on the enlargement of the freedom from hunger or the lack of clean water. Thus, in critically assessing the implementation of the rights approach, attention should be given to whether the RBA has actually contributed to enhancing these entitlements and freedoms. Before going into the practical issues around implementation and fulfilment of the rights to water and food, it is essential to introduce the main human rights debates. As noted earlier, the discourse on human rights is composed of various strands of arguments, including arguments for and against the existence of human rights. Thus, any assertion of, or argument for, human rights – and the rights to water and food in particular – needs to be located in these broader human rights debates.

The Human Rights Critiques

The human rights debates are not just about what meaning should be given to the term "right", or what should qualify as "human rights", but also about the ontological and epistemological foundations of the concept of human rights itself. As shall become apparent in this and in the next chapter, different aspects of human rights have been challenged and defended over the centuries. While human rights in general have attracted a great deal of public appeal and popularity in both domestic and international political fora (Sen 2004), the concept of human rights is noisily contested. Ardent critics of human rights, such as Jeremy Bentham, have long dismissed human rights as "simple nonsense" and natural rights as "rhetorical nonsense". Coming from a legal-positivist tradition, Bentham claims that "*Natural right* is simple nonsense: natural and imprescriptible rights, rhetorical nonsense, nonsense upon stilts" (1987 [1816]: 53).

Although these views were evidently a reaction to the French *Declaration of the Rights of Man and Citizen* during the last quarter of the eighteenth century, they influence debates on human rights even today. There are a number of authors who still question the theoretical foundations of human rights and the congeniality of the concepts (see MacIntyre 1985; C. Brown 1999).

Similarly, Duncan Kennedy, although focusing mainly on the legal discourse of rights in the United States, laments the dwindling of faith in the power of rights in general as an effective vehicle for articulating and bringing about desirable change in society. In an effort to defend his "loss of faith" in the legal processes as a route for reaching definitive sociopolitical goals, Kennedy (2001: 180) sees legal reasoning – including "rights talk" – as "whimsical rhetoric":

> Once I believed that the materials and the procedure produce the outcome, but now I experience the procedure as something I *do to* the material to produce the outcome I want. Sometimes it works and sometimes it doesn't, meaning that sometimes I get the outcome I want and sometimes I don't.

According to Kennedy, while rights may be an effective tool for reaching some desired social outcomes such as improving access to water and food for the poor, they have lost the ability to produce predictable and definitive ends – what he calls "closure".[13] It is crucial in the discussion of human rights to be aware of the different critiques which have been developed over time. To present an overview of these critiques here, they are grouped into five categories: the relativist, ontological, positivist, generational and Marxist critiques.[14]

The Relativist Critique

One of the major critiques of human rights is advanced by cultural relativists, whom I shall refer to here as the relativist school. Relativists, whether methodological, epistemological or ethical (see M. Brown 2008: 367),[15] are opposed to the principle of universal human rights on the basis of cultural diversity. In

13 Kennedy (2001) writes in the context of the American rights discourse, articulating his scepticism about the efficacy of legal reasoning in bringing about change – especially the empowerment of disadvantaged groups such as women, the poor, racially discriminated groups, gays and lesbians, the disabled, and minorities.

14 Of course some of the authors utilise elements of more than one critique. For example, MacIntyre (1985) seems to utilise both ethical relativism, as well as positivism threads in his argument. Brown's (1999) critique contains both ontological and relativist features.

15 Brown (2008) reports 20 different types of relativists recognized in the literature, but he groups them into three types: methodological, epistemological and ethical relativists,

general, relativists argue that given the diversity of cultures, customs, traditions, ethical and moral values, asserting a universal human rights system amounts to an imposition of certain values from some cultures ahead of those of other cultures. The basic argument of the relativists is that moral values, ethical principles and cultural practices differ from one culture to another, and therefore one has no grounds upon which to assert a universal system of values that can be called "human rights" (cited in Booth 1999: 32). As mentioned earlier in this chapter, the American Anthropological Association raised similar concerns during the debates leading to the adoption of the *UDHR*.

Cultural relativists therefore argue that since there are no universal cultural values, there is no universal (single) moral or ethical community that human rights regimes affirm (ibid.: 61). Based on this premise, human rights critics like Adda Bozenman argue that even "such documents as the *Universal Declaration of Human Rights*, passed by the United Nations in 1948, are futile proclamations, derived from moral principles valid in one culture and thrown out into the moral void between cultures" (cited in Vincent 1986: 38). More radical critics like Alasdair MacIntyre simply dismiss the intelligibility of such a concept, asserting that "there are no such rights and belief in them is [at] one with belief in witches and unicorns" (1985: 69). MacIntyre dismisses the notion of human rights on two grounds. First, the idea of human rights only came into fashion during the eighteenth century, and was founded on the concept of "natural rights". Second, that human rights are not universal because if they were, then they should have been recognised in the centuries before the rise of liberalism. Thus, MacIntyre (ibid.) argues

> the concept [of human rights] lacks any expression in Hebrew, Greek, Latin or Arabic, classical or medieval, before about 1400, let alone in Old English, or in Japanese even as late as the mid-nineteenth century. From this it does not of course follow that there are no natural or human rights; it only follows that no one could have known that there were.

Other critics have argued that that human rights, as such, "have no separate ontological status; they are a by product of a particular kind of society" (Brown 1999: 120). Brown builds his argument on the premise that there is no universal human nature or natural law which could be proposed as the foundation for universal human rights (ibid.: 119). This critique has inspired several positions which challenge the whole enterprise of human rights.

---

arguing that while the other two types are widely accepted and practiced among all sciences, ethical relativism is the least convincing.

The Ontological Critique

The other major critique of human rights comes from what is referred to here as the "ontological critique". This argument is not couched in terms of the uniqueness of cultural values, practices and ethical codes in different societies – rather, it is the actual nature of human rights that is questioned. In its simplified form the ontological critique states that human rights, conceived in universal terms, have no secure, or at least have an insecure, existence. In this argument the age-long problem of the ontological and epistemological status of "natural rights/ law" is at the centre of the argument. Simply put, the ontological critique denies notions of natural law, human nature, equality and inherent human dignity, on the basis that the existence of these concepts cannot be ascertained. In this sense the ontological critique is different from the cultural relativist one in that it questions the very heart of the concept of rights.

The Positivist Critique

The third major human rights critique is the positivist one – which focuses on *codification* and *enforcement* as the two defining elements of law and rights.[16] According to this school of thought, rights are only those that can be enforced (Sieghart 1983: 12). During the eighteenth century, Bentham was a fierce defender of legal positivism, arguing that there was no such things as laws that were not prescribed, or unenforced. Hence, in Bentham's view (1987 [1816]: 53), "no government, and thence no laws – no laws, and thence no such thing as rights". And the idea here is that laws, and therefore rights, are only those that are clearly prescribed and enforceable by a court of law. This view is based on the legal positivist principle, expounded by John Austin, that "law is a command of a sovereign backed by a threat".

Authors with a positivist persuasion ridicule the notion of natural or moral law, arguing that their foundation is "intuitive, non-determinable and metaphysical, hence unhelpful" (cited in Freeden 1991: 5). Principally, as a reaction to rationalism, positivists contend that belief in natural or moral law is not "objectively verifiable" and would therefore not be of much help in establishing truth or settling disputes in society (Sieghart 1983: 12; Smith 1996: 19).

Legal positivists such as Jeremy Bentham, John Austin and Edmond Burke, claim that codification of rules, together with the existence of enforcement structures, are necessary conditions for the existence of human rights – according to

16 Sometimes, positivism is interchangeably used with empiricism, but it is essential to distinguish between the two to avoid confusion. What seems clear is that positivism uses empiricist epistemology, but as a methodology positivism is different from empiricism (see Smith 1996).

them one cannot enforce uncodified rules. Following on from John Austin's "command theory of law" – which sees law as the command of the "politically superior" to the "politically inferior" – legal positivists view enforcement (threat of punishment) as an indispensable component of any regulative structure. For instance, endorsing the idea that state legislation or the domestic codification of international human rights instruments are the only legitimate ways through which human rights can be implemented, Brown (1999: 107) argues that human rights not only do not make sense to those who live in "societies" that have no culture of constitutionalism, such rights are non-existent in such places. To support his point, Brown argues that human rights would make sense to him as a citizen of the United Kingdom because he can take refuge in the "pieces of legislation" when his rights are threatened. Similarly, a citizen of the United States would find solace in the Bill of Rights; and a German citizen[17] in the *Grundgesetz* (ibid.). For proponents of legal positivism, "to establish that A has a right…it is necessary to demonstrate that there is or is not a rule which warrants, entitles or enables A to have or do the thing or act in question, [with] this warrant having specific legal consequences" (Freeden 1991: 5).

As such, legal positivism recognises a certain group of human rights; though it does *not* deny that there are *no* human rights. However, this school asserts that human rights are only those that can be enforced. For example, Brown (1999) has difficulties with international human rights regimes on the grounds that their implementation or enforcement is problematic at the national level. In fact, radical legal positivists deny the existence of international law in general – on the basis that there are no enforcement mechanisms at the international level.

The Generational Critique

The fourth major human rights critique is what I will refer to here as the generational critique.[18] Cranston Maurice is one of its main proponents. Although the argument is a partial critique of human rights, its implications can have far-reaching implications as far as human rights are concerned, especially ESCRs. In essence, this critique refutes the basic human rights principles of indivisibility and interrelatedness. Its main argument is that only civil and

17 See Sieghart 1983.

18 Chitonge (2005; 2007) refers to this as the Cranstonian critique, after the American supporter of civil and political rights, and ardent critic of socioeconomic and cultural rights. While Cranston Maurice is one of the most prominent critics of socioeconomic rights, there are many others who have rejected economic and cultural "rights" as being rights at all.

political rights – such as the "right to life, liberty, and a fair trial" – are the *genuine* human rights. ESCRs – such as the right to employment, an old-age pension, healthcare, food and water – are politically as well as philosophically bankrupt. According to Cranston (1973: 65), recognising economic, social and cultural rights does not only endanger the respected concept of human rights, such a move is absurd and "hinders the effective protection of what are correctly seen as human rights" (ibid.).

To defend what he calls "traditional human rights", Cranston uses a "three test" criterion which an alleged "right" should meet if it is to be regarded as a genuine human right. The three tests of the Cranstonian framework are that it has to be *universal*, of *paramount importance*, and *practicable* (Cranston, 1973: 66). In this framework, any purported right that fails any one of the three tests is excluded from being a *genuine human right*. Cranston, in his quest to "sanctify" the list of human rights, argues that a claim must only be called a right if it is possible to be correlated with a duty – arguing that affirming the so-called economic, social and cultural rights as human rights is to "push *all* talk of human rights out of the clear realm of the morally compelling into the twilight world of utopian aspiration" (ibid.: 68).

In this sense, then, like the positivists, the Cranstonian triad test does not fundamentally deny the existence of human rights, but does narrow the scale and scope of what can be accepted as human rights. The rights to water and food, for instance, would be in doubt on the grounds that they would not pass all three test of universality, practicability and paramount importance.

The Universality Test

What Cranston means by the universality test is that a genuine human right should be a right *of all*, and that it should impose the duty *on all*. In this sense, the universality test poses no major problem to the traditional conception of rights, since universality is an attribute of human rights in the sense of the right being granted to *everyone* who belongs the species, *homo sapiens*. However, Cranston argues that rights such as a right to rest, leisure, reasonable working hours and periodic holidays – recognised in the *ICESCR* Article 7 (d) – would not pass this test because such rights are only claimed by a group of human beings (employees) and not by *all* people. On this ground, then, Cranston excludes such rights from being genuine human rights, arguing that the right to a paid holiday – or to leisure or rest, for instance – is "a right that is necessarily limited to those persons who are *paid* in any case, that is to say, to the *employee* class". Cranston (1973: 67) further contends: "Since not everyone belongs to this class, the right cannot be a universal right, a right which in the terminology of the Universal Declaration, 'everyone' has."

The Practicability Test

This test, in essence, is based on the "generational" notion of human rights which classifies human rights into three generations: first generation (civil and political rights), second generation (socioeconomic and cultural rights), and third generation (solidarity rights, e.g., the right to development, the right to a clean environment). The generational approach to human rights usually categorises human rights into negative and positive ones, with *positive* rights seen as those that require the state to *do* something in order to fulfil the rights, and *negative* rights as those that impose a negative duty on the state such as the duty of the state *not* to interfere with the rights of citizens (see de Waal 2001: 432).

Using this classification, Cranston argues that since all ESCRs require *positive action* by the state, or at least by someone with a corresponding duty, in situations where there are no clearly identified duty-bearers it is practically impossible to claim these rights. And "[i]f it is impossible for something to be done, it is absurd to claim it as a right" (Cranston 1973: 66).

Like many authors who recognise civil and political rights as the only genuine human rights, Cranston sees a practicality problem which emanates from the view that the realisation of ESCRs depends on the availability of resources. According to Cranston, this is not the case with civil and political rights; all that is needed is simply to secure their enactment since these "rights are for the most part rights against government interference with man's activities" – which require no more than government to restrain itself from infringing individuals rights (ibid.).

In Cranston's view, since the realisation of ESCRs depends on the availability of resources, it is impractical to impose a duty to fulfil them on governments that have no resources to provide for them.[19] Consequently, rights such as the right to water, food, education and healthcare cannot be genuine human rights because they fail the practicality test.

The Paramount Importance Test

With regard to this test, although there is some ambiguity over what *paramount importance* means, Cranston seems to refer to the weight of the contribution to human well-being that a claim makes. For example, a claim to leisure weighs comparably less than a claim to healthcare or to food. It is in this sense that a claim should only be accorded a the status of a "right" if it proves to be of superlative

19 Paradoxically, economic, social and cultural rights have been very popular in those Third World countries that have limited resources; although Cranston (1973: 76) argues that this was a move by the developing countries to "squeeze economic aid out of rich ones".

importance. For instance, while it is a "paramount duty to relieve great distress", it is not a "paramount duty to give pleasure" (ibid.: 67). In this sense a claim qualifies as a human right only when its contribution to human well-being is not of a fictitious or frivolous nature. The rationale behind this test is that a claim of paramount importance is backed by a moral duty, while a frivolous claim does not have a compulsive *moral force*, but is rather a matter of *virtue* (ibid.).

In the Cranstonian schema, the *universality test* may not pose a great difficulty for many ESCRs – such as the right to water, food, healthcare, education, social security and employment – in that such entitlements can be said to belong to "everyone"; most of these ESCRs, however, would fail the *practicality* tests. In effect, the Cranstonian catalogue of rights systematically excludes most (if not all) ESCRs because the existence of these rights is strictly tied to the availability of the means to fulfil them.

At the heart of this critique is the assumed tension between ESCRs and political rights (Jones 1994: 157; Vincent 1986: 13). And the conclusion arrived at is that endorsing the former set of claims as human rights constitutes a confusion of rights with utopian ideals (Cranston 1973: 66). Having excluded ESCRs from "genuine" human rights, this argument leaves neither theoretical nor practical grounds for asserting solidarity rights such as the right to development or a clean environment.

The Marxist Critique

To the above critiques of human rights should be added the Marxist critique. Marx's critique of rights is stated in one of his earlier writings: *On the Jewish Question*. Marx's main critique is that rights promote individualism, which in turn leads to alienation or separation of individuals from the community (Waldron 1987). Thus, for Marx, rights were created to be the "servant of egoistic man, [and] the sphere in which man behaves as a communal being is degraded below the sphere in which man behaves as a partial being, finally that it is not man as a citizen but man as a bourgeois who is called the real and true man" (cited in Waldron 1987: 65). Thus, for Marx, human rights serve the interests not of all people, but of the bourgeoisie. However, as Waldron (1987) has noted, Marx's views on rights are not formulated with the degree of clarity that would merit them being analysed as a system of thought.

Implications of the Human Rights Critiques

The view expressed in the critiques summarised above do influence the thinking and practical action concerning various human rights, especially the ESCRs;

and as such these debates should not be dismissed as misconception or mere academic exercise – as many human rights activists often do. As would be expected, several defenders of human rights have responded to these critiques, debunking and clarifying some of the apparent misapprehensions manifested in them. The different rebuttals of these critiques are presented in Chapter 2. Here it suffices to note that the critiques mentioned above have done little to dilute the public appeal of human rights in many societies, at least at the level of campaigning and lobbying. Every day, millions of people around the world appeal to these concepts whenever their interests are at risk. At the practical level, people who use human rights to make their claims do not sit down first to determine if their claim is a universal human right, a justiciable right, or even a genuine human right for that matter; they simply assert through the courts, through public protest, and in their homes, that their right has been infringed and seek redress. As later examples in this book will show, many people – either as groups or as individuals – have found ways of asserting the claim that their rights to water and food are not fulfilled; and there have been several ways in which such people have initiated struggles in their bid to give effect to these rights. Practical expressions of the collective struggles for basic necessities such as water, food, electricity, healthcare and education include the Right to Food Campaign in India, the Citizen Action Against Hunger in Brazil, and the Treatment Action Campaign and The Free Basic Water Coalition in South Africa. As Amartya Sen has observed,

> Invoking of human rights tends to come mostly from those who are concerned with changing the world rather than interpreting it. It is not hard to understand their unwillingness to spend time trying to provide conceptual justification, given the great urgency to respond to terrible deprivations around the world.
>
> SEN 2004: 317

Nonetheless, it is essential to note that the various critiques, in their different forms, should not be seen as damaging the concept and practice of human rights. To the contrary, they help to clarify some of the grey areas, and also create greater awareness of them. Indeed, the human rights debates generated by these critiques must continue as a way of elaborating and clarifying issues, as well as a means of securing international support and attention for them. Second, human rights form an indispensable way of seeing and talking about the world we live in today. In other words, the human rights discourse is a significant way of bringing the human individual to the centre of national and international sociopolitical activities (Annan 1997: 24); a way of identifying essential human attributes to be enclosed in a "protective capsule" (Freeden, 1991: 7); a way of keeping justice in the foreground by emphasising that every person is a "locus of human flourishing" (Finnis 1980: 221); and a way of bringing about social change. Third, human rights are broadly seen as valuable "propert[ies] we own, and from which we may not even temporarily be dispossessed" (Feinburg 1973: 75); and valuable properties that people give to themselves out of a common understanding (Sengupta 2000: 553). In this sense it is the community (both national and international) which is the grantor, upholder, protector and enforcer of these entitlements, and as such these rights cannot be treated as private affairs (Delvin 1983: 57). Similarly, the community that grants rights is not homogenous – there are people who have different views about rights and they must be listened to.

Do Human Rights Make any Difference?

While the concept of human rights has huge public appeal, the experience with implementing ESCRs in particular, suggests that though there has been enthusiastic accession and ratification of the major international human rights laws – including the *ICESCR*, *CRC* and the *CEDAW* – the implementation of the basic responsibilities under these instruments has been disappointing, with many countries failing even to submit country reports (Horn 2009: 59). Further, although there are many people taking up the struggle for human rights, "an excessive amount of attention on the rights-based approach is currently directed at the rhetorical level rather than on the practical implementation of development policies" (cited in Banik 2008: 25). Many state officials and some civil society groups around the world are reluctant to take steps towards the implementation of some of the rights recognised – even in their own national constitutions and statutory laws. For countries in the Global South that receive significant donor aid, the push for human rights is from donors who, regrettably, underemphasise ESCRs and focus mainly on civil and political rights. Experience from different countries presented in this book point to this tension (between first and second generation rights) in the practical implementation of human rights. In the case of the rights to water and food, the available evidence from selected countries suggests that there are a lot of gaps that many states still need to plug before they can start to address even the minimum requirement of respecting and protecting such rights – particularly in Africa (Keetharuth 2009). In most cases the inadequate protection of civil and political rights – such as the right to freedom of expression, assembly and association – has constrained the spaces through which a vibrant civil society can emerge and play an important role in giving effect to ESCRs (Olowu 2009).

Human Rights and Development: The Rights-Based Approach (RBA)

Since the publication of the first *Human Development Report* in 1990, there has been a growing recognition, globally, that the realisation of human rights should be an indispensable objective of the development process. Although this integration of human rights and development has been an underlying concern since the French Revolution (1789), it is only in recent years that integration of human rights and developmental concerns has received considerable attention (Alston and Robinson 2005). The perceived value added by integrating these two concepts has spurred many development practitioners and agencies to adopt what is known as the "rights-based approach" (RBA)[20] to development (Nyamu-Musembi and Cornwall 2004: 1).

There has been a recent upsurge of rights talk in development discourse works, working from the assumption that integrating human rights and development adds value to development theory and practice by drawing attention to issues of equality, accountability, empowerment, participation, respect and protection of human dignity. Not only that, it is argued that human rights

> bring legal tools and institutions – laws, the judiciary and the process of litigation – as means to secure freedoms and human development. Rights also lend moral legitimacy and the principle of social justice to the objectives of human development. The rights perspective also helps shift the priority to the most deprived, especially to deprivations because of discriminations.
>
> UNDP 2000: 2

Although there are controversies as to what exactly a rights-based approach to development entails,[21] it is generally agreed that integrating human rights norms in development planning and policy implementation constitutes a new and distinct way of bringing human needs and aspirations to the centre of human endeavours. This approach has emerged from the realisation that

20 Up to now, there have been different views as to what this rights-based approach is. Different development agencies use the term to mean different things. However, what seems to be common among all the different development practitioners is that human rights are seen as an intrinsic part of the development process – highlighting the fact that both identify human beings as the centre of the development and human rights processes.

21 There are some scholars, for example Ferguson (1999), who argue that the "rights-based approach" is a distinctly new and different way of thinking about development; while others (cited in Univ 2002) issue a cautionary warning that this could be a new fashion that is "being used to dress up the same old development in what may amount to the Emperor's New Clothes" (see Nyamu-Musembi and Cornwall 2004: 1).

human development and human rights pursue common objectives; namely, improving human capabilities and well-being, and protecting human dignity and fundamental freedoms. While human rights seek to secure the protection of human dignity and basic freedoms, development seeks to advance people's freedom by improving their capabilities and well-being. In this sense, "[w]hen human development and human rights advance together, they reinforce one another – expanding people's capabilities and protecting their rights and fundamental freedoms" (UNDP 2000: 2). When viewed from this complementary perspective, the rights-based approach to development then suggests that "human development is essential for realizing human rights, and human rights are essential for full human development" (ibid.).

While there has been great hype and enthusiasm around the RBA as a practical way of giving effect to human rights, it has been noted that "[a] human rights based approach is not a magic formula: it cannot solve every issue... However, it provides an important guidance for decision-making...and gives a framework for accountability of state authorities" (SDC 2008: 8). Chapter 3 discusses in detail some of the opportunities, as well as the challenges of implementing a rights-based approach to development.

CHAPTER 2

The Human Rights Discourse

An Overview

As may be apparent from the discussions in Chapter 1, the concept of human rights is highly contested. This contest is not just an academic exercise on the meaning and the semantics around the term; it is also about defining power and social relations. Indeed, human rights are in essence about regulating power relations, which in turn affect how people interact with each other and how power is exercised in society. The various dimensions of power and how these relate to human rights are discussed in Chapter 4. Here, focus is on the fact that while human rights are widely invoked in different societies, times and settings,[1] they have been conceptualised differently, leading to the divergence of views on what human rights are and what they entail. Although every society has a way of assigning certain entitlements – such as life, reason, justice, citizenship or respect – to human beings as categorical attributes, the question of what these entitlements entail in reality has always been controversial. Whereas there have been strong assertions[2] that human beings have certain inalienable entitlements by virtue of belonging to the species *homo sapien*, the implications of these assertions tend to be interpreted differently and are consequently given different shades of meaning and value depending on the interpreter's interest and ideological orientation. For instance, as we shall see later, the assertion that everyone has the right to access water and adequate food often means different things to different people. The implication of this assertion is understood differently by state officials when compared to ordinary people who struggle to meet basic needs. In some countries, especially developed ones, access to water and food is not seen as a human right; it is largely perceived as a mere aspirational goal for social policy. As will be illustrated in subsequent chapters, efforts (mainly) by the United Nations to create a common understanding and standard of human rights have not gone far in resolving the differences. Thus, it cannot be taken for granted that when we talk about human rights we are all talking about, and mean, the same thing.

---

1 Ife (2002) has argued that although the same vocabulary of rights may not be used, the principle that human beings are endowed with fundamental "valuables" which should be protected and cherished is common in all societies or cultures.

2 For instance, the *American Declaration of Independence*, the French *Declaration of the Rights of Man and Citizen*, and more recent times the *United Nations Universal Declaration of Human Rights* (UDHR) in 1948 endows man with "*inalienable rights*" which are declared to be a 'self-evident.'

 | DOI 10.1163/9789004299559_003

In this chapter, we look at these different views of human rights, including the different meanings often attached the word "right". Some of the main responses to the human rights critiques (in defence of human rights) introduced in the previous chapter are also discussed in more detail. While many human rights activists, bent on bringing about social change, waste no time on abstract ideas such as the meaning of human rights and whether human rights exist or not (Sen 2004), it is important to recognise, understand and clarify the different meanings and usages of these concepts to avoid muddled thinking – which can be a great hindrance to clear reasoning and application of these concepts to concrete situations (Hohfeld 2005).

Morality and Law

To start with, it is essential to point out that the human rights discourse has largely relied on the moral and ethical reasoning that human beings have some inherently desirable value which should be protected – without exceptions. Of course certain members of the species *homo sapien*, such as prisoners, find themselves in situations where the enjoyment of these rights is restricted or regulated; but there is a strong belief that even in these circumstances people are endowed with inestimable value. In this sense the concept of human rights is largely built around what some have termed the "collective goal" (Dworkin 1977), as opposed to "*legal rules*" or "*primary rules*" (see Hart 1961). This distinction, as we shall see later in the chapter, leads to the delicate argument about the separation of morality from law. Many liberal jurists and legal philosophers assert that human rights are largely regulated by moral rules which often have no legal force – although they acknowledge that there is often no clear line separating the two. In a subtle way the separation of "the moral" from "the legal" is implied in the generational approach to human rights – whereby the first generation rights are seen to fall under the legal realm with clear duty-bearers and beneficiaries; while the second and third generations (such as the right to food, water, healthcare and development) are largely regarded as moral and social aspirations, devoid of clearly demarcated duty-bearers and distinctly identified beneficiaries. One example of this position in the case of the right to food is the view consistently adopted by the US government that "the attainment of any 'right to food' or 'fundamental right to be free from hunger' is a goal or aspiration to be realised progressively [and which] does not give rise to any international obligation" (cited in Cohen and Brown 2008: 138).

But the distinction between morality and law has been deemed an artificial partition which has no foundation in fact or in practice. Critics argue that there are actually no clear lines separating morality from law, especially when one moves into the field of jurisprudence. According to this view, separating morality from law ignores "the crucial fact that jurisprudential issues are at their core issues of moral principle, not legal fact or strategy" (Dworkin 1977: 7). Lord Delvin (1983: 57) goes even further, arguing that such a separation is not only wrong, but leads to impractical conclusions. However, the debate about separating morality from law is a much extended and broader one which has great influence on various policies and social and political programmes adopted in different countries. For a full discussion of this and related debates readers can refer to Feinburg (1973), Fletcher (1996), Hart (1961; 1963), Gerwirth (1982). We return later to this debate when discussing the practical implications of socioeconomic rights, particularly the rights to water and food.

Because many human rights, especially ESCRs, are often located in the moral and not legal realm, they are often given a *normative* rather than a *positive* interpretation, and this can influence the weight given to a particular right. For instance, the *UDHR* itself has been seen as a "common standard of achievement for all peoples", and as such "a source of inspiration" (see *Preamble to the Vienna Declaration and Plan of Action* 1993). While there is essentially nothing wrong with the normative approach to human rights, this has given rise to the view that such rights can only be given effect when it is possible; that they need not be given effect immediately; and that they can only be "progressively realised" depending on the availability of resources and capacity. Many governments in low income and developing countries have used this as an excuse to postpone the implementation of ESCRs, in some cases indefinitely.

However, it has been observed that the fact that human rights are perceived to fall in the realm of morality has not weakened their appeal to people everywhere in the world. The concept of human rights has become one of the most widely invoked and used concept in everyday life across the globe. "There is something deeply attractive in the idea that every person anywhere in the world, irrespective of citizenship or territorial legislation, has some basic rights, which others should respect" (Sen 2004: 315). Interestingly, this wide and strong appeal of human rights has been attributed to their moral persuasiveness – the prospect they hold in safeguarding basic human needs, dignity and collective aspirations.

Seen from this angle, human rights can be affirmed not on the basis of natural law or any semblance of universal human nature or culture, but on the basis of identified common values that a community decides to give itself. This is sometimes referred to as the "*rule of recognition*" (Hart 1994 [1961]). What is meant by the term "community" here may require further elaboration, but in the context of human rights it refers to the international community within the United Nations (UN) system that has largely recognised and elaborated most of them. The question that many commentators have raised about whether the UN system appropriately represents a *global* community is rather a different one that need not detain us here.[3] Whether the UN embodies a true global community is debatable, but it has been submitted that the UN has, in some sense, created a global moral community (Vincent 1986), imperfect though that may be. In this case, one could argue that the rights to water and food can be asserted on the grounds that they have been recognised by the international community as being valuable properties which the community seeks to protect and defend. However, that recognition of the rights to water and food as something valuable is only a first step in a complex process of giving effect to these rights.

What is a Right?

Although disagreements about human rights are rarely directed towards the meaning of the term "right", the way this term is understood has an influence on what meaning is ascribed to the term "human rights". It is therefore important to discuss the different meanings attached to this term, and what the different implications on the meaning of "human right" are. One of the key challenges in trying to clarify the term "right" – perhaps well known to philosophers but much less so to political and legal analysts – is the fact that the word takes up different meanings in different contexts; such that it becomes more difficult to define the term in an abstract context. A word of caution has been issued in this regard – attempts to formally define the term "right" often result in "making the commonplace seem unnecessarily mysterious, [and] we would be better advised not to attempt a formal definition of either 'right' or 'claim'"(Feinburg 1973: 64). Dworkin (1977: 90) makes the similar observation that while it is essential to ask the question, "what are rights?" it "is hard to supply any definition that does not beg the question", and this is mainly because any such definition "uses rather than explains the concept of right".

3 Of course the UN itself, at the time of adopting the *UDHR*, had only 56 members, and most of the world's peoples were not represented. However, subsequent instruments flowing from the *UDHR* – such as the *ICCPR, ICESCR, CRC, CEDAW, CRED*, etc. – have been adopted by a wider family of nations. The main issue is not about membership in the UN system, it is rather about how representative of the different values for the different communities the views that the UN system has adopted really are.

In common parlance, however, when people use the term "right" in expressions such as "you have the right to remain silent", or "I have the right to freedom of movement", they often understand a right as something that requires other people not to interfere with the prescribed or proscribed entitlement. In this sense many rights are understood as imposing a negative duty on all community members to refrain from interfering with the right-holder's exercise or enjoyment of the right and freedom in question. The arresting officer, for instance, should refrain himself or herself from anything that would violate the right of the arrested person to remain silent or the right to freedom of movement; except, of course, under specific circumstances when these restraints do not apply – for example, when interrogating the suspect or during a state of emergency when movement is restricted by specially applied laws.

But rights do not only impose a negative duty; there are also rights that carry a positive duty requiring an individual, a group of individuals, or a collective, to perform a specific act towards the right-holder – thereby generating a *positive right*. For example, a person's right to be heard requires that someone or some others perform the act of listening; and in certain circumstances a conducive environment (such as providing an interpreter) has to be created in order to afford a person the right to be heard. Another example is the right to water and food. People who are unable to secure access to clean water and adequate food have some expectation that someone (this could be the state, relatives, neighbours, religions groups or NGOs) will perform positive action that can help them meet these basic needs.

Rights and Duties

Formulating rights in this way, however, leads to another debate about whether rights necessarily need to be correlated with duties. While most jurists and legal analysts would argue that only those claims that have a corresponding duty, with a clearly specified duty-bearer (legal rights), should be regarded as rights, it has been contended that the correlation of claims with duties is neither logically necessary nor morally desirable since "there are numerous classes of duties both legal and non-legal, that are not logically correlated with the rights of other persons" (Feinberg 1973: 63). For instance, a person in need of the basic necessities of life is said to be "in a position to make a claim, even when there is no one in the corresponding position to do anything about it" (ibid.: 67). A good example of this is the French law of Criminal Omission – which applies when people neglect to help others in dire need (see Ashworth and Steiner, 1990). Although the people in dire need of water or food may not have a legal claim against the state, relative, or their neighbours, this law does generate a right to make the claim that an act of omission has resulted in their right not being fulfilled. On the contrary, those who assert the correlation of rights with duties argue that only those claims that can be linked to an explicit duty-bearer should be recognised as rights. Nonetheless, even if one was to take the latter meaning, most ESCRs – such as the rights to water and food – would still be affirmed on the basis that the state is explicitly recognised under *ICESCR* (for countries which have ratified this treaty) to have the duty to respect, protect and fulfil such rights. It is apparent, however, that the use of the word "right" can generate different meanings – which can be a source of contention.

The Versatility of the Term "Right"?

Although it has been argued that any attempt to define the term "right" is bound to be problematic, it is important to clarify the different meanings that the term assumes in different contexts. In conventional usage the term seems to be so obvious that it rarely calls for elaboration of what is meant when someone says X or Y has a right to A or B. The notion of rights at this level seems to carry a force that is so compelling to the listener that the value of such statements are taken to be self-evident. As Sen (2004: 315) has noted, "[f]ew concepts are as frequently invoked in contemporary political discussions as human rights" and there is no dispute that using the rights language can be "politically powerful".

At the theoretical level the power of such claims is not only questioned; their meaning is contested. Regardless of the strong assertions of human rights in declarations such as the *French Declaration of the Rights of Man and the Citizen* (1789), the *American Declaration of Independence* (1791), the *Universal Declaration of Human Rights* (1948), and the *African Charter of Human and Peoples' Rights* – which often take these rights to be self-evident – the meaning and practical implication of these seemingly 'self-evident truths' are fiercely disputed from different fronts. As noted earlier, while some critics are dismissive of the entire notion of human rights, others have taken a discriminatory approach – recognising some human rights and dismissing others as 'loose talk'. While human rights activists have been quick to dismiss such critics and continue to use the language of rights in their quest to effect change in the world (and they have little sympathy or time for those who engage in conceptual battles about human rights), it has been suggested that these conceptual issues should be addressed if human rights are to have a strong and defensible intellectual standing (Sen 2004: 317).

In a sense it should not be surprising that questions about what, exactly, human rights *are* have often attracted heated debates, given that the concept is widely applied and serves a diverse set of functions. In an analysis of the usage of the term "right", Corbin (2005) discovered up to 20 different meanings in different circumstances.[4] Although the fact that the term has multiple meanings does not necessarily imply that the term itself is vague, this situation can give rise to blurred meaning if used indiscriminately. There is, of course, no confusion between someone using the term "right" in a phrase like: "when you come to the T-junction turn 'right'", and someone who says "the 'right' thing to do is to pay your TV licence". In this instance, even though both expressions use the same word to mean different things, the two expressions do not give rise to ambiguities. But when someone uses the word in an expression like, "it is my 'right' to vote" and "I have a 'right' to be paid at the end of the month for the work I have done", the meaning that the word has now acquired can indeed be ambiguous. While both convey the same principle that there is something that is due to the right-holder, there are differences; in the first instance, the right imposes a duty on others not to do anything that may prevent the right-holder to accomplish the objective of the right to vote; while in the second instance it imposes a duty on another person(s) to perform certain actions (paying a salary) towards the right-bearer.

Because of the inherent versatility of the term "right", clarifying the meanings assigned to it is essential to avoid clouded conceptions and meanings that are capable of leading, in turn, to clouded thinking; "[o]ne whose own mind is cloudy and confounded is certain to convey only cloudy and confused thoughts to others" (Corbin 2005: viii).

Hohfeldian Categories of Right

Despite the fact it is not easy[5] to formally define the word "right" (and no attempt is made here), it is perhaps helpful to categorise the different usages that the word often acquires in different contexts. Wesley Hohfeld (2005 [1919]), in his famous book *Fundamental Legal Conceptions as Applied in Judicial*

---

4 For instance, in continental legal systems the word "right" can also be translated to mean "law" as in *droit, jus, Recht* and *dirrito*, see Kent (1970) and Feinburg (1973). H.L.A. Hart, although he is talking about legal rights, acknowledges the difficulties associated with the term: "The notion of a legal right has proved in the history of jurisprudence to be very elusive" (1982: 162).

5 A number of authors have noted the dangers of attempting to provide a formal definition of the word "right". Hohfeld also cautions against undue obsession with formal definition of such "*sui generis*" terms as *right*. In many instances "attempts at formal definition are always unsatisfactory, if not altogether useless" (Hohfeld 2005 [1919]: 36).

TABLE 2.1 *Hohfeldian Scheme of Jural Relations*

	Relation 1	Relation 2	Relation 3	Relation 4
Opposites	Right: No-right	Privilege Duty	Power Disability	Immunity Liability
Correlatives	Right: Duty	Privilege No-right	Power Liability	Immunity Disability

SOURCE: COMPILED BY AUTHOR, BASED ON HOHFELD'S SCHEME.

Reasoning, created categories for the different usages of the term "right" in an attempt to clarify the various connotations and uses attached to it. Although Hohfeld's categories are mainly concerned with "jural relationships" aimed at bringing some clarity to analytical jurisprudence, his scheme is an important one to bear in mind during the course of the discussion on human rights. Instead of formal definitions, Hohfeld (ibid.) proposed to categorise "the various relations in a scheme of 'opposites' and 'correlatives'" and apply these relations to individual concrete cases.

In his attempt to clarify what he called "Fundamental Legal Concepts", Hohfeld came up with a scheme containing four pairs of opposites and correlatives to signify the different relationships which are often described in the use of the term "right" – as illustrated in Table 2.1 above. Using this scheme, Hohfeld made a deliberate distinction between right in the "narrow sense" (referring to a right that is correlated with a single duty), and right in the broad sense (referring to the other relations where there is no clear correlation between a claim-right and a duty). In daily usage the word "right" can be used in relationships that, in actual fact, do not convey the meaning of a right in the "strictest" or "narrow sense". For Hohfeld, the only situation that merits being denoted by the term "right" is when a relationship involved is correlated with a duty – in other words, a *claim-right*. In this case, *privileges*, *powers* or *immunity* are not supposed to be confused with a right in the "strict sense" of the term.

In the example above, the person saying "I have a right to vote" is using that term to refer to the liberty to vote (Chitonge 2005), which implies that others have no right to obstruct his execution of the elements of the right (they have a liability to refrain from interfering with the right-holder). But the person who says "I have the right to be paid for the work I have done" has a *claim-right*, meaning that the other person has the duty to *perform certain actions* to the claimant. To clarify his scheme, Hohfeld uses the idea of opposites and correlatives which he thought would help avoid the indiscriminate use of the term "right" in legal or jural relations. Aware of the futility of attempting to formally define the term, Hohfeld argued that the "most promising" way to deal with the conflated use of the term right "seems to consist in exhibiting all of the various relations in a scheme of 'opposites' and 'correlatives' and then preceding to exemplify their individual scope and application in concrete cases" (Hohfeld 2005 [1919]: 36).

It is important here to realise that Hohfeld was primarily concerned with legal relations and how they are used in arriving at judicial decisions. Hence, the examples that he extensively cites are from judicial precedents in which the term "rights" had been used indiscriminately or indistinctly.

In Hohfeld's view the opposites and correlatives help to clarify the different relations which are often used indiscriminately as rights, but in actual fact denote *privileges, powers* or *immunities*. This indiscriminate use of the word "right", according to Hohfeld, is one of the greatest barriers to a clear understanding of legal and moral relations (ibid.: 35). Hohfeld believed that by presenting these relations as opposites and correlatives it would be possible to distinguish the different relations that are often conflated in the use of the word. For example, while the opposite of "right" is "no-right", the correlative of a *righ*t is a *duty*, implying that a *legal* or *claim*-right exists only when a *claim*[6] is correlated with a *duty*. Elaborating on this scheme, Hohfeld (ibid.: 60) asserts that a

> *right* is one's affirmative claim against another, and a *privilege* is one's freedom from the right or claim of another. Similarly, a *power* is one's affirmative 'control' over a given legal relation as against another; whereas an *immunity* is one's freedom from the legal power or 'control' of another as regards some legal relations.

The key terms that Hohfeld uses to construct his scheme of *correlatives* are: *right* (*claim-right*), *privilege*, *power* and *immunity*; and their corresponding opposites are: *no-right, duty, disability and liability*.

Claim-Rights

In the Hohfedian scheme, a right is correlated with a duty; while the opposite of a right is *no-right* – meaning that a right-holder creates a relation where everybody else has *no-right* against him or her with respect to the claim. An example of a claim-right is when two people enter into a contract – for example, A borrows money from B, undertaking to pay back on a specific date. In this case, A has a *duty* to pay B the amount he or she owes B, while B has a *right* to be paid the amount A owes him/her. In this case, a right imposes a positive

6 Hohfeld uses the term "claim" as a synonym of the word "right" (see Hohfeld 2005 [1919]: 38).

duty on A to fulfil the terms of the contract with B. In other words, B has a *claim-right* against A, meaning that A should pay him/her the money owed. In terms of the opposite relations created, by virtue of A having a claim against B, the latter has *no-right* against A – meaning that B has no claims against A under the agreed terms.

Privilege

As may be evident from Table 2.1, a *privilege* is the opposite of a *duty*, and a correlative of *no-right*. What this means is that when someone has a privilege, this generates a relationship where other parties have no duty towards the privileged person. For example, if A allows B to use A's car, the relations do not impose a *duty* on A to give his/her car to B; B has *no-right* against A, though he has a privilege to use A's car. In terms of correlatives, while B has the *privilege* to use A's car, B has *no-right* to claim the use of A's car in this relationship. The term "privilege" is used, in this sense, to mean that the guarantor of the privilege is under no legal obligation (or duty) to provide the granted privilege. It is in this sense that "a *privilege* is one's freedom from the right or claim of another" (ibid.). Hohfeld (ibid.: 39) contends that the meaning and

> the conception of a right (claim) and the conception of a privilege [are] quite distinct from each other [and] that seems evident, and, more than that, it is equally clear that there should be a separate term to represent the later relation. No doubt ... it is very common to use the term 'right' indiscriminately, even when the relation designated is really that of privilege.

Power

Power in the Hohfeldian scheme is correlated with *liability*, and its opposite is *disability*. What this means in terms of opposites is that a person with *power* (a power-holder) imposes a *liability* on those he or she holds power over; while in terms of correlatives it means that the power-holder imposes a negative relationship on the other party which *disables* them from acting against the power-holder in relation to that over which power is held. In this sense, *power* constitutes having the *liberty* to do or not to do something. In a narrow technical sense, power would imply the authority to create and extinguish legal and other relations, and, according to Hohfeld, examples of legal power in daily life interactions are many. It is specifically because of this understanding that Hohfeld asserts that "a *power* is one's affirmative 'control' over a given legal relations as against another" (ibid.). For example, "X, the owner of ordinary personal property, 'in a tangible object' has the power to extinguish his own legal interest (rights, powers, immunities etc.) ...and simultaneously and correlatively, to create in other persons privileges and powers relating to the abandoned object" (ibid.: 51).

The term "power" is more familiar to people in the legal profession in phrases such as the "power of attorney" or the "power of appointment". The opposite of power is *disability* and it is correlated with *liability*. The correlation in this instance signifies a relation between two or more parties in which the power-holder has authority when there is a corresponding person or group of persons who incur some *liability* if that power is exercised. In the case of the power of appointment, the power-holding party may exercise this power by refusing to make any appointment, and the other party may incur the liability resulting from the lack of exercising the power (for instance appointment is reserved).

Simply put, X, in exercising his power to extinguish and create new legal relations, generates negative relations with other parties by imposing a duty not to act against him/her in exercising his/her legal power. In its correlative form, by exercising his/her power, X generates a correlative *liability* on any party over whom he/she exercises the said power. As such, A has *power* relative to B, if, and only if, B has a *liability* to have his or her legal position changed by A (Finnis 1980). For example, if A owes B, US$500, and if B can waive A's duty to pay B the US$500, then we can say that B has the *power* relative to A, since B can effectively alter the *legal* relationship between the two. As Hohfeld clearly states, a power gives the holder a positive control over a legal relationship against another person's performance of duty. However, it has to be noted that in exercising one's power, the power can only be exercised in accordance with other prescribed rules. It does not mean an unlimited exercise of control over one's property.

Based on this understanding, L.A. Hart argues that *power* confers "ultimate sovereignty" to the *power-holder* (cited in Freeden 1991: 46). *Power* as a legal relation is different from a *claim-right* in that a *claim-right bearer* may be under obligation not to alter the relationship. For example, B's right to life may not be waived to absorb A when she or he commits murder. Inasmuch as B (though dead) may want to waive A's duty, she has no *power* to change A's legal position as a murderer. Similarly, judges have no *power* to set a criminal free insofar as they are constrained by the demands of justice, interpretative fidelity, legal rules, statutes and judicial review. In this case, *power* exists in connection with other rights and presupposes them (Jones 1994: 23).

Immunities

In the Hohfedian scheme, *immunity* is the opposite of *liability* and its correlative relation is *disability* – meaning that if I exercised my immunity, this exercise disables others from acting against me and imposes a *liability* on others to accept the consequences of exercising my immunity. For instance, in countries where the immunity principle is applied, the president is immuned from prosecution in matters relating to the discharge of his public office. In common parlance, it is often said that the president has the right to immunity, while in actual fact the president, by exercising his immunity, generates a corresponding relationship that *disables* other parties from acting against him/her – such as prosecuting him/her on matters related to the discharge of the duties of his office. The opposite of this relationship is that the president cannot suffer *liability* on matters relating to the course of discharging the duties of his office. For instance, if it happens that the president signs off a loan with a creditor (such as the IMF)[7] in his/her capacity as head of state, and if the loan is not repaid, the personal property of the president – even after leaving office – cannot be used to pay back the loan. The president's property is immuned from the *liability* of state loans.

In this sense, immunity resembles power in as far as it confers the freedom of the immunity-holder from the control or power of others. Just as power gives the power-holder a positive control over a legal relationship, "an immunity is one's freedom from legal power or 'control' of another as regards some legal relations" (ibid.: 60). For instance, a landowner has immunity from claims or control over his land by other parties. In exercising immunity over property, a person generates a correlated *liability* against other parties. In this sense "immunities include every respect in which I am not subject to another's power" (Jones 1994: 25). In our example, B has *immunity* as a right if, and only if, A has no *power* to change his/her relation with B. If, for instance, B's speech amounts to libel against A, B may have the *immunity* to exercise her right to speak constrained, relative to A. Thus, immunities, like power, are not absolute; they are relative to the specific relationship to which they apply.

The same applies to the common statement that the president has the right to appoint cabinet ministers – which in the Hohfeldian sense means that the president has the *privilege* to appoint his cabinet ministers and there is '*no-right*' against him/her doing so – unless of course the appointment procedures are not followed correctly, or if the person appointed is found unfit to hold the position he or she is appointed to. The opposite of this relationship is that the president has no duty to appoint any particular individual. Correlatively, there is no particular person who can claim, legally, to have a right to be appointed as a minister by the president; the president remains free to appoint anyone he

7 Often the minister of finance signs loan deals with the IMF, and he or she, as long as she/he is exercising the powers of his/her office, is immuned in his personal capacity from the liability which the incurred debt may entail.

or she thinks appropriate for the office. The Menzi Similane case in South Africa is one example where the president's appointment of a Director of Public Prosecution (director of the National Prosecuting Authorities, NPA) was declared by the Supreme Court of Appeal as "irrational and invalid", a judgement later confirmed by the Constitutional Court.[8] In this case it was not the president's privilege to appoint the director of the NPA which was nullified – the president still had the privilege to make the appointment; rather it was the constitutional requirement to appoint someone fit to hold the office of director of the NPA which was not met.

Looking at the four terms in Hohfeld's scheme it can be seen that he was bent on clarifying what should qualify as a *claim-right* by limiting the use of the term "right" to relations where claims are correlated with *duties*. Note that although Hohfeld seems to be concerned about individual claims and duties, this reasoning can be applied to claims and duties outside of individual relations, such that the state or any other collective can also be a *claim-holder* – just as it can also be a *duty-holder* – in a specific relationship.

Limitations of the Hohfeldian Scheme

Even though the Hohfedian classification of the different meanings of the term "right" helps to show that there are different ways in which the term can be used, it does not clarify the question of what meaning to adopt in different legal relationships. As Dworkin (1977) has noted, it seems that the term is used to explain *relations* rather than actually being explained itself. In fact to some extent the clarification is even more confusing and complex – as Hohfeld himself admits (see also Jones 1994: 13). Further, the Hohfeldian classification's narrow focus on *legal relations* leaves out other important meanings allotted to the term. In addition, the Hohfeldian analysis does not provide us with much help on the fundamental question of what having a right, in a broad sense, constitutes. Nevertheless, the Hohfeldian scheme is a useful reference point from which different usages of the term "right" – such as choice, power, privilege, title, benefit, sanctions, etc. – can be clarified.

Although the Hohfeldian scheme does not define the term "right", what is clear from it is that the term, if not properly distinguished, can stand in the place of a *privilege, power* or *immunity*. A right can be used to mean a *claim-right* (a right in the narrow sense), *privilege, power* or *immunity*; and in such cases confusion may arise. Although Hohfeld restricted his categorisation to legal relations and applications, his four categories help to illustrate the

8 See *Democratic Alliance* (DA) *v. President of South Africa & Others* (CCT 122/11) ZACC24: BCLR1297 (CC). (5 October 2012).

slipperiness of the term "right" – hence the need for a more guarded use of the term. However, these different meanings, to a large extent, reflect the "generous interpretation of the term *right* corresponding with its use in ordinary language" (Jones 1994: 13).

Application and Implications of the Hohfeldian Categories

Certainly, these different uses of the term "right" highlight the important fact that the way the term is understood influences the assertion made about rights; which in turn has a practical impact upon the fulfilment of human rights. Following on from this, it can be argued that the controversial nature of the concept of a *right* itself may be one of the factors that constrains the implementation of human rights – including the rights to water and food. It is for this reason that it becomes important to pay attention to the political and social meaning given to the term "right" at all levels of society. Here particular attention is paid to the meaning given to the concept of rights and to the understanding given to the term as "shared meaning" (Sederberg 1984). Though the meaning shared by a community may not be explicitly stated, it is often mediated or embodied in verbal – as well as non-verbal – responses, as well as actions taken and not taken.

In the context of the rights to water and food it is important to see if the use of the term "right" is applicable to the schemes discussed above. If one follows Hohfeld's strict sense of the term as a *legal claim* that is correlated with a duty, there is arguably some ground for regarding access to water and food as rights. The basis for the right to food is the Covenant (*ICESCR*), which has provided explicitly for the right to food; and since this Covenant is legally binding on all state parties (Courtis 2007), and since it also recognises the state as a duty-bearer with individuals and groups as beneficiaries (OHCHR 2004), it can be argued that the right to food, even in the strictest sense used by Hohfeld, is a claim-right – although this would only apply to citizens of the 166 UN member countries that have ratified the Covenant, including 49 African ones (see Horn 2009).

The right to water is not explicitly provided for in the Covenant, but its status as a *claim-right* can be affirmed indirectly on the basis of other international human rights instruments, specifically *CRC* and *CEDAW*. For countries that have recognised the rights to water and food in their Bill of Rights, there can be no question about the status of these two rights. We will come back to the implications of Covenant accession, signing and ratification in respect to the implementation of the rights to water and food in Chapter 7. For now it should be noted that although there has been a great deal of scepticism about the genuineness of ESCRs such as the rights to water and food, there are an amazing number of countries that have either implicitly or directly recognised them (Knuth and

Vidar 2011). As we shall see in Chapter 6, some 56 countries have explicitly recognised the right to food in their national constitutions, and an additional 106 countries have implicitly recognised this right. However, implementation has been slow in some and completely absent in most. Clearly the challenge is not only about the right being explicitly recognised; there is much more to the realisation of a right than mere recognition and legislation (Courtis 2007).

Theories of Rights

As noted in the previous chapter, the theoretical foundations of human rights have been questioned with some critics arguing that this is largely due to the lack of coherent, well-developed theories of rights. Some critics have argued that at the moment such a theory is underdeveloped or does not exist at all, and there is urgent need for "some theory and also for some proposed defense of any proposed theory" (Sen 2004: 317). Arguably, while theories of rights may clarify many issues and provide some defence of human rights, they may, however, not resolve all the debates surrounding human rights. Nonetheless, in the context of current human rights debates, there is need to elaborate theory or theories of human rights to provide the conceptual foundation. Amartya Sen, in "Elements of a Theory of Human Rights", sets out to outline what such theories would constitute and the key questions which need to be addressed. Although Sen describes his main task as presenting a theory and justification for a "general idea of human rights", he does not actually construct a theory of human rights as such; rather, he proposes elements what such a theory should contain. Further, contrary to Sen's assertion that there hasn't been a theory of rights as yet, there have been two major competing schools of thought on this topic: the *interest/benefit* theory of rights (Raz 1986) and the *choice/will* theory of rights (H.L.A. Hart 1982). Table 2.2 below summarises the key features of the two schools.

Interest/Benefit/Entitlement Theory of Human Rights

The *benefit* or *interest* theory of human rights asserts that a person will have a right only in matters that he or she has a strong interest or benefit, so as to reasonably merit assigning duties to other persons or parties. Joseph Raz (1986: 166), one of the main proponents of the interest/benefit theory of rights, argues that X has a right "if and only if X can have rights, and other things being equal, an aspect of X's well-being (his interest) is a sufficient reason for holding some other person(s) to be under a duty". Evidently, the basic claim of this theory deviates from the positivistic conception that sees rights as only those claims necessarily correlated with duties. As seen above, in the strict legal sense a person is said to have a right only

TABLE 2.2 *Two Theories of Rights*

Choice theory	Interest/Benefit theory
Components of the theory	
Main Proponent: L.A. Hart	Main Proponent: Joseph Raz
· Duty neither necessary nor sufficient	· Benefit/interest the condition for duty
· Duty implies ability to choose	· Focus on individual interest
· Right gives control over another's duty	· Focuses on well-being of the individual
· Protects individual autonomy	· Right prior to duty
· Right implies options/alternative	· Right without duty possible
LIMITATIONS	
· Unduly exclusive	· Leads to individualism
· Not all human beings can make choices	· Right and benefit not always joined
· Choice may be exercised wrongly	· No clear relation of duties and rights

SOURCE: COMPILED BY THE AUTHOR.

when there is a person(s) with a corresponding duty to the claim. According this strict legal view it will be absurd for a person to claim that he/she has a right when there is no one with a corresponding duty to ensure that the right-holder's claim is fulfilled. In a sense, the *interest/benefit theory* of rights goes beyond the right-duty correlation principle and recognises other possible situations where a person can have a claim – even in cases where there is not necessarily a distinct duty-bearer. Although analysts like Hohfeld would normally refer to such rights as privileges (Hohfeld 2005 [1919]: 41), there are many analysts, theorists and advocates of human rights who have been quite keen to use the term "right" and not "privilege" in such cases (see Feinburg 1973; Dworkin 1977; Raz 1986).

Rather than seeing duty as the basis for the existence of a right, this theory sees the identification of an important human interest as the ground for imposing duty (Jones 1994: 29). Recognising an important human interest/benefit in this theory is seen as the precondition for affirming a right and imposing duties, and not the other way round (Raz 1986: 166–7). In this school of thought, access to clean water and adequate food, to the extent that they constitute important vectors of human well-being, would be swiftly affirmed as genuine human rights.

Choice/Will Theory of Human Rights

The other theory of rights is the choice theory. This theory asserts that having a strong interest or benefit is neither a necessary nor a sufficient condition for the existence of rights (Jones 1994: 32). L.A. Hart (1961; 1982), one of the main proponents of the choice theory, argues that it is not always the case that a person's interest in something generates a right in that "thing". For Hart, a fundamental feature of a right is the ability to control a choice from possible alternatives – hence the *choice theory*. Operating within the legal positivist framework, Hart argues that the only time when we can assign someone a right is when that person is not under a duty to do or not to do what the duty stipulates (note that in the Hohfeldian scheme this relation amounts to a correlative of *power*, where the power-holder has control over the relationship). Hart argues that "it is inappropriate to speak of a right correlating with a legal duty where the beneficiary of the duty can exercise no choice over its performance" (in Jones 1994: 32). For instance, a crime victim cannot be said to have a right to pardon the offenders in the sense that the criminal offence falls under, and is controlled by, the criminal law procedures – regardless of what the victim may wish to do. According to this school of thought, in as far as a person has no control over something, even if one has the strongest interest or is envisioned to receive very important benefits, that person cannot be said to have a right. Thus, in the *choice theory*, a right exists only where an individual can exercise control over the performance of duty of another person. For instance, if A lends money to B, A has a right to what B owes him or her to the extent that A can choose to claim or abandon what B owes him or her. As Jones (1994) has observed, in the *choice theory* it is absurd to talk of rights under criminal law since it is only under civil law that people may have control over the performance of duties by other parties.

However, what is interesting in the *choice* theory of rights is that it is entirely possible to have rights independent of duties. But the narrow focus in this theory on the ability to make choices ignores one important aspect of rights understood as a valuable property which seeks to protect and enhance people's well-being (UNDP 2000). Further, attaching a right to the ability to make choices may exclude children and other persons whose ability to make choices is limited or impaired. Furthermore, even if an individual can make choices, the main question to be considered is whether those choices enhance the individual's well-being or have the potential to jeopardise other people's well-being in circumstances where choices made impact on other parties.

Although the *interest/benefit* theory may lead to individualism – where only the person's interest or benefit is taken into account – it seems to have a stronger argument that brings out the core values and goals of human rights; namely, securing the well-being and dignity of a person. Under the *interest/benefit* theory there is no doubt that accessing water and food would certainly qualify as rights in as far as people have strong interest in accessing these necessities. On the other hand, the practical implication of the *choice theory* on the rights to water and food is, at best, unclear. More importantly, the question of how these theories should be put into practice has been left hanging. Among the many brilliant authors on human rights, very few provide concrete ways by which, for instance, the rights to water and food can be turned into reality in the lives of people who find it difficult to secure these basic human needs. Debates so far have largely remained at the theoretical level, with little attention given to the practical implications of the different theoretical formulations of human rights (Banik 2008). In this instance, what is needed to elaborate on the question of rights is sharing the empirical experience of implementing them in different contexts. This experience will definitely clarify some of the theoretical debates, but also shed more light on how human rights can be used as effective instruments for social change.

Pre-conditions for Giving Effect to Rights

So far, there have been suggestions of conditions which need to be secured to facilitate the implementation of these rights. Gewirth (1996), for instance, suggests that there should be *suitable* institutions for the "effectuation" of rights in what he calls the "community of rights". In his view the effectuation of rights cannot, and should not, be left to the *market* or "private *charity*". Like Polanyi (1944), Gewirth argues that the market should be subordinated or embedded in society, and not society subordinated to the market.[9] According to Gewirth (1996: 59), when it comes to the effectuation of human rights, "markets cannot be relied on for this purpose because the persons in need of help do not have the economic resources to compete for the needed commodities".

Apart from proposing a social democratic welfare system as constituting a set of suitable institutions for the advancement and effectuation of human rights, Gewirth (1996) further argues that the state is the primary respondent to the rights of individuals. The proposed way in which the community of rights (the state) should achieve the *effectuation* of rights is through a "*political*" as well as an "*economic*" constitution, followed by the implementation of such constitutions (ibid.: 328).

9 Polanyi argues that the humane foundations of society require that the "self-regulating market" be subordinated to a "democratic society" (and not vice versa); that the market be embedded in society and not society in the market (1944: 234).

Gewirth's assertion that the state bears primary responsibility for respecting, protecting and fulfilling human rights – through the implementation of legislation and policies – has received widespread sympathy, especially within the UN human rights system. Gewirth defends this assertion on the basis that human rights, properly understood, logically imply that public attention be drawn to those who live in situations of severe deprivation. He calls this principle "*deprivation focus*", which, according to him, does not conflict with the principle of non-discrimination (ibid.: 110–11).

Human Rights Counter Critiques

The previous chapter introduced the various critiques of rights from cultural relativism to Marxist. In this section the counter critiques which attempt to defend the concept of human rights are briefly discussed. While for many legal and political philosophers and analysts defending human rights requires elaborating on the nature, scope, meaning and foundation of such rights, human rights advocates are mainly concerned with giving meaning to the entitlements contained in them. For human rights activists all over the world, rights are something they find attractive as tools for drawing political and moral attention to human suffering, and as tools for social change. They see human rights as instruments they can use to achieve some desirable social change; as tools for reframing, reimagining and contesting social, economic and political priorities. For such activists human rights are taken as "self-evident truths" which need little debate about what they are and what they imply.

However, this enthusiasm for human rights among activists overlooks the importance of debating various aspects of them – including the debate about the efficacy of rights as tools for social change. As noted in the preceding chapter, there are many critics of rights from many different angles – and these debates are not just about what meaning should be given to the term "right", or what should qualify as human rights. They are also about the basic foundations of rights and how they should be translated into practice. Fundamentally there are four main areas of debate: the legitimacy, relevancy, coherence and practicality of human rights. Below are some of the common counter critiques or responses to the critiques of human rights. The counter critiques below are discussed according to the five critiques outlined in the preceding chapter.

Universalism v. Relativism

In view of the relativist critique of human rights (see Chapter 1), the counter critique targets the relativists' main assumption that there are no universal human values, cultural practices and moral codes. The counter critique acknowledges that while cultural practices and moral values differ among different societies/communities even in the same country, there are some moral values and practices that are common *across* cultures. Proponents of this view argue that it is these common human values and practices which should be the basis of a human rights system. In cases where there is a fundamental clash of values between cultures (for instance the practice of polygamy and feminist discourse), it has been suggested that we should focus on what is common to all rather than dwelling on the differences (Hinz 2009). In this regard, some advocates of this view have observed that the cultural relativists often exaggerate the differences and underplay the commonalities that exist between cultures and societies (see Brown 2008). Most human rights advocates argue that a rigidly relativist position is just as untenable as a rigidly universalist one.

Furthermore, those who defend human rights argue that cultural relativism is built on the supposition that culture is static and impervious. It has thus been argued that an empiricist approach to culture, which the cultural relativists appeal to, reveals that cultures are neither static nor impervious; rather they are dynamic creations modelled and shaped by people's multiple experiences. Thus, if culture is seen as a dynamically evolving phenomenon it is possible to create space through which cultures can influence each other in the course of human interaction, thereby establishing an intersection which would be common to all interacting cultures. Such an interplay of cultures need not essentially entail disregard, disrespect, domination and disappearance of certain cultures; on the contrary, interacting cultures can enrich each other, consciously or unconciously, in a fruitful exchange (Harvey 2000: 88).

Despite the fact that the interacting cultures are different and need not be homogenised, there is also evidence that they do have many values in common – such that one cannot ignore the differences, just as one should not exaggerate the commonalities. In this debate, regretabbly, it seems that relativists and universalists "traffic in exaggeration, 'with relativists denying the possibility of cross-cultural understanding and their opponents denying the possibility of systematic untranslatability'" (Brown 2008: 368). An authentic evaluation of the relativist position begs the question of whose interest such a position defends. Is it the interest of the ordinary poor widow or some political ideology or class? As Booth (1999: 39) rightly observes, often defending culture serves "power interest" and "has very little to do with the interests of the poor peasants or serfs, the weak children, the oppressed women and the marginalized minorities". For example, whose interest does denying people access to water or adequate food serve?

Often the relativists' displeasure with the principle of universal human rights lies in the claim that much of what we have today as human rights is in fact a codification of Western cultural values. To pronounce such values as universal therefore amounts to cultural imperialism (Donnelly 2003: 41; Jones 1994: 214; Booth 1999: 54). This argument, in a purely logical sense, seems to be misleading in that it discharges an argument on the basis of geography and not the cogence or soundness of the premise. Surely an idea should not be dubbed morally repugnant because of its geographical origin. As Booth (1999: 52) points out, "[t]he most trivial point anybody can make about human rights is that they come from 'somewhere'", implying that geography is destiny. True, the values may have been articulated or have originated in the "West" but that is not the main issue; rather, the two key questions are: Do these values enhance human well-being in society? Are they useful in protecting the values which the community sees as important?

Similarly, the relativists' claim that universal human rights have no foundation – since there is no such thing as universal culture upon which the universality of human rights can be anchored – underplays, if not ignores, the empirical evidence. While it is undeniably true that there is no such thing as a universal culture in the sense of all cultures having a convergence of values, customs and moral beliefs, common aspirations among these different cultures are evident. To mention only a few obvious ones: love; charity; hospitality; compassion; care for the weak, the sick, the young, the elderly. These are just some of the examples which can be found across cultures, though their specific expressions may take various forms. As the *Human Development Report 2000* argues, all regions and cultures strive and celebrate respect for human dignity: all regions and cultures struggle against oppression, injustice, discrimination, inequality and other "human wrongs" (UNDP 2000: 12).

Universal-Particular Dialecticism

At this point, the relativists' position may be saved by turning to the dialectics between the particular and the universal; or to use Harvey's (2000: 83) terms, the *commonalities* and the *differences*. In this dialectic, the *particular* can help to understand the *universal* just as the universal defines and gives meaning to the particular. In other words, we allow the particular to flourish in order to enrich the universal; just as we allow the universal to broaden the particular. Such cultural cross-fertilisation, inevitably driven by the incessant waves of globalisation – though seeming riven with paradoxes and contradictions – "create opportunities and potentialities for progressive forms of political action" (Harvey 2000: 86). While globalisation, on the one hand, offers us "market value indexes" instead of humanity, emptiness instead of hope, international terror instead of life, and globalisation of misery and hopelessness instead of dignity, it has offered opportunities for global mobilisation of political action as evidenced in the surge in international campaigns concerning various human rights issues, environmental justice, poverty and the enslaving effects of capitalist development (ibid.: 73). Thus, it would be erroneous to conclude that the universal swallows up the particular, or that the particular obstinately resists the emergence of the universal. Such a configuration of the dialectical process between the particular and the universal, which the relativists propose, is not only simplistic but untenable in the current sociopolitical arrangement. What we know for sure now is that "what happens at one scale cannot be understood outside of the nested relationship that exists across a hierarchy of scales" (ibid.: 75). In this current social dynamism, commitment to one of the scales at the expense of the other is not as sufficient as it once might have been. Harvey (2000: 82), for instance, argues that in the current situation, focusing on the particular while disregarding the universal "appears far too simplistic to capture the intricacies of uneven spatiotemporal development as these now exist" (ibid.).

While recognising that human rights, due to their emphasis on the "universal", can easily become a vehicle for repression and domination, Harvey (ibid.: 91) still sees the universal human rights project as offering "spaces of hope" in the current stage of globalisation. He suggests three reasons why the universality of human rights offers hope in the context of the eminent contradictions and paradoxes brought about by globalisation. The first is that human rights create a platform for demanding institutional reform and overcoming deepening economic inequalities. The second is that environmental problems that require global regulations can seek refuge in the universalisation of concerns. The third is that the emergence of *common* voices protesting against social, economic and cultural frustration can only be pegged on the hooks of universal concerns. From the fact that uneven geographical development constrains and limits what we can become, Harvey (2000) contends that those who argue against universals are regrettably misguided. Although some leftists criticise the human rights project as a mere reformist strategy – since it relies on the tools of litigation rather than genuine revolution – throughout history human rights have provided a strong force for mass mobilisation, drawing on the politics of "memory solidarity" inspiring significant social changes and political commitments (Roithmayr 2001: 8–10).

Legal Positivism Counter-Critique

Most human rights activists agree that the legal positivist critique raises a fundamental question about what constitutes a *right*. However, human rights advocates note that because of its preoccupation with the punitive functions or aspects of law, legal positivism leaves out other basic functions and aspects of a legal system. In a critical way, taking such a narrow view of law or rights undermines the social purpose of law, and amounts to a grave mismatch with social realities. First, limiting "rights" to mere claims that can be legally enforced or institutionalised, overlooks the complexity of the social order. Thus, the simplistic view taken by mainstream legal positivists suffers from both inadequacy and incongruence with reality. In contemporary times, even authors with a strong positivist inclination, such as L.A. Hart, have acknowledged the practical limitations of positivism in its crusade to distinguish law from morality:

> Contemporary voices tell us we must recognize something obscured by the legal "positivists" whose day is now over: that there is a point of intersection between law and morals, or that what *is* and what *ought* to be are somehow indissolubly fused or inseparable, though the positivists denied it.
>
> L.A. HART 1983: 49–50

As will be illustrated in subsequent chapters, while codification and explicit statement is an important step towards the realisation of a given right, realisation of rights is not just about their institutionalisation, and nor is it just about parliamentary processes. The actual realisation of rights involves going beyond parliamentary proceedings and assertions. Unfortunately, as Baxi observes, many policy-makers and government officials "still insist on silly, or at times even wicked ways, that rights which do not prescribe 'a legal sanctions for non-performance' are not rights properly so-called" (2006: 9).

Ontological Counter-Critique

Counter critiques of the ontological critique focus on the validity of the claim that there is no such thing as *universal* human nature, *natural law*, or *human dignity*. Critics observe that it is one thing to deny the existence of human nature, but quite another to prove its non-existence. At the centre of this critique is the empiricist ontological argument that everything that is inaccessible empirically is ontologically void because it is intuitive, mythical and unascertainable, and therefore a "figment of human fiction" (Freeden 1991: 5). Simply stated, the argument essentially postulates that since we cannot prove nor disprove the existence of human nature, we cannot assert its existence either. But a quick look at this line of reasoning reveals the lop-sidedness of the argument; simply because we cannot prove something does not mean that such a thing does not exist. The only logical conclusion that is tenable here is that the argument is inconclusive.

More importantly, social values such as human rights do not have the same existence as physical objects in the universe – like black holes, tables or even mango trees. Social values are given a *derived existence*. Consequently, it is absurd to try to prove the existence of human rights in the same way as one would prove the existence of a black hole or dark matter or neutrons. Human rights exist because "they are recognized by a community of people, flowing from their own conception of human dignity, in which these rights are supposed to be inherent. Once they are accepted through a process of consensus building" they become *real* – at least they do for those who are party to that process (Sengupta 2000: 555). Dworkin makes the same point when he argues that rights are creatures of history and morality (1977: 87).

Cranstonian Counter-Critique

The generational approach to human rights seems to be attractive and influential within political and policy circles. Although some enthusiastic defenders of ESCRs are quick to dismiss the generational approach – arguing that it "has lost its critical, and as some will say, ideological edge" (Baxi 2006: 8) – the critique continues to provide "asylum" for many politicians who want to escape the responsibility of promoting the general welfare of their citizens. Giving the excuse of non-availability of resources continues to be an appealing and convincing rhetorical manoeuvre in many countries, particularly in the Global South.

However, at the theoretical level, the force of this critique is slowly being neutralised by recent international community pronouncements that have repeatedly reaffirmed human rights as indivisible, interdependent, inalienable and mutually re-enforcing. Among others, the *Vienna Declaration and Programme of Action* has unequivocally dismissed the notion of "classes" or "generations" of rights by stating that "[a]ll human rights are universal, indivisible and interdependent and interrelated. The international community must treat human rights globally in a fair and equal manner, on the same footing, and with the same emphasis" (1993: para. 5).

Further, as Harvey (2000: 87) has highlighted, the current stage of globalisation makes the split between civil and political rights and ESCRs impossible to sustain. In recent years it has been observed that even countries which were initially opposed to the adoption of these rights have begun to recognise and support them. For example, the US voted against the rights provisions contained in both the *1966 Covenant* and the 1986 *Declaration on the Right to Development*; but at the 1993 Second Vienna World Conference on Human Rights it was reported that the US supported these rights (Sengupta 2004: 179). As Mbaye (1991: 1054) has observed, the view that only civil and political rights are genuine human rights is obsolete: "Economic, Social and Cultural rights are not only recognized, but the emphasis placed on them has increased as international law has come to pay greater attention to the problems of decolonization and development." Even Cranston (1973: 75) acknowledges the growing attention that the international community has been paying to economic, social and cultural rights, noting that since 1945 the "[h]uman rights question has come to turn more and more on discussion of economic and social rights and less and less on political and civil rights". However, at the practical level the arguments of this critique hold a firm grip over many policy-makers and politicians, part of the reason for which is its being a remnant of the Cold War political and ideological tension.

Regarding the view that realising ESCRs requires a lot of resources, it has been pointed out that even civil and political rights require resources for them to be given effect (Sengupta 2000: 559). In practice it is not true that civil and political rights only require state forbearance or the state refraining from interfering with individuals' rights. For instance, the right to vote requires huge amounts of resources to organise elections to enable an individual to realise his or her right to vote. Similarly, the right to fair trial implies that the government has to spend money (in wages and salaries) to provide for legal services that make such a right possible. In addition, it has been observed that there is no automatic link between resource availability and the realisation of socio-economic rights (UNDP, 2000: 9). While the HDR 2000 acknowledges that the availability of resources creates an enabling environment for realising these rights, it is not always the case that countries with more resources realise them more than those with less.

Further, arguing that ESCRs are not genuine human rights on the grounds that the *ICESCR* does not have an individual complaint mechanism whereas the *ICCPR* does, is actually trivialising the issue (Dennis and Stewart 2004). Surely it is the case that the "absence of an individual complaint mechanism under the International Covenant on Economic, Social and Cultural Rights does not prevent these rights from being recognized and treated as human rights. Furthermore, a number of ESCRs (such as labour rights) are already protected in national law, and are justiciable before national courts" (Sengupta 2000: 558).

As for the argument that ESCRs are constrained by, or that their realisation is dependent upon, the availability of resources, there are two counter arguments. One is the position stated in the *Limburg Principles*: that resources should not be an excuse for not realising progressively the obligations that the rights engender. The *Limburg Principles* state that "[T]he obligations of progressive realization of rights exists independently of the increase in resources; it requires effective use of resources available"(para. 23). The other counter argument comes from the observation by the *HDR* (UNDP 2000) that there is no automatic link between resource availability and the realisation of ESCRs. Using the Human Development Index (HDI) as the proxy indicator of progressive realisation of these rights, it is apparent that resources, while they constitute a necessary condition, do not automatically translate in realising such rights (UNDP 2000). If that were the case, countries with the highest Gross National Income (GNI) per capita in 2013 (Qatar with US$133,713 and Liechenstein with US$86,587) would be top of the HDI rankings. But these countries are ranked 31 and 21 respectively on the HDI for 2013 (see UNDP 2014: 160, 196). The first ranked country according to HDI in 2013 was Norway, whose GNI per capita (US$62,858) was three-quarters that of Liechtenstein and Qatar; while the second ranked country (Australia) had a GNI per capita of just US$42,278 – less than a third that of Qatar. If the resource argument were to hold, we would expect Norway to be ranked far below Qatar and Liechtenstein.

Nonetheless, the Cranstonian critique continues to influence many policies that are adopted by governments around the world, especially in the Global South. But the current wide international recognition of ESCRs provides a starting point for both international and local civil society to lobby the international community and institutions to accord these rights the attention they deserve. Certainly, there is an emerging international political will which creates an enabling environment for lobbying the international community and individual states to give meaningful attention to ESCRs such as the rights to water and food.

Notwithstanding the Cold War politics under which the debate on the generational approach to human rights flourished, it has come to be widely acknowledged that if civil and political rights are to acquire any appreciable meaning, they have to be accompanied by ESCRs. Jones (1994: 163), for instance, points out that for people to enjoy civil and political rights, a certain level of material well-being, education, health and nutrition is indispensable. In more compelling terms, Vincent argues that the rights to basic human essentials such as the right to education, food, healthcare, clean water and sanitation are a prerequisite for enjoying civil and political rights: "A person deprived of subsistence, it has been often said, is insulted rather than dignified by a right to vote" (Vincent 1986: 78). To some extent, the motto of "one man one vote" should be preceded by "one man one bread" as a way of drawing attention to ESCRs (Shivji 1989).

The question that emerges at this stage is whether the controversial nature of the concept of human rights renders its implementation problematic. In other words, can the challenges of implementing human rights norms be attributed to the complexity or controversial nature of the concept of human rights?

Do the controversies discussed above pop up in the actual implementation and effectuation process? Such questions are difficult to answer in the abstract. Answers will only be provided by exploring the experience of implementing these instruments in particular cases. The next chapter looks specifically at one of the practical ways of giving effect to human rights, particularly ESCRs.

CHAPTER 3

Human Rights and Development

Building Bridges

The primary focus of human rights is to secure human dignity and promote human well-being. While the objectives of development vary, depending on the ideological orientation of the practitioner or implementing agent, there is some agreement that the ultimate goal of economic growth and development is the improvement of living conditions of all the people, especially the poor (Alston and Robinson 2005). In more recent times, there has been a convergence of views among theorists, policy-makers and practitioners that economic growth is not an end in itself, but a means to an end. Securing economic growth is now widely understood as creating an environment where human life can flourish, an environment where freedoms of people can be expanded. Seen from this angle, human rights and development strategies have a common ground, though in the past and in practice these two realms operated with a huge gulf between them, especially when it came to the practice of rights (UNDP 2000). However, since the 1990s, due to widespread dissatisfaction with the outcome of policies that adopted a narrow focus on a few economic variables, there has been a process of widening horizons beyond the traditional human rights and economic growth concerns within the human rights community and among development practitioners. "In the mid-1990s the human rights community began to engage more directly with their counterparts working on development issues and a movement began to promote [a] rights-based approach [RBA] to development" (Alston and Robinson 2005: 2). While commentators have applauded this merging of rights and development, some analysts are critical of such a marriage, noting that this may mean little in terms of the radical changes needed (Univ 2002; Slim 2002). In this chapter we look more closely at the origins, principles, value added and practical implications, as well as the challenges of, the RBA.

In the last two decades there has been a growing realisation and agreement that the "full realisation of human rights should be a vital goal of development" (Olowu 2009: 16). However, it is important to note that although many international organisations – especially within the UN system, as well as the NGOs and bilateral development agencies – have adopted and implemented the RBA in their operations, very few governments have actually adopted this approach explicitly. With particular reference to African governments, it has been observed that there is very low awareness of the RBA in particular, and ECSRs in general. A general observation has been made that the uptake of the RBA has been slow and far from being straightforward. This lack of awareness and

 | DOI 10.1163/9789004299559_004

slow uptake has been attributed to the fact that ESCRs have been "under-theorised and under-explored" in Africa (Olowu 2009: 6).

What is a Rights-Based Approach to Development?

Most ESCRs – such as the right to water, food, education, health, housing etc. – are often articulated within the rights-based approach (RBA) framework. While the RBA in its conception seeks to apply general human rights principles (which includes civil and political rights), this strategy is widely associated with ESCRs in both theory and practice. Many human rights activists and development practitioners who operate within the RBA framework conceive their work mainly as a struggle for the creation of a society where human dignity is upheld through the fulfilment of basic human needs such as access to water, food, education, healthcare, etc. (Offenheiser and Holcombe 2003). As the name suggests, the RBA is not a theory but a practical strategy for integrating human rights principles in development policy, programming, implementation, monitoring and evaluation. Although there have been efforts to develop common understandings and principles of the RBA, there is no single RBA framework; different organisations have conceptualised, and consequently applied, the RBA differently.

From the available body of literature and practitioners' experience, it is apparent that there is no single definition of the RBA. Although there appears to be an increase in the number of organisations, including government agencies, that are endorsing the RBA, there is no common understanding of what the RBA is among the different organisations and individuals who adopt this approach (see Nyamu-Musembi and Cornwell, 2004).[1] Even among the United Nations agencies, prior to the adoption of a common understanding document in 2003 there was (and maybe still is) a divergence of views about what the RBA essentially is and what its practical implications are (UNFPA 2004). For

1 For example, Care International defines the RBA as supporting "poor and marginalized people's effort to take control of their own lives and fulfil their rights, responsibilities and aspirations" (A. Jones 2005: 81). For other organisations, the RBA essentially means holding the state accountable (Robinson 2005); to other organisations such as Action Aid, the RBA is largely seen as a means of empowering people through participation. In fact, some development practitioners use the *rights based approach* interchangeably with the *human rights approach*. Eyben (2005) argues that the two are actually not the same in the sense that the human rights approach is more focused on international legal pronouncements while the rights-based approach is more flexible, encompassing general and broad human rights norms and a more practice-oriented approach (see Nyamu-Musembi and Cornwell 2004: 13).

example, Nyamu-Musembi and Cornwell (2004: 13) compiled a list of ten different international development agencies' understanding of the RBA, and all of them came up with a different notion. Jonsson (2005: 52) also observes that when it comes to what, excactly, constitutes an RBA, "there is a plethora of concepts that are very seldom explained, including human rights approach to development, rights-based approach to development, programming in human rights perspectives…and programming through a human rights lens".

Some analysts see the RBA as a component feature of the *Declaration on Right to Development* (DRD) such that it is listed as one of the "four basic operational elements of the DRD", which include Poverty Reduction Strategies (PRS), Development Compacts (DC) and Monitoring Strategies (Sengupta 2003: 235). Others see the RBA not just as a tool for poverty reduction, but as a way of comprehensively redefining the "aims and approaces to development" (Banik 2008). Still other analysts see the RBA as a new vision that broadens the conception of both human rights and development to the extent that this pushes human activists, development theorists and practitioners alike, "to think outside the box" (Offenheiser and Holcombe 2003: 74). For some donor countries and agencies, the RBA is often taken to mean that aid-receiving countries should show serious commitment to human rights; the recipient countries or communities, on the other hand, have understood the RBA as meaning that they have a right to be helped to meet the challenges they face (Thiis 1996; Arts 1996). There are other practitioners and analysts who see the RBA as a strategy for creating a platform on which people can collectively launch struggles for social change, a platform for challenging the structures and relations of power in society (Chapman *et al.* 2005).

As may be evident from the above discussion, not only are there differences in the way the RBA is conceptualised, the approach is loosely used to encompass many other things. This diversity in the way the RBA is conceptualised poses a challenge when it comes to isolating its main features, and, more especially, when it comes to translating the RBA into practical programmes and interventions. A study that examined the experience of an RBA among practitioners from different organisations and countries observe that "[w]hile interest in rights-based approach and participatory approaches is widespread, nearly all of the organisations and individuals we spoke with seem to be struggling with the practical implications" (VaneKlasen *et al.*, 2004: 2). Differences in views about what the RBA actually is, are not just limited to the conceptual debates, but extend to the practicality of operationalising the approach. Nonetheless, there have been efforts to identify some of the main features that are common among these different conceptions and practice of the RBA.

Within the UN system, efforts have been made to adopt a common understanding of the RBA. In 2003, at a meeting of several UN Agencies, a *Common Understanding* document and definition of an RBA was adopted.[2] However, in this document the RBA is so broadly defined that it can convey different things to different people. Be that as it may, there seems to be some common sympathy that the RBA is a practical approach that seeks to adopt and integrate human rights standards, norms and principles derived from international human rights instruments into development cooperation, programming and technical assistance.

Broadly, the RBA within the UN system means that all UN specialized agencies take into account human rights, and incorporate human rights norms and principles in their operations (Univ 2004). For example, whether the agency is the Food and Agriculture Organisation (FAO), the World Health Organisation (WHO), UNESCO, UNDP or UNICEF, each are required to incorporate human rights principles within their respective programmes and policies from formulation through to implementation, monitoring and evaluation. The RBA in this instance is not just limited to incorporating human rights norms and principles; it also means that each agency has to review its development efforts within the framework of fulfilling basic human rights. This requires asking questions like: has the work of FAO enhanced the realisation of the right to food among the people affected by its policies and programmes? Adoption and implementation of human rights norms, and promoting and fulfilling of human rights among UN agencies, is expected to be monitored by the Human Rights Council (Formerly the Commission on Human Rights); and in the case of the rights to water and food, monitoring and reporting any violations of these rights by UN agencies should be directed to the Committee on Economic, Social and Cultural Rights (CESCR).

Whether these agencies implement the RBA as defined in the *Common Understanding* document is beyond the scope of this chapter. Here it suffices to note that according to the document, UN agencies should apply the principles of accountability, participation, equality, progressive realisation and non-discrimination in their work; and that compliance with these should be monitored by civil society organisations.

Within the UN system it has been observed that the most distinctive feature of the RBA – whether it applies to poverty reduction, HIV/AIDS, orphans, food production, women's health, water services, education, social development programmes etc. – is the anchoring of all these works on the norms and values contained within the international human rights instruments. In this framework:

2 The *Common Understanding* is available at: www.hreoc.gov.au/social_justice/conference/engaging_communities/un_common_understanding_rba.pdf.

> A human rights approach is explicit about its normative framework: international human rights. Underpinned by universally recognized moral values and reinforced by legal obligations, international human rights provide a compelling normative framework for the formulation of national and international policies, including poverty reduction strategies (PRSS).
>
> OHCHR 2004: 1

Defining the RBA in this way begs the question: what are these international human rights norms? Within the UN system a list of what constitutes the fundamental human rights principles has been compiled – although there are, sometimes, differences in the composition of the list. The common five fundamental human rights principles adopted by the UN HRC include empowerment, accountability, non-discrimination and equality, participation, and progressive realisation. Each of these principles is discussed in more detail later in the chapter.

Why the RBA?

At this stage, it is perhaps important to ask the question: why the RBA? As would be expected, different organisations give different reasons as to why they adopt the RBA and not other approaches like the basic needs approach, the capability approach, and the legal empowerment approach, etc. One of the common reasons cited for adopting the RBA by many organisations is the view that incorporating human rights into development work changes both the process and the goals of development; meaning that the RBA changes the way of thinking about, doing, and delivering, development. Other analysts have argued that bringing human rights into the development discourse forces one to shift from state-centric approaches – which see the state as the guarantor and protector of rights – to an approach that focuses on changing the way individuals perceive themselves vis à vis the state and other actors (Jochnick 1999). Other analysts argue that adopting the RBA challenges neoliberal extremism and that it provides a framework for holding actors such as the state and multinational corporations accountable for their actions (Offenheiser and Holcombe 2003). It has also been observed that the RBA provides space for the spontaneous emergence of social movements concerned with gender issues, landlessness, indigenous people and minority rights, etc. (IDS 2003).

Generally there seems to be wide endorsement of the idea that integrating human rights and development policy provides more effective ways of giving attention to issues of poverty, inequality, human suffering and deprivation – although this view has been contested by many who are critical of the RBA (Univ 2002). As noted above, since the mid-1990s there has been a strong shift towards integrating human rights principles in development strategies as a way of creating synergies that did not exist when the two approaches operated separately (Hunt *et al.* 2003).

Looking at development literature prior to the 1990s, it is evident that human rights and development were regarded as separate and distinct realms. Although it is not at all clear what motivated the initiative of integrating human rights within development planning and programme implementation, the *Human Development Report* (HDR) 2000 summarises the underlying justification:

> [T]he ideas of human development and those of human rights are linked in a compatible and complementary way. If human development focuses on the enhancement of the capabilities and freedoms that the members of a community enjoy, human rights represent the claims that individuals have on the conduct of individual and collective agents and on the design of social arrangements to facilitate or secure these capabilities and freedoms.
>
> UNDP, 2000: 2

During the 1990s many organisations began to accept the view that human rights are an indispensable ingredient of the development process. The rationale for this was that often impoverishment, indigence and deprivation lead to denial of people's freedom and dignity; just as human rights abuses often lead to similar outcomes. In this context it has been argued that where human rights are integrated within development efforts, the two complement each other to enrich the strategy.

While human rights seek to protect human dignity and basic freedoms, development seeks to advance people's freedom by improving their capabilities and well-being. In this sense, "[w]hen human development and human rights advance together, they reinforce one another – expanding people's capabilities and protecting their rights and fundamental freedoms" (UNDP 2000: 2). When viewed from this complementary perspective, the RBA is founded on the idea that "human development is essential for realizing human rights, and human rights are essential for full human development" (ibid.). In principle, this view can have few detractors; but in practice, the practicality of forging these linkages is far from being realised (Robinson 2005). This becomes more evident when we look at the specific case of the rights to water and food.

The RBA: Background and Origin

Struggles for human rights and freedoms have a long history in many societies. In Africa, human rights were central to the liberation struggles across the continent (Zeleza 2006). However, the linking of human rights to issues of poverty, deprivation and underdevelopment is something that arose out of the search for alternative ways of dealing with widespread poverty and widening inequality during the 1980s and 1990s. As noted earlier, the RBA evolved from a search for alternative development strategies during the 1990s once it became clear that the conventional model of "growing the economy first" had proved unable to address the many social issues including hunger, the widening gap between the rich and the poor, as well as a lack of basic services for the majority of the people in the Global South. However, as an alternative strategy, the RBA does not have a particular date when it started or when it was officially proclaimed.

Some authors point to the reliance on human rights by the liberation movements of the 1950s and 1960s, as well as the appeal to human rights by those who were trying to change the international economic order though initiatives such as the New International Economic Order (NIEO) of the early 1960s and 1970s, as examples of an RBA (Mohan and Holland 2001; Nyamu-Musembi and Cornwall 2004). Other analysts trace the origins of the RBA back to the 1948 *Universal Declaration of Human Rights* (*UDHR*). Analysts writing about the African experience in particular have noted that the adoption of the RBA among NGOs and donors working on the continent can be traced to the 1990s when activists began to draw attention to the deplorable conditions in which many people lived (Mohan and Holland 2001).

However, the common view is that the RBA became dominant as a development framework that links human rights to issues of poverty, inequality and vulnerability during the course of the 1990s. Hunt *et al.* (2002) observe that the UN Secretary General's announcement in 1997 that all UN agencies and organisations should integrate human rights into their work, marks the official beginning of efforts to integrate human rights in development work. Similarly, Alston and Robinson (2005) trace the practice of mainstreaming human rights in development programming and policy-making to the former UN Secretary General, Kofi Annan's 1997 appeal for UN agencies to integrate human rights principles and values in their work. Nyamu-Musembi and Cornwall (2004) speak of the rights-based approach emerging in the 1990s, and gathering momentum on the eve of the World Summit on Social Development in 1995. Belinda Calaguas (1999) also recalls the RBA "gaining ground" among donor countries and development NGOs during the 1990s.

Factors Attributed to the Emergence of the RBA

One of the many reasons offered in the literature to account for the emergence of the RBA during the 1990s was the growing concern around poverty and human suffering in many low income countries occasioned by programmes and strategies which focused purely on promoting economic growth as the best way to overcome poverty and underdevelopment. Policies which were broadly formulated under the *Washington Consensus* framework during the 1980s are seen by many as responsible for increasing poverty and human suffering, particularly in the Global South. Serious concerns about poverty, hunger, growing inequality and the failure of public policies in the Global South to provide basic services and welfare to vulnerable groups led many to question the efficacy of the *Washington Consensus* paradigm (Stiglitz 1998). Other factors that are attributed to the emergence of the RBA during the 1990s include the series of UN summits, mainly: the World Summit on Sustainable Development in Rio de Janeiro in 1992; the Vienna Conference on Human Rights (1993); the World Conference on Women in Beijing (1994); the World Summit on Social Development (1995); and the World Food Summit (1996) – all of which were seeking to respond to the crisis of the 1990s.

More pertinent was the growing critique of the mainstream economic policies promoted by the World Bank and the IMF in poor countries during, the 1980s. As a result of this dissatisfaction with mainstream development strategies, many organisations working in the Global South started to seek ways to secure economic growth while at the same time protecting the lives of the vulnerable and weak in society. Criticisms such as those expressed by UNICEF (1987) – which called for "adjustment with a human face" – prompted the search for alternative development paradigms. Other UN agencies such as the UNDP's work and focus on human development and the capability approach also gave impetus to the idea that human development and economic growth are in fact two sides of the same coin. The publication of the first *Human Development Report* in 1990 (UNDP 1990) drew attention to the fact that economic growth could be enhanced by focusing on human development; that economic growth without solid human capital is difficult to achieve in a sustainable manner.

Broadly speaking, it has been noted that although the principles underlying the rights approach are not new, the adoption and integration of these principles into the development processes began in the early 1990s, gaining ground during the mid-1990s in the build-up to the Copenhagen Social Development Summit of 1995 (see Nyamu-Musembi and Cornwall 2004; OHCHR 2002; Andreasson 2003).

Some human rights practitioners and analysts link the RBA to the 1986 UN *Declaration on the Right to Development* (see Sengupta 2003), and in particular *Article 1*, which clearly indicates the link between human rights and development. This is often cited as the foundation of the RBA:

> The right to development is an inalienable human right by virtue of which every human person and all peoples are entitled to participate in, contribute to, and enjoy economic, social, cultural and political development, in which all human rights and fundamental freedoms can be fully realized.

Prior to the 1990s human rights and development were seen as unrelated fields, as the *Human Development Report* 2000 notes:

> Until the last decade human development and human rights followed parallel paths in both concept and action – the one largely dominated by economists, social scientists and policy-makers, the other by political activists, lawyers and philosophers. They promoted divergent strategies of analysis and action – economic and social progress on the one hand, political pressure, law reform and ethical questioning on the other.
>
> UNDP, 2000: 14

At this point it is important to note two things. First, this approach did not start as a deliberate, official, planned strategy – it was started as a result of experiences of working in developing countries, mainly by international development agencies, multilateral development institutions and NGOs. Second, the initiative to integrate human rights and development was not started by the "mainstream international human rights organisations" but rather by a caucus of "development" and "humanitarian" NGOs (Nyamu-Musembi and Cornwall, 2004: 10). It has been observed that many mainstream human rights NGOs were reluctant to adopt the RBA for fear that such a move would compromise their support and funding (Offenheiser and Holcombe 2003). However, the RBA is a predominantly NGO-driven development strategy. Very few governments and bilateral development agencies in both the developed and developing world actually talk about, let alone, implement the RBA.[3] Similarly, the World Bank and the IMF, until recently, were reluctant to integrate human rights in their activities (Danino 2005).

3 For instance, at the DFID meeting of 2003, out of a staff of 25 development practitioners only two had heard of the Right to Development and the RBA (Nyamu-Musembi and Cornwall 2004: 9).

Broadly speaking, integrating human rights into development planning, programming, monitoring and evaluation has a strong appeal to the many development and human rights practitioners who are looking for new ways of doing and delivering development. As mentioned earlier, UNICEF's (1987) idea of "adjustment with a human face" is just one example of the attempts to refocus the objectives of development from narrow preoccupation with macroeconomic fundamentals to taking stock of the consequences of development strategies. At the UN level, the adoption of the *Declaration on the Right to Development* (*DRD*) in 1986 by UN General Assembly *Resolution 41/128* represented a recasting of development with a focus on human development as the ultimate objective of economic policy and sociopolitical reforms.[4] However, some critics doubt whether an RBA is radical enough to constitute a credible alternative to mainstream development thinking. Critics of the RBA often argue that "little more than the language of development has changed" (Tsikata 2004).

The RBA Principles: Finding the Common Thread

The fact that there are various conceptions and definitions of the RBA does not mean that the water is muddy; there are common elements that are widely acknowledged to be at its core. As noted above, what seems to be common to many conceptions of the RBA is the use of human rights norms as the standard on which development programmes, projects and policies should be conceptualised, implemented and assessed. Mary Robinson (2001), former UN High Commissioner for Human Rights, captures the core of the RBA when she argues that "[t]he rights-based approach integrates the norms, standards and principles of the international human rights system into the plans, policies and processes of development". Emphasis here is laid on integrating human rights norms in development planning, process, programmes, implementation, monitoring and evaluation. While the norms that have been adopted as the core components of an RBA differ from organisation to organisation, as stated earlier, five human rights principles are common in most RBA formulations and applications. These are: accountability, empowerment, equality and non-discrimination, participation and progressive realisation, and I will now look at each of these in more detail below.

4 Arjun Sengupta (2003), the UN independent expert on the Right to Development (RTD), sees the RBA as one component of the RTD framework.

Accountability

Accountability is not a new concept in development discourse and practice. Earlier approaches to development such as the basic needs approach, livelihood approach, and the redistribution and growth strategies all mentioned accountability as an important ingredient in the development process. In developing countries in particular, accountability of states and other actors – including NGOs (local and international) – has been a defining concept in development practice. Accountability as a human rights principle in the RBA is thus not limited to public institutions; it includes NGOs, CSOs, multinational corporations, UN agencies, bilateral and multilateral development agencies, etc. The Office of the High Commissioner for Human Rights (OHCHR) clearly states that "monitoring and accountability procedures should not only extend to states, but also to global actors – such as the donor community, intergovernmental organisation, international NGOs and TNCs – whose actions bear upon the enjoyment of human rights in any country" (OHCHR 2002).[5]

The main thrust of this principle is that these actors should be held to account for their decisions, lack of decisions, actions and non-actions in accordance with international human rights norms and values (OHCHR 2004). The principle of accountability's main focus is not to find fault in the implementation of norms but to draw attention to the duties and responsibilities of various actors under international human rights rules and standards. In this sense the principle of accountability seeks to assist actors to fulfil their duties and responsibilities under various international human rights instruments.

Robinson (2001) refers to accountability as the "defining attribute of human rights in development". Similarly, the OHCHR notes that "the most important source of added value in the human rights approach is the emphasis it places on the *accountability* of policy-makers and other actors whose actions have an impact on the rights of people" (OHCHR 2002: 23). The basic reasoning behind the principle of accountability rests on the notion of government as trustee – entrusted by citizens to oversee public resources, welfare, security and public order. Essentially, the state administers public resources gathered through various

5 Despite the insistence by the UN on having the IFIs consider the impact of their policies and programmes on human rights, the World Bank and the IMF have consistently denied that human rights are part of their mandate. Justification for this position is based on the famous Article IV (10) of the Articles of Agreement – which the Bank has interpreted as prohibiting any involvement in issues that are political in nature: such as human rights. Most especially during post-MacNamara era, this position has been defended viciously by the Bank's legal advisors. However, contradictions have been noted – especially in recent years when the Bank has been championing the Good Governance campaign (see Gathii 2001; Nyamu-Musembi and Cornwall, 2004: 24).

sources – mainly taxation of individuals and private sector operations – on behalf of the public. Thus, it is only right that the public know how the resources entrusted to the state are utilised (Diokno 1999: 28). But this is just one level at which accountability is required. At a more fundamental level, accountability entails transparent public conduct and procedures. Accountability in this sense is a pillar of democracy and good governance. Mark Brown, for instance, asserts that "accountability in the use of funds and accountability to people's needs are also an integral dimension to pro-poor governance" (in Hunt *et al.* 2003: 12). Thus, accountability as a human right principle or norm emphasises not only accountability in the use of public resources, but also the duty to account for public conduct – including decision-making processes which may not necessarily involve the use of resources. What the norm of accountability presupposes is a set of adequate institutions and mechanisms which make it possible for the public to hold all public actors accountable. Otherwise the duty to account becomes no less than "window-dressing" (OHCHR 2002: para. 8). Institutions essential for effective accountability include an active civil society, and independent media, and autonoums statutory bodies like the public protector/ombudsman – which can all be effective vehicles for giving meaning to the process of accountability.

There are different mechanisms though which the principle of accountability can be implemented. While the nature of the mechanism for implementing it depends on many factors – such as the nature of the issues concerned, and whether the actors involved are municipal, national, regional, state, non-state or bilateral, or multilateral institutions or corporations – there are four common types of mechanism for implementing accountability. These are:

> judicial (e.g. judicial review of executive acts and omissions), quasi-judicial (e.g. ombudsmen, international human rights treaty bodies), administrative (e.g. the preparation, publication and scrutiny of human rights impact assessments) and political (e.g. through parliamentary processes).
>
> OHCHR 2004: 16

In this regard, a rigid conceptualisation of human rights as legal claim-rights (in the Hohfeldian sense) can lead to frustration; and often stifles any creative way of giving effect to rights such as the rights to water and food. Mechanisms for giving effect to human rights should be flexible depending on the prevailing circumstances. Which mechanism to adopt can only be decided after due consideration of all the relevant facts, and the context in which the principle is to be applied. In certain circumstances a judicial mechanism may be necessary; in other situations, scrutinising the actions and omissions of the actors may be all that is required. As we shall see later, for many human rights the UN

Human Rights Council is open to hearing and receiving complaints from individuals, civil society groups, and even state institutions.[6] In most cases civil society groups initiate the process of checking the actions and omissions of state institutions and other actors. For instance, in the case of the right to food, the CSO may request the state to provide information about the steps it has taken to ensure that it has met its stipulated obligations under the Covenant. A good example is the Indian case of the right to food (see Ahluwalia 2004). Effective implementation of the principle of accountability requires active participation of civil society in its broadest sense (Chitonge 2006).[7] Civil society's role in securing a development process that ensures people's human rights are not sacrificed for pursuit of narrow social and political interests is an indispensable notion of the RBA. As Olowu (2009) has observed, it is difficult to give effect to ESCRs without an active civil society.

Here it must also be stressed that accountability in the RBA should be distinguished from its rhetorical forms embellished in the good governance propaganda (Univ 2002) that often implies developing countries are accountable to donors, creditors, or the international financial institutions in a top-down manner. Accountability as a human rights principle does not just impose an obligation on the outcome of a development process; it also imposes obligations on the conduct of the policy-makers and development agencies (Salomon 2003; Thiis 1996). The importance of this point lies in the view that accountability offers individuals, NGOs, and other civil society groups in general, an opportunity to assess the extent to which duty-bearers have fulfilled or not fulfilled their duties.

6 Both the *ICCPR* and the *ICESCR* provide guidelines on complaints procedures and requests for information and reporting mechanisms; which are further elaborated upon by the specific committees and *General Comments*. Most of the complaints procedures, however, are included under the optional protocols, and the relevant treaty bodies act as quasi-judicial bodies that receive and investigate complaints.

7 The term "civil society" can have different meanings. In this work, I use the liberal Hegelian notion of civil society as any form of organisation between the family and the state; any organisation including opposition parties, trade unions, social movements, and other associations that are non-governmental in nature (Veltmeyer 2004). Using this view of civil society fits well with the rights approach, which emphasises participation of any organisation in any activities in society (Tabbush 2005). A similar notion of civil society is evident in the neo-Gramscian conception of civil society (ibid.). Under this notion of civil society, the main function of the "civil", in general, is to act as the conscience of society in socioeconomic and political matters. Demand for accountability of state officials has become the main way that civil society pushes for social and political reform – not only at the national level, but also at the global level, especially since the beginning of the 1990s (Veltmeyer 2004).

In general, genuine accountability challenges the way power is configured and exercised in society (Gready and Ensor, 2005). This is probably one of the reasons why accountability in particular, and the RBA in general, are often unpopular principles in most corridors of power. Most importantly, this is the reason why most governments – although having committed themselves to human right norms – are unwilling to implement the actual meaning of what they have committed themselves to.

Participation

Like accountability, participation has been part of the *realpolitik* of development discourse and practice since the 1970s. However, in mainstream development politics, participation has been advanced as a way of appearing politically correct. Since the early 1970s, with the advent of Participatory Rural Appraisals (PRAs) and the Participatory Poverty Assessment (Chambers 1983), participation has been used as a currency for performing many functions. For instance, the Basic Needs Approach[8] of the late 1970s, the drawing up of PRSPs in the developing world, as well as many of the development policy documents, have all ridden on the wings of participation. A sister word to participation, in some discourses, is community ownership – which often mean different things to different people. For example, the World Bank in the PRSP emphasises participation and local ownership of programmes (Craig and Porter 2003), despite the fact that the programmes themselves are drawn up by Washington DC-based development "experts" (Jubilee South 2000).

Participation as a human rights principle goes beyond the mere *formalism* that is often exhibited in the various official processes by which people are asked to participate in discussing something that is already decided. As a human right principle, participation requires "active and informed participation" of the poor, especially "in the formulation, implementation and monitoring" of public decisions that affect their lives (OHCHR 2002: para. 10). So the right to participate generates a duty on policy-makers to ensure that people are not just consulted, but that people's contributions are reflected in policies, programmes and decisions taken.

From a human rights point of view, participation becomes a way through which rights can be asserted, articulated, contested and claimed. For it is by participating in the sociopolitical processes that the participating individual or members of the community create *space* in which they can express, advocate,

8 Ghai *et al.* (1977) have described participation as one of the "basic elements" of the basic needs approach. People were asked to participate in the selection of basic needs, although the process of how to identify such needs was not integrated into the strategy.

lobby and claim their interests. Participation, in a sense, is a way of reinforcing the old idea of citizenship (Gaventa 2002); it is a means to radical democratic politics. Fulfilment of other human rights – such as the right to freedom of speech, or freedom of expression – creates an environment in which the right to participation can be given effect.

The principle of participation in the RBA is justified on the understanding of human beings as *agents* endowed with dignity and the freedom to make choices. In this sense, participation is not just a social activity to be valued as a means to some end, but rather as a fundamental human right that enhances basic human rights values such as equality, human dignity, freedom and self-worth. Understood from this angle, participation becomes critically important – not only as a means to achieving the goals of development, but as a safeguard against decisions and policies that may be harmful to the interests of members of the community, especially the poor (OHCHR 2002).

Of course, this is a challenge for any government that takes this norm seriously since it will certainly involve going back and forth to the people and the community more generally at every level of decision-making. Further, for people to be able to participate effectively, information, discussion fora, knowledge of the policy or programme being discussed, and other enablers, should be made accessible. In other words, the realisation of the right to participate is contingent upon, and influenced by, the realisation of other rights[9] such as the rights to information, education, freedom of speech, assembly, conscience, etc. Participation in the absence of these enablers often turns out to be a mere talk shop in which bureaucrats seize the opportunity to fulfil their job descriptions. Thus, implementing the principle of participation in an RBA requires that people, especially the poor, are treated not as "objects of charity" but as "active participants" and beneficiaries of the process of development (Offenheiser and Holcombe 2003: 4).

Progressive Realisation

A rights-based approach to development does not create an obligation that requires an immediate realisation of all human rights; realistically, it is impossible to realise some of them immediately. This, however, does not make human rights, especially ESCRs, idle claims. The principle of progressive realisation does not mean that the rights in question should be left to a time when resources are "abundant". Rather, it requires the state to take *immediate* necessary measures towards the realisation of the right in question, though within

9 It is in this sense that human rights are interdependent, indivisible and complementary (See *Vienna Declaration and Programme of Action* 1993).

the means and resources available to it. *General Comment 3*, which outlines and explains "the nature of the duty of states parties" to *ICESCR* expands on the meaning of this principle:

> The concept of progressive realization constitutes a recognition of the fact that full realization of all economic, social and cultural rights will generally not be able to be achieved in a short period of time. Nevertheless, the fact that realization over time, or in other words progressively, is foreseen under the Covenant should not be misinterpreted as depriving the obligation of all meaningful content. It is on the one hand a necessary flexibility device, reflecting the realities of the real world and the difficulties involved for any country in ensuring full realization of economic, social and cultural rights. On the other hand, the phrase must be read in the light of the overall objective, indeed the *raison d'être*, of the Covenant which is to establish clear obligations for State parties in respect of the full realization of the rights in question. It thus imposes an obligation to move as expeditiously and effectively as possible towards that goal. Moreover, any deliberately retrogressive measures in that regard would require the most careful consideration and would need to be fully justified by reference to the totality of the rights provided for in the Covenant and in the context of the full use of the maximum available resources.
>
> CESCR 1990: para. 9

Contrary to the argument common among critics of ESCRs that progressive realisation can be an escape route for the state to delay serious commitment to these rights, the state has a clearly defined duty *not* to delay the formulation, adoption and implementation of relevant measures and programmes. In this instance, the lack of a programme or measures that address the right to water or food cannot be justified by hiding behind the principle of progressive realisation.[10]

Regarding measures that a state party to the Covenant should take, *General Comment 3* stipulates that they "should be *deliberate, concrete* and *targeted* as clearly as possible towards meeting the obligations recognized in the Covenant" (*CESCR* 1990: para. 2). Accordingly, when implementing the RBA the question that should be asked about any right is whether there is a programme that aims at realising that particular right – such as the right to water or food – and whether that programme is concrete, deliberate, targeted and reasonable.

---

10 Critics of socioeconomic rights have often pointed to *progressive realisation* in the *ICESCR* – which is absent in the *ICCPR* as a major difference between these two sets of rights.

In reality, however, the obligation to realise ESCRs is often side-tracked by the generational or Cranstonian type of argument, i.e. that there are no resources available to give effect to these rights. In terms of the progressive realisation principle, inadequacy of resources should not be an excuse for failing to comply with the obligations under the Covenant – which includes the obligation to take measures. The *Limburg Principles* clearly refute the ploy utilised by many state parties to the Covenant (especially those in the Global South), to hide behind the curtain of scarce resources: "[T]he obligations of progressive realization of rights exists independently of the increase in resources; it requires effective use of resources available" (*Vienna Declaration and Programme of Action* 1993: para. 23). Progressive realisation, therefore, is not something that should be targeted when there are enough resources to do so; rather it is something that should be started with what ever is available. Taking concrete, targeted and deliberate steps can be started with as little as $100, just as it can be done with $750 zillion.

What should be stressed in the RBA, though, is that the steps taken should be reasonable, concrete, and pertinent to a given right, considering the resources available. In addition, the principle of progressive realisation demands effective monitoring of selected indicators and national benchmarks (Hunt *et al.*, 2002: 17), such that it not only creates an obligation of a *process* or *measure*, but also an obligation of an *outcome*[11] (Osmani 2003). The monitoring of progress made on agreed indicators and benchmarks creates a background upon which the principle of accountability can be applied. In this sense, accountability is intricately linked to progressive realisation as well as participation.

Equality and Non-Discrimination

The principle of equality is central to the concept of human rights (Hunt *et al.* 2002). Equality as a human rights principle is affirmed by all major international human rights documents, including the *Universal Declaration of Human Rights* (*UDHR*) and the *Declaration on Right to Development* – such that little explanation is offered as to what the equality principle means in the real world where people are actually very different and unequal in many respects (Sen 1992). Arising from the principle of equality is the norm of non-discrimination.

11 The independent expert on the right to development argues that the it does not generate the obligation to a particular outcome – it only creates an obligation of a *process* of development; that is, an obligation to adopt and set in motion a particular development process (see Sengupta 2003). But, as a number of writers have highlighted, a right to a process is almost meaningless unless it is coupled with the right to an outcome of some sort (see Osmani 2003).

Justification for equality and non-discrimination are based on the natural law notion of human rights mentioned in Chapter 1. The argument is that although people are different in size, height, age, gender, wealth, income, ability, intellectual capacities, social status, property ownership, etc., they all have some *inherent* dignity and worth by virtue of being members of species *homo sapiens*. Consequently, the equality referred to is not the equality of external or physical qualities; it is based on a moral value attributed to every human person regardless of their physical or social disparities.

As a human rights principle, equality refers to equality of opportunity in the distribution of resources; as well as a means of livelihood (Rawls 1971). However, the principle adopts a bias towards the poor and the vulnerable, without prejudicing other groups. OHCHR points out that the "international human rights normative framework has a particular preoccupation with individuals and groups who are vulnerable, marginal, disadvantaged or socially excluded" (2002: para. 9). In this regard equality entails equity in that the most deprived would have a weightier claim on public resources. The justification for this bias is that often it is the poor whose rights are not likely to be realised; it is often the vulnerable groups that are discriminated against and marginalised (OHCHR 2002; Hunt *et al.* 2003). Diaz (2002) makes the same point, arguing that the RBA focuses on the marginalised, the poor and the powerless because these are the groups (or individuals) whose rights are most at risk and their development prospects are low. Theoretical justification for taking a bias towards the poor has been elaborated though the "*deprivation focus*" principle discussed in Chapter 1. Similarly, the Rawlsian "*difference principle*" also supports the approach of focusing on the poor while not disadvantaging the non-poor (Rawls 1971: 68).

Adopting an RBA demands that attention be given to poor and vulnerable groups, such that policies and programmes focus on those sections of the population whose rights are more likely to remain unrealised. RBA strategies, therefore, should develop programmes that are more likely to benefit the poor such as primary healthcare, food and education programmes, low cost housing, and water services to low income areas, etc. In cases where a particular programme results in the poor being disadvantaged, discriminated against or ignored (which is often the case), then that programme fails to incorporate the norm of equality and non-discrimination. In general, the right to equality "lends moral legitimacy and the principle of social justice to development objectives, and helps shift the focus of analysis to the most deprived and excluded, especially to deprivations caused by discrimination" (Robinson 2001). In view of this, the RBA focuses on preventing discrimination on such grounds as race, gender, social status, religion, culture, ethnicity and many other superficial distinctions.[12]

Empowerment

Related to participation and accountability is the principle of empowerment. For human beings to effectively participate in public affairs that affect their lives, they need the space to participate. According to the OHCHR (2002), the most effective way of empowering people is through the introduction of the concept of rights which then translate the entitlements guaranteed in international human rights norms into matters of moral and legal obligations, taking into account the fact that rights bring with them the notion of obligation. Empowerment in the RBA is a way of enabling people to take control of their own development, as well as a way of securing their livelihoods (Thiis 1996: 11). Empowerment as a human right principle is double-sided: on the one hand, it seeks to enable the right-holder to claim their rights; and on the other, it seeks to build the awareness and the capacity of the duty-bearers to fulfil their obligations and responsibilities. In a sense, empowerment is realised when all the above principles are implemented. People become empowered when their rights are progressively realised; when they can hold other actors accountable; when they are not discriminated against; when they are able to have a voice in policies or programmes; and when their suggestions are taken seriously. However, it is important to note that how far people are empowered depends on a number of factors including the securing of conditions favourable to genuine participation. It is in ensuring that people have the capacity to effectively claim their rights that civil society has a vital role to play in the RBA.

In brief, the five principles outlined above are widely regarded as the core principles of the RBA. There are other principles which are included as essential components of the RBA, such as the principle of explicit recognition of international human rights law, international cooperation, international minimum threshold and transparency (Hunt *et al.*, 2003). Other principles mentioned as components of the RBA include the principle of "indivisibility and universality" (Gready and Ensor, 2005: 21). But the five principles considered above are commonly found in most formulations of the RBA.

---

12 Interestingly, many national constitutions have actually decreed against discrimination on these grounds to the point that equality and non-discrimination do not appeal only to international human rights instruments, but are grounded in domestic legislation.

Value Added by the Rights-Based Approach

Having discussed the core principles, this section looks at the value added by the RBA to development discourse and practice. The discussion below focuses on identifying the difference between the RBA and other development approaches, to identify the value added element of the RBA.

There are several ways in which other approaches, such as the basic needs approach (BNA), are similar to the RBA. For instance, the BNA has also a bias towards the poor. Paul Streeten (1981: 9) makes this clear when he argues that the "basic needs strategy is concerned with removing mass deprivation, a concern that has always been at the heart of development". Like the RBA, the BNA also deploys the language of rights by noting that the "satisfaction of basic needs is a human right: freedom from want is like the right not to be tortured" (ibid.: 26). For example, BNA literature asserts that the "satisfaction of an absolute level of basic needs as so defined should be placed within the broader framework – namely the fulfilment of basic human rights" (Ghai *et al.* 1977: 9). Similarly, BNA literature suggests that the principle of participation is also recognised as fundamental. This is emphasised mainly in regard to the identification of what constitutes BNA (Streeten 1981: 25). Further the equality principle has also been acknowledged as one of the pillars of the basic needs approach (ibid.: 12). Nevertheless, the BNA differs from the RBA in four fundamental ways.

While BNA recognises the satisfaction of basic needs as a human right, it does not expand the concept of human rights beyond the mere satisfaction of these needs. Once they are satisfied – no matter in what manner – the BNA has achieved its objective. In contrast, the RBA has extended the notion of obligations beyond merely meeting the vegetative functions – to also include principles of accountability, participation and empowerment, as discussed above.

Here there is a *real* difference between seeing the obligation as extending to the way or process of satisfying the need, and the obligation that has satisfaction of basic needs as its objective. Thus, one could argue that under BNA, accountability, empowerment and participation cannot be demanded as a matter of right.

Second, BNA, especially in its earlier forms, was not concerned with structural injustice – the main focus was to keep the poor person's soul together with his or her body. Structures at the national (as well as the international) level that render people unable to meet their basic needs, were of no concern to the BNA. Similarly, BNA is often silent on power relations and the politics of change. For this reason BNA has been criticised as a ploy to distract developing countries from focusing on real structural issues at the international level – where poverty and deprivation seem to emanate. Gathii (1999), for instance, critiques both the *weak* as well as the *strong* versions of BNA, arguing that focusing on the basic needs of the poor prevented radical changes such as those suggested by the NIEO. In this view Gathii contends that the BNA "cushioned popular challenges to both the capitalist states and also to capitalist development" (1999: 129). Some critics of BNA have noted that due to its overemphasis on meeting basic needs, the approach is paternalistic and narrowly focused (in Streeten 1981). Oxfam, for instance, rejects the BNA on the grounds that it often focuses on meeting the basic needs of people "as passive recipients of charity" (Brouwer *et al.* 2005: 64). Further, the narrow focus on meeting basic needs in the BNA pays little or no attention to the institutional capacity-building that is necessary to ensure that the objectives set out are achieved.

On the other hand, the RBA requires just this: that attention be paid to those structures and processes that lead to some people's rights being denied – including the denial of rights through poverty and deprivation. In a sense, a serious commitment to the principles of equality and accountability that the RBA affirms at both the national and international level, cannot afford to be silent on structures that produce and perpetuate inequality or the deprivation and denial of human rights. However, critics of the RBA have also noted that this framework has harped on Millennium Development Goals and PRSPs, but has remained almost silent on the key issues of economic liberalisation, unfair trade practices, and the bullying of poor nations by international financial institutions such as the World Bank, the IMF and other multinational actors (see Tshikata 2004).

Holistic Approach

Third, the RBA differs from the BNA in that the latter focuses on meeting basic needs "mainly" for survival, without paying attention to people's sense of worth, freedom or capability. To the contrary, the RBA seeks to address the non-physiological needs of people as well as paying attention to notions of capability, freedom and a sense of self-worth (Hunt *et al.* 2003); it thereby strives to enable people become active participants and controllers of their own struggles for their livelihood and empowerment. Related to this is that the RBA clearly deploys the language of rights, especially with regard to the duties of the state. Of course this may largely be mere rhetoric, but a clear stipulation of duties is a perquisite for realising rights, empowering people, and also creating political and social space in which the proclaimed rights can be articulated and contested. Creating this space is essential for making human rights a part of the process which produces the social spaces in which some people are able to realise their rights and others are not.

Last, a fundamental way in which the RBA differs from the BNA is the orientation of the strategies. The BNA overtly depended on external aid to meet its objectives. During the 1970s the BNA was almost synonymous with international aid. Commenting on the question of where the resources to meet basic needs would come from, Streeten asserted that the approach, due to its political appeal, was capable of mobilising international resources (1979: 174). While the reliance on international aid is implied in the RBA with its emphasis on bilateral and multilateral cooperation, the primary duty rests on individual states to ensure that they effectively allocate available resources within their boundaries (Sengupta 2000). As indicated above, the RBA emphasises that even the poorest of nations should take concrete, deliberate and targeted measures towards the realisation of rights. Thus, the responsibility is at two levels: the international community should commit resources, but the individual states should take measures to realise the rights. More fundamentally, the RBA recognises and seeks to promote the agency in each and every human being; the NBA, with its emphasis on meeting basic needs, has often disregarded the human agency elements.

Repackaging Old Wine in New Wine Skins? RBA Critiques

Like the BNA[13] and indeed any development strategy, the RBA has been criticised on many grounds – including the fact that international law, upon which the human rights instruments and treaties are based, is toothless. Rieff (2002), in particular, argues that the human rights approaches championed by NGOs lack focus. He argues that the multifaceted work of human rights approaches has an over-reach tendency which in the end amounts to everything yet nothing in particular. Chandler (2002) makes a similar point, arguing that the all-encompassing approach associated with humanitarianism shoots in all directions – from relief, to advocacy, to long-term development issues – and in the process fails to address any one particular target (cited in Rieff 2002). Univ (2002) is also critical of the RBA, arguing that it assumes many things, including the capacity of the state to meet the claims.

More radical critiques of the RBA include the argument that it gives a false hope in a world where legal enforcement of human rights has produced very disappointing results, especially at the international level. For example, Reiff

13 Paul Streeten lists eight criticisms directed at the BNA, including that the approach tampers with market fundamentals, that it is a communist Trojan horse, that it leads to welfarism and state intervention, and that there is nothing new about it (1978: 180).

(2002) argues that realisation of human rights requires the existence of an "international community" – which according to him does not exist. Chandler (2005) echoes similar concerns, arguing that the RBA is "rhetoric without responsibility"; that the pronouncements made on paper are rarely applied in the real world.

Admittedly, the RBA has an inherent weakness stemming from the fact that international human rights norms on which it is based are often given a rhetorical commitment at the domestic level.[14] A detailed discussion of the relationship between international and municipal law is provided in Chapter 7. A key point to note in this regard is that while governments enthusiastically sign international treaties, documents, and plans of action, there is little enthusiasm in translating the obligations generated by these instruments into programmes; and, later on, into concrete actions which make a difference in the lives of ordinary citizens. In this sense it can be argued that while the RBA is strong on rhetoric, it is weak when it comes to matters of *realpolitik*. Consequently, the greatest challenge facing RBA is ensuring that governments move beyond rhetorical commitment to actions and more towards ensuring tangible entitlements. However, in spite of these daunting challenges, RBA possesses the potential of ensuring that states, as duty-bearers, take reasonable measures towards fulfilling these obligations.

Competing Interest among Rights

A more substantive critique that Reiff (2002) raises is that rights often conflict and compete with each other. This is particularly relevant to human rights, which require the state to allocate resources to give them effect. For instance, realising the right to water may compete with the need to realise other rights such as the right to food, education, healthcare, the right to vote or to a fair trial, etc. However, not all rights simultaneously require the same attention and resources – prioritisation can help balance the conflicting demands (Sengupta 2000).

The RBA has also been criticised for fostering superficial political engagements – with the result that it often fails to make the kind of radical political claims that can result in genuine social change. Duffield (2001), for instance, points out that the RBA often adopts an *apolitical* discourse in development (cited in Gready and Ensor 2005: 33).

Other critics of the RBA have observed that it represents nothing new from earlier strategies; arguing that it is nothing more than a change of name and an invention of new acronyms. Univ (2002), in particular, cogently argues that the

14 This point is discussed in detail in Chapter 4.

incorporation of human rights norms in development is "little more than thinly disguised repackaging of old wine in new bottles". With particular reference to the right to water, Bakker (2007: 439) argues that deployment of rights is not effective when it comes to access to water because such a strategy fails to separate human rights and property rights; fails to distinguish the difference between property rights and service provision; and as a consequence of these two failures, the right to water campaign fails to "foreclose the possibility of increasing private sector involvement in water supply".

While most of the critiques are valid and should be taken into account, it is important to note that an approach only presents a *framework* for doing something. The outcome of implementing an approach therefore largely depends on the manner in which it is implemented. If little or no commitment is given to the RBA norms, it is unlikely that any desired results will be obtained no matter how strong its appeal to the public. For example, the right to water cannot be expected to prevent privatisation of water services merely by recognising it as a right in a national constitution or framework law. How effective the use of the right is in achieving this objective depends on how it is utilised.

To a large extent, implementing the RBA is haunted by the Cranstonian paradigm of rights. This is mainly because the RBA is largely seen to be advocating for ESCRs (Offenheiser and Holcombe 2003) – which are often seen as rights only when there are "enough" resources. Like Maurice Cranston, many policy-makers believe that these ESCRs are not actually rights at all; but rather moral aspirations which only rich nations have the luxury to be able to fulfil. Unfortunately, governments in the Global South also tend to fall prey to this kind of thinking. For instance, when one government official was asked about whether access to water was a human right in Zambia, his response was immediately directed to the issue of resource scarcity: "I think government seems to be reluctant to pronounce that...again it all comes to the limited resources. I think the bottom line is that the cake is small. I think that is basically the economic situation of our country" (Chitonge 2007).

Challenges of Implementing an RBA

Certainly, most of the anti-RBA critiques can be attributed to implementation challenges. One has to ask serious questions about the practical challenges it poses. As noted earlier, while the RBA has been adopted widely by some NGOs and UN development agencies, very few governments have adopted it. The biggest challenge is to get states to move away from mere manifesto-level commitment to more concrete implementation of the principles that they have so enthusiastically subscribed to. Effective implementation of the RBA, especially in developing countries where investment in key areas that benefit the poor will have to come from public resources, requires serious commitment from the state. Although most states affirm the importance of these principles, the commitment to them is highly questionable in many countries. Given the current lack of commitment and political will to implement a rights-based approach, it is important to identify the different levels of commitment that should be secured to improve its implementation and impact.

Levels of Commitment

Acknowledgement

For the RBA to be implemented, a state must formally acknowledge a particular human right to which the state subscribes. For instance, a state must acknowledge that there is a right to water or food prior to any attempt to give effect to that right. This level of commitment is often expressed by either signing or ratifying a relevant international treaty, or declaration, or inclusion in national framework law. While there can be other forms[15] of acknowledgment other than signing or ratifying international instruments, signing or ratifying an instrument has traditionally been seen as the official way of making a commitment or expressing consent. Acknowledgment is the first level of commitment to a particular right or value. But that is not enough to realise a particular right.

Proclamation

The right concerned has to be given content relevant to the local circumstances, by various means – including incorporating core values of the treaty into the domestic legal framework. This level of commitment requires that a particular right be proclaimed publicly, and recognised as making a significant contribution to humanity and in the realisation of the norms and values to which society aspires. It indicates a deeper commitment on the part of the state to take more seriously the rights it has recognised. But recognising a right by incorporating it into domestic statutes or policy is only a step towards realising it; more needs to be done.

15 For instance, the *Vienna Convention on the Law of Treaties*, states that consent to be bound by a treaty can be by signing, ratifying, acceptance or approval, accession or by exchange of instruments. However, the commonest way of expressing consent to be bound by an international or bilateral treaty is by signing or ratification.

Taking Concrete, Deliberate and Targeted Measures

To give effect to a proclaimed right, there must be programmes or measures that outline how the recognised right is to be implemented or realised. It is one thing to acknowledge and proclaim that access to water or food is a human right; it is quite another to elaborate on what this entails in concrete terms. Taking measures requires that the content of that right, the entitlements that people can claim, and the duties that the state embraces, be made as clear as possible. Thus, taking measures by designing a programme or strategy indicates a deeper commitment to a right.

Giving Effect

Having a programme or taking measures may not be enough to ensure that a particular right is given effect. A programme must be concrete, specific and reasonable, with measurable time-bound targets. Such a programme should find concrete expression where its contents are translated into appropriate actions directed towards the realisation of a given right. The attention at this stage should be on the outcomes or measurable impact of the measures or steps taken. It is at this level that rights that have been acknowledged, proclaimed, and acted upon, can become a reality in the lives of the people. A programme that does not have measurable targets, one that is not reasonable, not concrete and not targeted, may not realise the rights of many people.

So, in determining whether a project can be classified as RBA, one has to ask not only whether the project or policy has incorporated the basic principles of human rights, but also whether the level of commitment has gone beyond mere acknowledgement. It is also apparent from the discussions above that although the RBA is a relatively new approach in development theory and practice, it suffers from the deeply entrenched notions of human rights. In spite of all its weaknesses, however, the RBA has the potential to fulfil the dual roles of enabling the state as duty-bearer to fulfil its obligation while at the same time providing opportunity for the right-holder to effectively claim the rights concerned.

CHAPTER 4

Human Rights in Democratic Politics

The business of rights is a deeply political affair. Claiming and asserting human rights is at the very heart of democratic politics to the extent that this entails a contest over the organisation and exercise of power. Claiming human rights, whether it is the right to vote or the right to food, entails a challenge to the existing power relations. Understood from this angle, a human rights approach entails an active engagement in democratic politics; it also entails constant engagement in creating and shaping spaces and relations which make it possible to give effect to the core human rights values. In seeking to create spaces and relations through which rights can be given meaning and effect, a genuine rights approach requires radical thinking about – and engagement with – structures and relations of power. In this sense, giving effect to human rights is not just a matter of having an explicit clause on the right to water or the right to food contained within the Bill of Rights; it involves a radical approach that seeks to transform existing structures and relations of power into spaces where the rights to water and food can become a reality. To realise this requires going beyond having a free basic water policy, and beyond having a school meal programme. In this sense, any strategy that seeks to give effect to human rights cannot afford to be apolitical. Genuine human rights struggles cannot afford to adopt a depoliticised stance (Chapman *et al.* 2005).

Human Rights as Basic Politics

We saw in the preceding chapter that human rights essentially embrace the values that seek to protect human dignity from various forms of abuse and neglect. In striving for this, a rights approach implicitly acknowledges and affirms that human dignity is a valuable asset that deserves to be defended and protected. Further, in seeking to protect human dignity, a rights approach is diametrically opposed to anything that militates against human dignity – such as chronic hunger, severe deprivation, scandalous inequality, structural injustice, corruption, manipulation, political and economic oppression, and exploitation, etc. Thus, human rights in general and the RBA in particular are fundamentally political; and the degree of success in protecting human dignity depends, to a large extent, on how the approach engages in the local, national and international power dynamics and structures. A "rights-based approach is

 | DOI 10.1163/9789004299559_005

inherently a political approach – one that takes into consideration power, struggle and a vision for a better society as key factors in development. It opposes a depoliticised interpretation of development which portrays problems 'as purely technical matters that can be resolved outside of the political arena'..." (ibid.: 6).

The mechanisms of engagement should not be limited to the formal political arenas of parliaments, courtrooms or round table politics; as noted in the previous chapter, they can take various forms including: legal, paralegal, social mobilisation, public protest, legislative campaigns, public awareness campaigns, documentation of abuses, monitoring, capacity-building, active participation in public processes such as budget debates, etc. The appropriate type of engagement ultimately depends on the nature of the issues and the context in which the rights are being asserted and contested.

Seen from this angle, it becomes clear that protecting human dignity and rights is something that is not given on a silver platter; it involves a continuous struggle to create spaces where human dignity and rights can be asserted, contested for, and given meaning and effect. In some instances the engagement starts with the struggle for recognising and proclaiming a particular right such as the right to water or food; whereas in other cases the engagement is taken at another level where the struggle is about ensuring that the recognised rights are given effect. This chapter introduces some concepts which are central to the view of human rights as radical politics.

The Primacy of Political Engagement

To the extent that human rights are about securing and giving meaningful effect to various human entitlements such as the right to vote, the right to freedom of conscience and choice, the rights to water and food, strategies aimed at giving effect to human rights cannot avoid political engagement at the local, national and international levels. For human rights strategies to be successful and relevant, it is necessary to continuously engage with the very same power structures and relations that often create barriers to attempts aimed at giving effect to basic human entitlements and collective aspirations. The main reason why engagement with power structures and relations at every level of human association (from the family to the UN) is indispensable in a human rights approach is that it is almost impossible to give meaningful effect to human rights of any kind without contesting existing power structures and relations. Whether the right in question is about electoral rights or the rights to water and food, meaningful protection and respect of these rights, for all people, can only be secured by transforming power structures and dynamics. Because of its inclination to challenge existing structures and relations of power, human rights strategies can be "messy" at times; they can be painfully slow, frustrating, psychologically taxing, and, in some cases, highly dangerous.

One of the main reasons why the business of claiming and securing human rights tends to be messy and dangerous is because power structures and relations are constantly changing, and this dynamism is never a clearly defined linear process. It is always an open-ended process with a certain degree of uncertainty. It is in this open-endedness and uncertainty where the opportunity, but also the challenge for human rights, lies. For example, a movement that seeks to profoundly change the existing arrangements around access to water and food may be outmanoeuvred by making concessions which prevent a more radical transformation to existing relations and exercise of power regarding the way water and food are accessed. As Steven Lukes (1974) observes, different forms of exercising power need not be conflictual in nature; power can be exercised in a way that appears as if it is done in the interest of the powerless.

The other reason why asserting and securing human entitlements often appears murky is because genuine human rights are the outcome of a contest, and as such the actual outcome is never predefined.

> Rights do not come in neat packages, but rather are part of dynamic, sometimes messy, processes of resistance and change that work to engage and transform relations of power. Despite the existence of the internal human rights system, the terrain of rights remains an ever-changing, political arena where some groups' rights compete and conflict with others.
>
> VANEKLASEN *et al.* 2004: 4

For many human rights it is not just the competing claims of different groups that creates the messiness; the way these rights are understood can sometimes be a source of contest as illustrated in Chapters 1 and 2. Nevertheless, one cannot escape the basic idea that "rights cannot be truly realized without changes in the structure and relationships of power in all their forms. Changes in who makes decisions, whose voice is heard, what topics are seen as legitimate" (Chapman *et al.* 2005: 7).

From this point of view a rights strategy will only be effective in bringing about the desired change in society if it constantly engages in the political and social dynamics to create spaces where rights can be given meaning and effect; spaces where the rights of some people, especially the poor, can be translated into tangible entitlements. For those deploying a rights strategy it is always important to be aware that genuine rights are never given freely; they are always the product of a contest in space and time. Thus, human rights activists bent on changing the world must be prepared take into account the existing power structures and dynamics surrounding a particular contested right when they design their engagement strategies. This requires that they be aware of the potential setbacks, the possibility of being co-opted, and the possibility of the contest dragging on endlessly: "Organisations therefore, need to be clear about how power operates in their context, what combination of strategies are most appropriate, and what sources of support they can tap to counter and transform backlash and conflict" (VaneKlasen *et al.* 2004: 4).

Often, changing the existing power dynamics involves identifying the basic values that many people can identify with and support. Historically speaking, it is this ability to identify collective values that human communities aspire to (whether it is freedom from colonial occupation, or freedom from thirst and hunger) which makes "human rights a force to be reckoned with" (Heyns 2006: 15). It is for this reason that such a collective process needs to be rooted in the local experiences and expressions of collective values and aspirations. This is another reason why a rights approach cannot afford to be politically disengaged and socially alienated. Creating politically engaged solidarities that can produce an effective force for changing existing power structures and relations cannot be achieved without being rooted in people's daily life experiences and struggles. Forging solidarities built upon the realisation that giving effect to human rights will not come cheaply will always rely on the local politics. Local solidarities around particular rights can be built through creating the awareness that "rights are not bestowed from on high. They are part of a never-ending human struggle to improve people's lives drawing on both visions of a better future and a desire to prevent reccurrences of past atrocities and abuse" (Chapman *et al.* 2005: 4).

The starting point for this kind of active engagement is the realisation that the failure of people to fulfil their basic rights, such as the right to water or food, is a product of social and power relations and not a naturally occurring phenomenon. As Sen (1999) observes, even in times when nature seems to impose constraints on food production – such as during drought or famine – death from starvation can still be prevented. When reflecting about how situations such as starvation or lack of access to clean and adequate supplies of water arise, one has to go beyond the actual situation itself and reflect on the *processes* which give rise to it. Thinking about these processes can lead to a deeper analysis of institutions, power configurations, and the context in which these arrangements function; as well as relations that produce, reproduce and sustain these structures (William 2004). Here, Henri Lefebvre's (1994) concept of the *production of space* becomes a useful idea for conceptualising and analysing power dynamics and social change.

The Production of Space

In Lefebvre's conception of *social space*, social space is understood not as a physical space but simply as an outcome of interactions between two or more people or groups of people (Lefebvre 1994). In Lefebvre's view, social space is both a *product* as well as a *means* of producing more spaces. It is important to emphasise here the word "product" for two reasons. First, a product is something that is brought forth – produced, created, manufactured – for a purpose. Human beings, unlike nature, do not produce in "vain". Production often involves a deliberate action or activity. Second, a product is different from a naturally occurring object. A product results from purposeful activities while a naturally occurring object surges forth without human intervention. Lefebvre makes this point clear when he argues that "nature creates and does not produce"[1] (ibid.: 70).

The importance of these two points is that they help to illuminate the idea that *social space* is not a naturally occurring thing; rather it is a socially produced order – often as a result of deliberate action, although sometimes as an unintended outcome. Using the concept of production Lefebvre goes further to argue that *space*, like any other product, is produced for a purpose which is sometimes not explicit. For instance, a situation where many people have no access to water, or inadequate access to food, is not a naturally occurring phenomenon; rather, it is often the outcome of social interactions and exchange between people. While such situations may not be the outcomes of the sort of neatly calculated actions that one might expect in, say, a shoe factory, they can, nonetheless, be directly or indirectly linked to the deliberate actions or non-actions of individuals and groups in society. Individuals and groups, through a variety of interactions, produce the *space* where some individuals are able to meet all their water and food needs, while others are not.

To distinguish between produced space and physical space Lefebvre refers to humanly produced spaces as *social spaces*. Because produced space is often the result of deliberate and calculated actions it serves very specific purposes. For example, in the case of the right to food, there are reported cases of millions of tonnes of food being dumped in the ocean to prevent the price of food commodities such as wheat, rice and maize from falling on the global market. In the case of water, social spaces are created where certain individuals are charged

1 Of course Lefebvre's concern here is to show that *production* is a socially conditioned phenomenon which has substituted nature's *use value* with *exchange value*. Using Marxian concepts he seeks to expose the deceptive (or fetishness) nature of *exchange value*. His point is made clear in the following sentence: "A tree, a flower or a fruit is not a 'product' – even if it is in the garden" (see Lefebvre 1994).

more than others (in some cases even 10 times more, see UNDP 2006). Thus, a more socially engaged approach to development needs to pay attention to the spaces produced, how these spaces are produced and reproduced, why they are produced and reproduced, as well as the intended and unintended consequences of such spaces being produced.

But what is this *social space*? Lefebvre looks at it as an active arena of contestation. Thus, "social space is constituted neither by a collection of things or an aggregate of (sensory) data, nor by a void packed like a parcel with various contents"; rather it[2] "incorporates' social actions over which the state imposes itself, occupies and rules" (Lefebvre 1994: 21). But this social space over which the "state occupies and rules" is rife with competing interests – mainly because "the rationality of the state, of its techniques, plans and programmes, provokes opposition" (ibid.: 23). Because the state is not the only actor in the social space, its actions, programmes and intentions often conflict with those of other actors. Human rights practitioners, activists and advocates are examples of the sorts of actor who *contest* in social spaces for meaningful protection and fulfilment of human rights such as the rights to water and food. But not all human rights practitioners contest in this social space; some have adopted a depoliticised position that only seeks to attend to the welfare needs of the poor, without reflecting on or analysing the root causes of the situations they seek to ameliorate.

What is of interest in this view of society is that social relations are not seen as a given, but as a product of human interactions which the state seeks to normalise and control. In this view, the sociopolitical and socioeconomic conditions in a given context are outcomes of certain processes – processes that produce the social space within which people seek to make sense of their lives; spaces in which some have access to water while others do not; spaces in which some have adequate food while others do not; spaces in which some are heard while others are not; spaces where some have concrete rights while others have *abstract* rights; spaces in which some are power-*ful* while others are power-*less*.

From "Issues in Space" to the "Actual Production of Space"

Lefebvre's idea of social space as something purposefully produced is relevant to the current discussion in that in order to clearly comprehend the product

---

2 Lefebvre tries to make his concept of social space clear by distinguishing *social* space from *physical* or *natural* space, and *mental* or *abstract* space. He blames the confusion surrounding the concept of space on Cartesian dualism and Kantian absolutism. According to Lefebvre, when these two confusions are put together the result is the "fetishization of space" (1994: 21).

(*social space*, e.g. a lack of water or food for some individuals in communities), it is first essential to understand the processes that lead to the production of the *product* itself. In this instance, instead of simply focusing on the fact that close to a quarter of the population in Africa are undernourished and often experience hunger (FAO 2014), it becomes essential to understand the *processes* which produce this situation. As one would imagine, there are myriad processes that contribute to the production of spaces where some have access to safe and secure sources of water and adequate food while others do not. Understanding such processes entails unlocking matrices of social, economic and political relations between individuals, between individuals and institutions, between state institutions and cross-national corporations, between the state and NGOs, and between the state and bilateral and multilateral institutions, etc. Human rights activist, practitioners and scholars ought to reflect on these processes at different levels and seek to understand the real processes that produce the situations in which they work, and the situations in which they collectively struggle.

Beyond the Unmet Basic Need

Experience from many human rights struggles suggests that there are many structural constraints that act as barrier to the realisation of human rights (CARE International 2007). Most of these are directly linked to unequal power relations that constantly produce and reproduce spaces in which the dignity and plight of the poor are often ignored (Chapman *et al.* 2005). Using the production of space framework it becomes essential for the analysis to go beyond unfulfilled rights or unmet basic needs – and move towards an examination of the processes that lead to the production of these spaces. For one reason or another many development NGOs, and some human rights activists and practitioners, adopt a welfarist paradigm in which they fight for clean water or access to adequate food for the poor – yet do little to reflect on and engage with processes that lead to the actual production of the conditions they seek to change.

In most cases the outcome of such an approach is disempowerment, where local agency gives way to passiveness, and many citizens become cases of charity rather than active agents struggling to shape processes and spaces that bring about social change (William 2004). Consequently, the mainstream approach to issues of human rights, poverty and development – even by development NGOs and some human rights activists – has often been to focus on the "actual spaces produced" (e.g. the lack of access to water or food, for instance), with little attention given over to the processes that produce these spaces. While understanding the spaces produced is essential, such an understanding is incomplete without a grasp of the processes that produce these spaces. In order to comprehend these social spaces the focus has to "shift from *things in space* to the actual *production of space*" (Lefebvre 1984: 37, emphasis added).

When this approach is applied to human rights it becomes apparent that a better way of giving them effect would be to shift emphasis away from the fact that hundreds of millions of people in the Global South have no access to clean water and inadequate food, and towards an examination of the processes that produce these phenomena. But this is a more demanding and challenging mode of struggle.

As noted earlier, failure to secure access to clean water or adequate food is not a naturally occurring phenomenon; it is a product of complex human actions, interactions and omissions. To respond more effectively to these challenges a deeper understanding of the processes, and how they operate, is indispensable; especially when it comes to identifying effective ways of radically transforming the processes, and changing the outcomes. When processes are understood, it becomes obvious, for example, that treating water as a public or private good is itself a product of a particular process of reasoning and human interaction. In this sense, *public-ness* or *private-ness* is a socially created and assigned attribute for very particular reasons.[3] Understanding this leads to an appreciation of the fact that the phenomenon of low budgetary allocations for water infrastructure is not just a matter of the "size of the cake" or the "resource envelope" – it is also an indication of the underlying sociopolitical relations between institutions. So the fact that many people have no access to safe sources of drinking water, or an inadequate supply of food, cannot be explained solely in terms of a lack of funding – as is often the case.

Power as a Resource

Up to this point reference has been made – several times – to the word "power", without elaborating what "power" actually means. Like the word "rights", the term "power" is a delicate concept – mainly because it manifests itself in different forms, and often in subtle ways even in situations where there is no trace of threat, authority, coercion, manipulation or open conflict. As has been observed, "the most effective and insidious use of power is to prevent...conflict from arising in the first place" (Lukes 1974: 23). In terms of the struggle for human rights and basic needs, power is a central pillar around which the contestation for rights occurs – with some groups asserting their entitlements, against others

3 McDonald and Ruiters (2005) have posed a similar argument – that essentially, water is neither public nor private; privateness or publicness is a socially ascribed feature of water.

who resist the asserted claims. When power relations are unequal (as is often the case) the realisation of human rights and fulfilment of basic needs becomes contested along the faultlines of inequality. Indeed,

> poverty and the denial of people's rights are directly linked with unequal power relations. This may seem obvious but it is remarkable how many organisations claiming to take a rights-based approach in their work ... ignore the question of power in their analysis and planning, except on a very superficial level.
>
> CHAPMAN *et al.* 2005: 9

Power relations are also at the centre of the production of social space, and significantly influence the notions and practice of rights. But power conceptualised and analysed in isolation is a cold idea that seems harmless and neutral. It is only when power is linked to *control* over resources and ideas that it becomes a dynamic shaper of relations, views, values, agendas and actions. Table 4.1 below illustrates the different dimensions of power and their corresponding manifestations.

From Table 4.1 it is clear that there are different forms of power – and that these give rise to different relations. For instance "power over" is often the sort of power that is concentrated among a few individuals or actors. Its main operational mechanism is domination – which creates patrimonial relations – and it is manifested most distictively in authoritarian attitudes and behaviour.

In contrast, "power with" is a collective manifestation of power; it operates in a cooperative manner, generating relations of solidarity and manifested in collegiality. Thus it can be seen that power can be exercised in different ways; the effect of this exercise of power depends on how power is configured. It is important to note, however, that the above types of exercise of power are not mutually exclusive. In some instances a combination of two or more forms of power can be exercised in a single act.

Power, Meaning and Politics

Control over *power resources,* broadly understood, not only influences social relations but also *shared meaning of* citizenship and human rights. Here Sederberg's notion of the interplay between *power resources* and *shared meaning,* or *political control,* is useful. In Sederberg's view, resources are not just material or physical; they include non-physical resources such as status, authority, information, privilege, knowledge and skills. Sederberg argues that "[t]hrough

TABLE 4.1 *Types and dimensions of power*

Type	Attributes	Mechanism	Relations	Manifestations
Power over	Concentrated	Domination	Patrimonial	Authoritarian
Power to	Diffused	Resistance	Assertive	Egalitarian
Power with	Collectivised	Cooperative	Solidarity	Collegial
Power within	Internalised	Empowering	Respect	Assurance

SOURCE: ADAPTED FROM CHAPMAN *ET AL.* (2005).

the manipulation of our available resources, we engage in the deliberate effort to control *shared meaning*, that is, politics" (1984: 69, emphasis added). Therefore, people with more control over *power resources* participate more effectively in public life in society, and are likely to have a more heightened sense of belonging (citizenship) than those with less control over *power resources*. At the root of this differentiated sense of citizenship is the unequal power dynamics mediated through unequal access to, and control over, *power resources*. For example, the unequal access to water and food which we see throughout the world is not a product of chance, but a direct outcome of the unequal access to, and control over, other *power resources* – not just money, but ideas and meaning. This inequality is reflected in the subtle control of power resources that are entrenched in defending the discourse about whether water should be treated as a private or a public good; it manifests through the production of knowledge and meaning which categorically affirms that securing food or water is the private affair of each family and should not be a matter of public interest.

There is an even more subtle exercise of power resources which makes mass hunger appear perfectly normal. This is the most fundamental way of exercising power: the shaping of people's "perceptions, cognitions and preferences in such a way that they accept their role in the existing order of things, either because they can see or imagine no alternative to it, or because they see it as natural and unchangeable" (Lukes 1974: 24). A particular way of controlling the shared meaning and public discourse has made the abnormal appear normal – such that thinking about a world where every person can have their basic needs for water and food met is not only seen as utopian, but as something that is frightening, even. A critical assessment of how we get to this point suggests that control over the construction and deployment of shared meaning – through a dominant discourse – has played a decisive role.

Meaning as a Power Resource

Critical to gaining an understanding of these processes of power is an understanding of the state (and related institutions); the state subsumes all these relations as it seeks to *impose* normalcy and homogeneity. The most obvious way in which the state seeks to impose *normality* on social space is through the enactment of laws, rules, policies and programmes. For instance, in the case of access to water, national legislation and ministerial promulgations which elaborate on the practical implications of the legislation are put in place to regulate interactions around food and water. The same is true about rules and legislation regarding food production, distribution, marketing and consumption. There is another subtle way in which these regulations impose control, and hence normalcy, on the social spaces. This is often achieved through what Sederberg (1984) calls "shared meaning". Like the production of space, construction of *shared meaning* is also tailored towards – and results in – the exercise of control over sociopolitical realities; including the realities around access to water and food. Here, Steven Lukes's three dimensional view of power is illuminating.

Lukes (1974) conceptualises three dimensions of power which correspond to the three levels at which power operates (i.e., at the level of decision-making, agenda-setting and control of behaviour, perception, desires, values, meaning and wants etc.). In Lukes's view, power can be exercised through brutal coercion, through threat of force, or through presiding over certain processes such as the formulation of policy or rules. This he calls the one dimensional view of power.

But this is not the only way in which power is exercised. Power can also be exercised through controlling what makes the agenda for public debate or policy discussion. Lukes refers to this as the two dimensional view of power. In this view, power is exercised by controlling what finds its way into public debate, policies, programmes and laws – including what gets recognised as "genuine" human rights. Controlling the agenda often leads to non-decisions on matters that those in control feel uncomfortable about. Hence, "non-decision is a means by which demands for change in the allocation of benefits and privileges in the community can be suffocated, kept covert or prevented from gaining access to the relevant decision-making arenas" (Lorenzi 2006: 91). In this instance the decision *not* to explicitly recognise the right to water may not be an innocent omission. Setting an agenda is indeed an exercise of power since it is through such an agenda that one can potentially restrict the public debates to "safe issues" which do not challenge the resources or power of the dominant actors (Lukes 1974: 18).

Apart from power exercised through decision- and non-decision-making, and controlling what gets on the agenda, Lukes also argues that power can be exercised by controlling people's perceptions, values, wants, aspirations, views, beliefs, shared meaning and choices. According to Lukes, this form of exercising power – which he refers to as the three dimensional view of power – is more subtle and often deeply entrenched in political and social exchange. In this three dimensional view of power, power is "exercised when A devotes his energies to creating or reinforcing social and political values and institutional practices that limit the scope of the political process to public consideration of only those issues which are cooperatively innocuous to A" (Lukes 1974: 17). At this level the exercise of power becomes more covert; it is often manifested in the capacity to elicit compliance – even on issues that are not exactly favourable to the complying party. It amounts to the capacity to alter another party's way of thinking or doing. Power at this level is exercised by influencing the way people think, and the meaning they attach to things. Shared meaning, and public discourses on issues such as the right to water or food, are shaped and entrenched in this way. People who have no access to clean water or an adequate supply of food are made to believe that they are in such a situation as a result of their own actions; that their failure to access the necessities of life is purely a private affair which has nothing to do with local or national politics. Of course it is often those with access to clean water, and adequate food, who sponsor, control and sustain this shared meaning – thereby exercising power in a very subtle way.

Power as a Relational Property

For this reason, discussing the way power is structured and exercised is central in a strategy that seeks to bring about social change. In the analysis of power it is essential to realise that that "[p]ower is never the property of an individual; it belongs to a group and remains in existence only so long as the group keeps together" (ibid.: 29). This view emphasises the relational nature of power as something that exists between two or more parties, whether this be at the family level, or at the UN level. The key point is that power remains a property of all the parties involved – which leaves room for contestation and change as long as the parties have the means and the willingness to engage in the contest. This is the point at which strategies such as the rights approach, in striving to protect human rights, often make a politically and morally appealing claim – though the actual navigation of the contest is often not that clear. But the potential to alter the configuration of power by using the language of rights and citizenship is widely acknowledged.

When analysing power in a given context, it is also essential to bear in mind that power and shared meaning are not always imposed by the mighty over the weak – they are often the product of a contest in social spaces; a pulling back and forth.[4] This is the dynamic part of power and social relations, and it presents an opportunity to initiate and call for social change – as long as there is a politically and socially engaged strategy. Although the power-*ful* often triumph in the contest for power, the characteristic feature of power as a relational property is that it is in a constant state of instability. It is in this context that social change becomes possible, and the use of the rights language seems to have the potential to rearrange the relations and structure through which power is exercised – including shared meaning.

This entails that meaning is context-dependent, or what Paul Rocoeur calls *locality*. Contestation of meaning, and therefore its vulnerability to manipulation, lies in the fundamental feature of language – *polysem*: "that is, the feature by which our words have more than one meaning when considered outside of their use in a determinate context" (Ricoeur 1981: 44). Thus, the politics of change is deeply rooted in the struggle over meaning. A dominant interpretation directs and determines both response and action in a given direction. For Sederberg the competition over shared meaning is translated into the competition over scarce resources. Put another way, conflict over shared meaning manifests itself through competition over power resources. The party that controls the power resources, broadly understood, imposes the shared meaning over others. And in most cases this imposition is neither obvious nor permanent.

Citizenship, Rights and Social Change

Debates about human rights are intricately linked to the notion of citizenship. Since the early Greek city states, the concept of citizenship has been closely linked to the notion of entitlement or privilege.[5] The critical link between the two is the principle of participation. For instance, Aristotle in *The Politics*, defines citizenship in terms of being able to participate in the administrative deliberations of the state: "[H]e who has the *power* to take part in the deliberative or judicial administration of any state is said by us to be a citizen of that state" (Aristotle 2000: 95).

---

4 Sederberg rejects both the coercive and consent theories of shared meaning. He rejects the former on the grounds that it overlooks the existence of meaning independent of the interest of the power-*ful*; and the latter on the grounds that it overlooks the influence of the power-*ful* over shared meaning. "Coercion theories tend to underestimate the possibility of consensually-based meaning, and consent theories overestimate its likelihood" (1984: 59).

5 The concept of rights as we understand it today did not emerge during the time of Aristotle. Conceptual development of rights was a later phenomenon that started to take shape during the thirteenth century with the enactment of the *Magna Carta*. However, elements of rights were already present in early Greek society in the form of privileges and powers.

Reference to power in this definition does not imply acquired abilities through social processes; rather power in the sense of the entitlement that comes by virtue of being a bona fide member of a society. Though Aristotle's notion of citizenship was limited to property-owning men, his basic idea of active participation as the defining feature of citizenship is still tenable in contemporary societies. In fact, even today there is a subtle way in which the notion of citizenship as being able to actively participate in one's society, is still largely dependent on one's control over resources. It could be argued, for instance, that poor people's participation in social and political processes that affect their lives is seriously undermined by poverty and lack of opportunity. It is often the case that poor people are excluded from critical deliberations about water supply systems, or the productive resources for food such as land and water; it may therefore be less than surprising that the same people have a voice that is either not heard, or ignored. As noted in Chapter 3, one of the fundamental norms of human rights is participation, with a particular emphasis on the participation of the poor who are often at risk of being excluded. It is in this sense that taking human rights seriously entails taking a radical stance against the status quo – this is why serious human rights struggles cannot afford to be apolitical.

Furthermore, with its emphasis on empowerment, accountability, non-discrimination and participation, the human rights approach is intricately linked to notions of active citizenship; and in its radical form offers a unique opportunity for transforming unequal power and social relations (Offenheiser and Holcombe 2003). It is for this reason that human rights have immense potential to play a significant role in the politics of social change. Connecting human rights to strong notions of citizenship reinforces the struggle view of human rights in as far as active citizenship implies a contest for rights and entitlements through social spaces. Understood from this point of view the rights approach does not ask favours from the state – rather it provides tools for defining, formulating and structuring the contestation in social space. However, in doing so the rights approach is not anti-state as such; rather it "in fact endorses the state but claims that the protection of [human] rights is a primary obligation of the state and holds the state accountable to this standard" (Heyns 2006: 16).

It is in this context that the notions of citizenship, struggle, and the rights approach tend to converge and reinforce each other. If these concepts are properly integrated they can create a rallying point for change, beyond the superficial level of "naming and shaming" human rights abusers (Univ 2002). But as other analysts have observed, the process of integrating these strategies has been slow. Notions of rights and citizenship are seen as separate and delinked from the aspirations of development and social change – with citizenship and rights seen as belonging to the *political* realm, while development and social change belong to the *economic* realm.

Citizenship has historically been an idea married to the concept of a state. Onuma, for example, argues that in the post-Second World War era, the notion of the state came to be defined largely in terms of citizenship or nationality. And the reason is that since the state as a "political entity cannot exist without people and territory, it follows that a people within the territory be presumed as a basic unit of the emerging state" (Onuma 1981: 26). A state exists because there are people within it who share the same culture, territorial boundary, history, and central authority. With this concept of a state comes the idea that anyone who meets the prescribed conditions for becoming a member of this common body of people is entitled to citizenship. In this way the state is built on citizens, just as the notion of citizenship has no independent existence or meaning outside the state.[6]

Because of the frustration of many ordinary citizens in their relationship with the state, various groups – especially civil society groups – have started to challenge the notion of representative or indirect democracy, preferring more direct forms of governance (Gaventa 2002). One of the results of this has been the growing trend towards decentralisation or devolution of "power" to local authorities as an effective way of giving meaning to true citizenship and democracy. This has been reinforced by the growing trend towards a more participatory approach to development and poverty issues. Rampant failure of the top-down approaches to development inherent in classical development theories led to a rethink that emphasised the notion of development *with* the people and not *for* the people.

This view has been reinforced by the *Declaration on the Right to Development*, which states that people should be active participants and beneficiaries of the process of development. Issues such as access to clean water and adequate food are clearly vehicles through which citizenship can be enhanced and concretised. In line with the view that social space is a product of human interactions,

6 Onuma sketches a brief evolution of concepts of nationality and citizenship during the pre- and post-Second World War eras. His main point is that the acquisition of independence by many states after 1945 posed a challenge to the ascription of nationality status in a number of newly independent states. Decolonisation in some cases meant changes of nationality, and the main focus within international law was to prevent people from becoming "stateless" in the emerging national order. However, while nationality or citizenship would be assigned to individuals in accordance with existing domestic laws dealing with nationality (mainly based on the domicile doctrine), in the later period more emphasis was put on the autonomy of the individual to choose his or her own nationality in cases where this was in dispute (see Onuma 1981).

notions of citizenship can be an important and powerful vehicle through which social change can be achieved – by actively engaging in the processes that produce these spaces. The rights approach can be an effective way of engaging and shaping the processes as well as the spaces produced; and it can be an important way of exerting influence over democratic politics. The next chapter looks more specifically at the right to water as an example of the potential role that the human rights discourse and its related struggles can play in fostering social change.

CHAPTER 5

The Right to Water

Foundation, Content and Scope

Though many human rights are widely acknowledged and formally recognised in domestic as well as international human rights law, the implementation of these rights – especially ESCRs such as the rights to water and food – remains a challenge in many countries. This is not only because of a lack of commitment from governments; it is also due to the controversial nature, content, meaning and implications of these rights. Even though there exist clear standards and guidelines outlined by international human rights law and which elaborate on many of these rights, applying such standards to concrete cases in specific countries is not always a straightforward matter. As elaborated in this chapter with specific reference to the right to water, giving effect to the right is a complex issue that requires much more than an explicit recognition of the right in domestic or international law. In most cases the international human rights standards and norms are often sidelined or completely ignored, leading to some analysts questioning whether such norms actually make a difference in reality (Hathaway 2002). As noted in Chapter 4, clarifying the nature of these rights – including the obligations and benefits entailed by them – is not something that is automatic; it requires sustained contest and engagement about what these entitlements mean and how they are to be given effect, especially for those whose right to water is unfulfilled. It is argued in this chapter that formally recognising the right to water is only the first, and perhaps the easiest, step; while giving effect to the right, especially for the poor, can only be meaningfully achieved through constant engagement in democratic politics.

This chapter looks more closely at the content, scope and implications of the right to water to illustrate the intricacies and challenges involved in giving effect to the right to water. The first part of the chapter provides an overview of the state of current global water resources – highlighting the fact that although there is rising pressure on global resources, there is still enough water to meet the basic needs of everyone as long as such resources are shared fairly and managed prudently. The second part of the chapter discusses the right to water in international human rights law, stressing the point that, unlike other ESCRs, the right to water is not explicitly recognised in major international human rights instruments, or national constitutions or framework laws. This lack of explicit recognition is a major challenge in the struggle to give meaning and effect to the right to water for the more than 1.2 billion people in the world who have no access to clean water – most of them in low income countries. The last

 | DOI 10.1163/9789004299559_006

part of the chapter provides some of examples of the practical challenges involved in giving effect to the right to water.

The Right to Water and Collective Human Aspirations

In the discussions that follow it becomes apparent that human rights are not given freely by a benevolent state, a progressive constitution, or by judges and lawyers; they are a product of a collective struggle driven by the fundamental human aspiration of a better world for all. As such, human rights "are not a cold legalistic formula to be arbitrated by well-meaning, well-educated and sophisticated experts on behalf of the majority. Rather they are a manifestation of what the human spirit aspires to and can achieve through collective and positive struggle" (Chapman *et al.* 2005: 4–5). This view of human rights underscores the idea that they are values that a society cherishes and gives to itself; thus making human rights (whether political and civil, or economic, social and cultural) essentially political and contestable. It is this contestable feature of human rights which makes their realisation possible, even in situations where everything seems hopeless.

However, for these struggles to be effective they have to be rooted in, and appeal to, the basic aspirations of the most-affected people. For instance, while people from outside can assist in mobilising communities that do not have access to water, the struggle to realise the right will have little impact if the members of the community itself are not at its heart. It is demonstrated in this chapter that there are many international human rights instruments that have *implicitly* recognised water as a human right, but in order to safeguard the right to water more effectively, to focus policy on access to water, to address the environmental concerns related to access to water, and to raise awareness about the deplorable state of access to water in many countries, there is a need for sustained engagement by affected communities in radical democratic politics in order to elaborate on the value of the right and come up with a practical means of giving it effect. This process is essential to the institutionalisation of the right, but also to generating wider support for a more explicit recognition of access to water as a human right.[1] The importance of a formal and wider

1 To date there are only two international human rights instruments that explicitly recognise access to clean water as a basic human right: the *Convention on the Rights of the Child* (CRC 1989), and the *Convention on the Elimination of all Forms of Discrimination Against Women* (CEDAW 1979). In both instruments the rights apply to a special group of people: children and women respectively.

recognition (beyond the constitutional and parliamentary) lies in the fact that "the ethical force of human rights is made more powerful in practice through giving it social recognition and acknowledgement status, even when no enforcement is instituted" (Sen 2004: 343).

Global Water Resources

Water resources, globally, have come under increasing pressure for a number of reasons, including population growth. In terms of demographic pressure on water, the global population more than doubled between 1950 and 1990. A *United Nations Population Division Report* shows that the global population increased from 2.52 billion in 1950 to 5.27 billion in 1990: an increase of 109 per cent. The global population in 2014 is estimated at about 7.3 billion (DESA 2014), representing a 38 per cent increase since 1990.[2] This increase in population, as would be expected, implies rising demand for fresh water – a situation that has led to what has being widely termed the "water crisis" (Saleth 2002). The impact of this increase in the world's population can be seen in the change in water availability per capita over the 60-year period (1950–2010). In most regions of the world, water availability per capita has dropped; with the highest drops recorded in Europe, Africa and Latin America – where availability per capita in 2010 was about a third of what it was 60 years earlier (Figure 5.1).

Apart from population growth, climate change – in its different forms – is said to be impacting on the availability of fresh water resources around the world; and more acutely so in water-scarce regions such as North Africa and the Middle East. However, water availability analyses suggest that population growth, alongside increased industrial and agricultural activities, are more responsible for declining per capita water availability than climate change. This situation is not expected to change (Parish *et al.* 2012). Available evidence also suggests that per capita use of water for domestic purposes has dramatically increased in all the regions of the world (see Figure 5.2), and this trend is likely to continue. Sharp increases in water withdrawal are expected in India, China and Africa as standards of living for the majority of people rise due to the sustained economic growth being experienced in these regions. Figure 5.2 also illustrates the fact that water resources are shared in a scandalously uneven manner.

---

2 Population growth has slowed down, globally, from an average of 2.5 per cent per annum during the 1970s and 1980s, to an average of 1.2 per cent per annum between 2010 and 2014 – lower than the predicted growth rate of 1.5 per cent (UN, DESA 2014). However, even at this low rate, the pressure on water resources will continue to build.

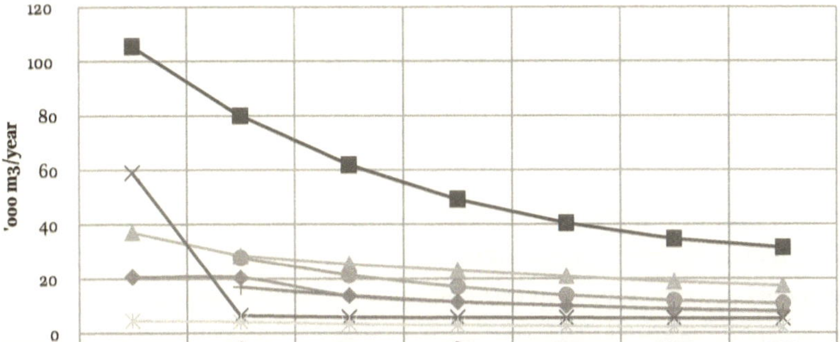

	1950	1962	1972	1982	1992	2002	2010
Africa	20.6	20.4	13.8	11.4	10	8.7	7.9
L. America	105.6	80	61.9	49.2	40.5	34.7	31.5
N.America	37	28.4	25.3	23	20.8	18.7	17.3
Europe	59	6.4	5.8	5.6	5.5	5.4	5.4
East Asia	4.5	4.2	3.3	2.9	2.5	2.3	2.2
South Asia		27.7	21.3	17	13.8	11.9	10.8
World		16.9	13.8	11.4	10	8.7	7.9

FIGURE 5.1 *Global Water Availability Per Capita (1950–2000)*
Note: Figures for 1950 are from Ayibotele (in Webb and Iskandarani 1998: 16).
SOURCE: AUTHOR, BASED ON DATA FROM HTTP://WWW.UNESCAP.ORG/STAT/DATA/STATDB/DATAEXPLORER.ASPX.

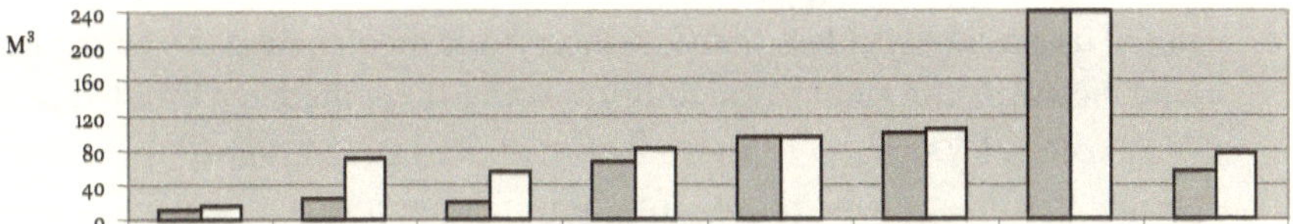

	Sub-Saharan	China	India	Latin America	Western Europe	Eastern Europe	USA	World
1995	11	25	20	65	94	98	240	56
2020	15	71	54	82	94	103	240	75

Regions

FIGURE 5.2 *Global Per Capita Water Withdrawal (Domestic 1995/2020)*
Note: Figures for 2020 are estimates based on population growth projections.
SOURCE: AUTHOR, BASED ON DATA FROM ROSEGRANT (IN WEBB AND ISKANDARANI 1998: 17).

Unevenness in the distribution and consumption of water is not only limited to the regional level; huge disparities exist within countries and cities, such that people in the same city can have very different access and consumption levels (see UNDP 2006). The disparity is not just in the way resources are distributed, but also in the quantities that people access. While, on average, a person in Sub-Saharan Africa was consuming only 11m³ per year in 1995, an average American was consuming 240m^3 per year – 21 times more water – and similar proportions are projected for 2020. In-country and -city analyses of the distribution and consumption of water, across the globe, reveals similar inequalities. Disparities of this magnitude in the use of resources highlights the point that the nature of the water crisis is not so much that of absolute scarcity, but rather that of uneven geographical distribution and consumption – a matter that relates to governance and social justice.

Looking at the projected estimates of water consumption per capita for 2020, the disparities are glaring – the figure increases by about 35 per cent in Africa and Latin America compared to more than 250 per cent in China and India. It must be noted, though, that these consumption disparities largely reflect the differences in the level of industrialisation and development, and, as such, recent economic growth reported in many countries in the Global South is expected to push consumption levels up. However, regardless of the anticipated rise of water consumption per capita in the Global South, it can be argued that if the water resources were to be shared more evenly, no one would lack access to basic clean water. Webb and Iskandarani (1998: 16), citing Rosegrant (1997), observe that,

> As with food, the world still has sufficient water at an aggregate level to meet everyone's minimum needs. Against estimated annual renewable freshwater supplies of between 9 and 14 trillion cubic meters, current global usage stands at less than 4 trillion cubic meters. As is the case with food, however, the global availability of water is *not* matched by adequate local access. Freshwater is unevenly distributed geographically and temporally, resulting in surpluses for some people and a threat of severe water insecurity for others.

The unevenness in access to water is not just a matter of uneven geographical distribution; it is also a function of social construction – which results in some people, in the same geographical location, having access to clean water, while others do not. Inequalities in the distribution and consumption of water globally are largely a socially produced space, which a rights approach strives to reconfigure by engaging the power structures and dynamics that produce and reproduce these spaces.

Pressure from Expanding Economic Activities

In terms of economic activities, the growth in global GDP can be used as a proxy indicator of the growing pressure on natural resources, including water.

In this regard, while the "global" economy in 1950 was producing goods and services worth slightly more than US$17 billion a day, by 2000 this figure had risen to US$107.5 billion per day (Institute for International Economics 2004: 5);[3] and by 2010 it was estimated at US$158.8 billion per day,[4] rising to $181.9 billion in 2014 (World Bank 2014). Thus, the water crisis that is increasingly receiving international attention needs to highlight the mismatch between demand[5] for, and the supply of, water (Saleth 2002). While the supply has remained constant (almost), demand is growing rapidly. Paradoxically, it is this seeming imbalance between supply and demand that has helped to draw attention to the issues that surround water, including access to water for domestic use (Webb and Iskandarani 1998).

In terms of sectoral water consumption, Table 5.1 below gives a rough idea of how water consumption is shared by the major water-consuming sectors. At

TABLE 5.1 *Water consumption by sector (%)*

	Domestic	Agriculture	Industry
Africa	10.9	84.2	4.9
Latin America and Caribbean	21.4	66.3	12.4
North America	14	38.9	47.1
East Asia	12.2	64.8	23.1
Average[a]	14.6	63.5	21.8
World[b]	8	69	23

Note: Figures for Africa, Latin America and the Caribbean are for 2000; the figures for East Asia are for 2005.
a = this is the unweighted mean for the four regions with data.
b = the weighted mean for the world including Europe, South and South East Asia and Pacific.
SOURCE: HTTP://WWW.UNESCAP.ORG/STAT/DATA/STATDB/DATAEXPLORER.ASPX.

3 The figures are converted to the 1993 dollar Purchasing Power Parity price.

4 If this production was shared evenly, the average per capita income per day would be around US$23 – but we know that in 2010 more than 60 per cent of the population survived on less than US$2 per day (see World Bank 2010).

5 Although it has been argued that improvements in technology have meant that resources are now used more efficiently than previously (see Saleth 2002; Roger 1997), this has not translated into efficient use of water, especially with regard to agriculture and mining which consume vast amounts.

the global level, agriculture in all its different forms (irrigation, fish farming, livestock, etc.) uses more than two-thirds of the world's fresh water. For this reason, agriculture has often been cited as the most inefficient user of water at the global level (Mollinga *et al.* 2007).

The unevenness between distribution and consumption of water at the global level is also reflected at the continental level. In African countries, renewable fresh water resources are unevenly distributed – ranging from 286km^3/year in Nigeria and Cameron, to just less than 1km^3/year in Djibouti and Libya (Table 5.2). Water use per capita also reflects high disparities – ranging from the highest of over 800m^3/year in Sudan and Egypt, to just 7m^3/year in the Central African Republic. Differences in the amount of water used are strongly influenced by the main economic activities of each country. Countries where irrigation-based agriculture is well developed tend to use more water. The average figures reported at regional and country level also hide the huge disparities that exist within countries.

With regard to the proportion of people with access to clean water sources, the overall picture for most of the selected African countries shows great improvement, especially for the period 2000–08 (see Table 5.3, below). The lowest percentage of people with access to improved sources of water in 2008 was reported in Ethiopia at 38 per cent, but the overall trend from 1990 shows a steady increase. The country with the highest proportion of people with access to improved water sources in 2008 was Egypt – with 99 per cent. While most countries registered a steady increase in the proportion of people with access to safe drinking water between 2000–08, the ratio in countries such as Algeria, Angola, Mali, Mozambique, Sudan, Niger and Lesotho declined by between 5–11 per cent over this same period. Declining levels of access to clean water is often an indication of the non-fulfilment of the right to water for some people. According to international norms on the right to water, declining access to it, as discussed below, is an indication of the state failing to progressively meet the right to water obligation.

Table 5.3 reveals a worrying gap with regard to the ratio of people with access to water in urban and rural areas. In countries such as Sierra Leone, Togo, Zambia, DRC, Niger, Ethiopia, Madagascar and Mozambique, the proportion of the rural population with access to improved sources of water was 50 per cent or less in 2008, reflecting the severe constraints on rural populations when it comes to accessing safe water. In most countries the access ratios for urban areas are 20 per cent more than the ratios for rural areas – except in Tunisia, Namibia, Algeria, Cape Verde and Gambia, where the gap between rural and urban access ratios is much smaller.

From a rights-based approach point of view, such huge disparities between urban and rural provision raise concerns and may be seen as unequal

TABLE 5.2 *Water resources and use profile for selected African countries*

Country	Renew-able fresh water (km^3/yr)[a]	Total fresh water w/drawal (km^3/yr)[b]	Per cap. w/drawal ($m^3/capita/yr$)	Dom. use (%)	Ind. use (%)	Agric. use (%)	Dom. use/capita ($m^3/capita/yr$)	Ind. use/capita ($m^3/capita/yr$)	Agric. use/capita ($m^3/capita/yr$)	2010 Pop'n (mill.)
Algeria	11.6	6.07	171	22	13	65	38	23	111	35.4
Angola	184	0.35	18	23	17	60	4	3	11	19.0
Botswana	14.7	0.19	96	41	18	41	39	17	39	2.0
Burkina Faso	17.5	0.80	49	13	1	86	6	0	42	16.3
Burundi	3.6	0.29	34	17	6	77	6	2	26	8.5
Cameroon	285.5	0.99	50	18	8	74	9	4	37	20.0
Cape Verde	0.3	0.02	39	7	2	91	3	1	36	0.5
CAR	144.4	0.03	7	80	16	4	5	1	0	4.5
Chad	43	0.23	20	17	0	83	3	0	17	11.5
Côte d'Ivoire	81	0.93	43	24	12	65	10	5	28	21.6
Djibouti	0.3	0.02	23	84	0	16	19	0	4	0.9
Egypt	58	68.30	809	8	6	86	62	49	695	84.5
E.Guinea	26	0.11	159	83	16	1	132	25	2	0.7
Gabon	164	0.12	80	50	8	42	40	6	34	1.5
Gambia	8	0.03	17	23	12	65	4	2	11	1.8
Ghana	53.2	0.98	40	24	10	66	10	4	27	24.3
Guinea	226	1.51	146	8	2	90	11	3	132	10.3
Lesotho	5.2	0.05	24	40	40	20	10	10	5	2.1
Liberia	232	0.11	27	27	18	55	7	5	15	4.1
Libya	0.6	4.27	652	14	3	83	91	20	541	6.5

TABLE 5.2 *Water resources and use profile for selected African countries* (cont.)

Country	Renew-able fresh water (km³/yr)[a]	Total fresh water w/drawal (km³/yr)[b]	Per cap. w/drawal (m³/capita/yr)	Dom. use (%)	Ind. use (%)	Agric. use (%)	Dom. use/capita (m³/capita/yr)	Ind. use/capita (m³/capita/yr)	Agric. use/ capita (m³/capita/yr)	2010 Pop'n (mill.)
Madagascar	337	14.96	743	3	2	96	21	12	710	20.1
Malawi	17.3	1.01	64	15	5	80	9	3	51	15.7
Mali	100	6.55	492	9	1	90	44	5	442	13.3
Mauritania	11.4	1.70	505	9	3	88	45	14	446	3.4
Namibia	17.7	0.3	136	24	5	71	33	6	96	2.2
Niger	33.7	2.18	137	4	0	95	5	0	130	15.9
Nigeria	286.2	8.01	51	21	10	69	11	5	35	158.3
Rwanda	9.5	0.15	15	24	8	68	4	1	10	10.3
South Africa	50	12.50	248	31	6	63	77	15	156	50.5
Sudan	64.5	37.32	864	3	1	97	23	6	835	43.2
Tanzania	91	5.18	115	10	0	89	12	0	102	45.0
Togo	14.7	0.17	25	53	2	45	13	1	11	6.8
Tunisia	4.6	2.64	254	14	4	82	36	10	209	10.4
Zambia	105.2	1.74	131	17	7	76	22	9	100	13.3

Note: All the figures, except population figures, are for 2005.

a Renewable freshwater includes surface and underground water stock, and reflects the water endowment levels.

b Water withdraw refers to water taken out of its natural environment for various uses including agricultural, industrial, commercial and domestic use. [pop] = population.

SOURCE: AUTHOR, BASED ON DATA FROM GLEICK *ET AL.* (2011).

TABLE 5.3 *Access to improved drinking water for selected African countries (1990–2008, %)*

	Urban				Rural				Total			
	1990	2000	2005	2008	1990	2000	2005	2008	1990	2000	2005	2008
Algeria	..	88	88	85		94	81	79	..	94	85	83
Angola	73	34	54	60	20	40	39	38	35	38	47	50
Benin	73	74	82	84	43	55	65	69	54	63	72	75
Cameroon	42	82	90	92	45	42	48	51	44	62	71	74
Cape Verde		64	86	85		89	82	82		74	84	84
CAR	19	80	89	92	26	43	50	51	23	60	65	67
DRC	68	89	82	80	24	26	28	28	36	45	45	46
Côte D'Ivoire	57	90	92	93	80	65	67	68	71	77	79	80
Djibouti		100	95	98		100	55	52		100	89	92
Egypt	95	96	100	100	86	94	96	98	90	95	98	99
E. Guinea	65	45	45		18	42	42		32	43	43	
Eritrea	..	63	74	74	..	42	57	57	..	46	60	61
Ethiopia	..	77	95	98	..	13	24	26	..	24	35	38
Gabon	..	73	95	95	..	55	43	41	..	70	86	87
Gambia	100	80	94	96	48	53	83	86	60	62	89	92
Ghana	63	87	89	90	..	49	68	74	21	64	78	82
Guinea	100	72	89	89	37	36	57	61	53	48	68	71
Guinea-Bissau	..	29	82	83	..	55	48	51	..	49	58	60
Kenya	..	87	85	83	..	31	48	52	..	49	56	59
Lesotho	..	98	96	97	..	88	79	81	..	91	83	85

TABLE 5.3 *Access to improved drinking water for selected African countries (1990–2008, %)* (cont.)

	Urban				Rural				Total			
	1990	2000	2005	2008	1990	2000	2005	2008	1990	2000	2005	2008
Madagascar	..	85	71	71	..	31	27	29	..	47	40	41
Malawi	..	95	94	95	..	44	70	77	..	57	74	80
Mali	41	74	77	81	4	61	40	44	13	65	51	56
Mauritania	..	34	49	52	..	40	43	47	..	37	45	49
Morocco	100	100	97	98	18	58	60	60	56	82	80	81
Mozambique	..	86	76	77	..	43	29	29	..	60	45	47
Namibia	90	100	99	99	37	67	82	88	52	77	88	92
Niger	98	70	89	96	45	56	37	39	56	59	45	48
Nigeria	100	81	76	75	22	39	40	42	49	57	57	58
Rwanda	84	60	80	77	67	40	63	62	68	41	66	65
Senegal	65	92	91	92	26	65	51	52	42	78	68	69
Sierra Leone	80	23	82	86	20	31	33	26	39	28	51	49
South Africa	..	92	99	99	..	80	75	78	..	86	89	91
Sudan	..	86	68	64	..	69	53	52	..	75	59	57
Tanzania	..	80	82	80	..	42	45	45	..	54	54	54
Togo	..	85	86	87	..	38	40	41	..	54	58	60
Tunisia	..	..	99	99	..		84	84	..	..	94	94
Uganda	60	72	89	91	30	46	60	64	33	50	64	67
Zambia	..	88	87	87	..	48	42	46	..	64	58	60
Zimbabwe	95	100	99	99	80	77	72	72	84	85	82	82

Notes: Safe drinking water was defined to include distance (source within 1km) and quantity (20 litres/person/day).
[..] = no data available.

SOURCE: AUTHOR, BASED ON DATA FROM *GLEICK ET AL.* (2011).

treatment – unless there is clear evidence that efforts are being made to address the problem. Article 37 (e) of *General Comment 15*, identifies the obligation "to ensure equitable distribution of all available water facilities and services" as one of the core obligations for states parties to the Covenant; and further, that this obligation is non-derogable (see *General Comment 15*: para. 40). Huge disparities in access levels between rural and urban areas may be a sign of the failure to ensure equitable distribution of water services, and the onus would be on the state to demonstrate that appropriate measures to address this discrepancy have been, or are being, implemented.

What is presented above constitutes the context in which the debates and struggles surrounding the right to water should be situated. This context is one in which almost one billion people (most of them living in the Global South) have no access to improved sources of water. Although there are indications that the situation is improving in all regions, including Africa, almost 40 per cent of the total population of that continent still has no access to safe water (WHO/UNICEF 2010).

Myriad Conferences and Policy Documents, Paucity of Programmes

Arguably, at the international level, attention to issues of fresh water resource management and development have only begun to feature prominently during the last two decades. It might be argued that the concern to address issues of water resources only surfaced in the 1990s at the time of an imminent water crisis (Rogers 1997). The increased attention directed towards issues of water can be inferred from the number of international conferences that have been dedicated to the subject, especially during the 1990s. Since the Mar del Plata Conference in 1977 – which was the first international conference specifically dedicated to discussing water issues – there have been myriad water conferences as shown in Table 5.4 below. However, while many of these conferences focused on water and made a number of solemn declarations, progress in realising a world where everyone has access to a basic clean water supply has been painfully slow (Biswas 1997; Falkenmark 1997). Assessing the impact of Mar del Plata, Biswas (1997: 114) makes the observation that

> [w]hile the *Mar del Plata Action Plan* provided an excellent road map, it would be true to say that we have not succeeded to follow this map to any significant extent. There have been many global meetings and discussions on water issues, ranging from Dublin and Rio in 1992, to New York in 1997. All of these have contributed marginally so far in terms of:

- putting water firmly on the international political agenda
- making governments aware of the real urgency of the water crisis facing mankind, so that they are forced to take immediate and concrete actions; and
- where do we now want to go, and how do we get there.

Evidence of the failure to follow up on the principles of Mar del Plata include the fact that 37 years after the conference there are still close to a billion people living without access to clean water, and more than 2.6 billion people living without adequate sanitation (WHO/UNICEF 2012). Despite most governments having committed themselves to the responsibility to ensure that "all people" have access to basic clean water, this commitment has meant little for many people the world over, especially in the Global South.

Water in the Global Political Economy

As one might infer from the number of conferences on water highlighted in Table 5.4, water seems to be attracting immense political attention, globally.[6] This upsurge of interest in water may be attributed to many factors, but emerging awareness of a "looming" water crisis is one of the main ones (Mollinga *et al.* 2007). While the magnitude of the crisis is not fully understood, there seems to be a growing awareness that the current rate of water resources consumption at the global level is unsustainable. Although much of the water crisis campaign literature has focused on issues surrounding sustainable use of resources, it is essential to note that much of the crisis – especially with regard to the domestic water supply – is related to management (second order scarcity) and allocation of water resources, rather than being a first order scarcity problem.[7] In reality, as Global Water Partnership notes, "the water crisis is mainly a crisis of governance" (cited in Mollinga *et al.* 2007: 700). The world has enough water resources, just as it does other resources, like food. The Second *United Nations World Water Development Report* (UNESCO 2006: 3) also confirms this when it states that "[t]here is enough

6 This is clearly evident from the number of international conferences on water in the last decade-and-a-half, but also from the deepening controversy about how water management, delivery, pricing and conservation should be handled.

7 First order scarcity is often defined as the natural or physical deficit of water resources resulting from natural occurrences such as low annual rainfall, geological formation and uneven distribution; second order scarcity is seen as a result of capacity and technological constraints which are linked to prevailing macroeconomic conditions and political institutions (see Chileshe *et al.* 2005; Perret 2002). Third order scarcity is mainly attributed to social and political arrangements around water usage, governance and management (Brooks 2006). Often, second and third order scarcities are intricately linked and reinforce each other.

TABLE 5.4 *International Water Conferences (1972–2012)*

Conference	Year	Statement
UN Conference on the Human Environment, Stockholm	1972	"We must shape our actions throughout the world with a more prudent care for their environmental consequences"
UN Conference on Water, Mar del Plata	1977	"All peoples, whatever their stage of development and their social and economic conditions, have the right to have access to drinking water in quantities and of a quality equal to their basic needs"
International Drinking Water and Sanitation Decade	1981–90	
International Conference on Water and the Environment, Dublin	1992	"Fresh water is a finite and vulnerable resource, essential to sustain life, development and the environment"
UN Conference on Environment and Development (UNCED Earth Summit), Rio de Janeiro	1992	"The holistic management of freshwater… and the integration of sectoral water plans and programmes within the framework of national economic and social policy, are of paramount importance for action in the 1990s and beyond"
Ministerial Conference on Drinking Water Supply and Environmental Sanitation, Noordwijk	1994	"To assign high priority to programmes designed to provide basic sanitation and excreta disposal systems to urban and rural areas"
World Summit for Social Development, Copenhagen	1995	"These efforts should include the provision of…safe drinking water and sanitation"
UN Fourth World Conference on Women, Beijing	1995	"Ensure the availability of and universal access to safe drinking water and sanitation and put in place effective public distribution systems as soon as possible"
World Food Summit, Rome	1996	"To combat environmental threats to food security"
1st World Water Forum, Marrakech	1997	"To recognize the basic human needs to have access to clean water and sanitation"

TABLE 5.4 *International Water Conferences* (1972–2012) (cont.)

Conference	Year	Statement
2nd World Water Forum, the Hague	1997	"Massively increase investments in water"
Millennium Declaration	2000	"We resolve...to halve, by the year 2015... the proportion of people who are unable to reach or to afford safe drinking water"
International Conference on Freshwater, Bonn	2001	"Water plays a vital role in relation to human health, livelihood, economic growth as well as sustaining ecosystems"
World Summit on Sustainable Development, Rio +10, Johannesburg	2002	"Integrate sanitation into water resources management strategies"
3rd World Water Forum, Japan	2003	
Rio +20, Rio de Janeiro)	2012	"We reaffirm our commitments regarding the human right to safe drinking water and sanitation, to be progressively realized for our populations"

SOURCE: ADAPTED FROM UNESCO'S *WORLD WATER ASSESSMENT PROGRAMME: "FROM STOCKHOLM TO KYOTO"* (AVAILABLE AT: WWW.UNESCO.ORG/WATER).

water for everyone. The problem we face today is largely one of governance: equitably sharing this water while ensuring the sustainability of natural ecosystems. At this point in time, we have not yet achieved this balance".

Popular predictions of "water wars" in hot-spot areas (water-stressed countries and regions), while they highlight the challenges of water scarcity in specific regions, overlook the unequal distribution of global water resources. This focus on the imminent water crisis distracts attention away from the current unevenness in distribution and access to water; and this, in turn, distracts efforts aimed at addressing these disparities.

Interestingly, at the same time that global political interest in water has been growing, private sector interest has been too – specifically after the *Dublin Statement* and the Rio Earth Summit of 1992. This growth of private sector interest in water post-Rio Summit is seen by some analysts as no mere coincidence. The *Dublin Statement* and the Rio Summit mark significant turning points. One of the key statements made by both the Dublin and Rio summits is the ambivalent recognition of water as both an *economic* and a *public good*. For many analysts, this recognition of water as an economic good further opened the door for moving water services deep into the bosom of the market. Prospects for making profits from the water business have been high for large multinational water corporations such as Suez, Vivendi, Sauers and Thames Water. However, this growing private sector interest in water supply services is largely limited to major cities, where high demand can guarantee a sustainable market for, and lucrative returns from, water services. Provision of water services to the smaller, and poorer, cities has been left to the hard-pressed local municipalities (Chitonge 2011).

It should also be noted that private sector involvement in water did not begin in the 1990s. The private sector has been part of the water delivery arrangement for a long time, especially in Europe and America. Swyngedouw (2005) identifies four major phases in the configuration of the water service delivery system.[8] A common feature of all of them is that private sector actors have been part of water services provision from the very inception of reticulated water systems. However, it was during the 1980s that an aggressive private sector participation policy was adopted globally, supported by the view that the private sector was more efficient and therefore better positioned to address the growing problems of water service delivery (see Prasad 2006). This view became widespread during the 1990s, and was followed by widespread attempts to privatise water services in many countries (Hall and Lobina 2006).

The Right to Water and the Commodification of Water

With regard to the right to water, there are possible dangers arising from its commodification. This has triggered a counter-force, in many parts of the world, that seeks to block the expansion of the market into water supply services (Bond 2005; Hall and Lobina 2005). Apart from the possible negative implications of treating water as a commodity, the risks of exploiting and depleting water resources have been widely acknowledged. Anti-privatisation movements all over the world have mobilised against the move to treat water just like any other commodity (Hall and Lobina 2006; Bond 2004). A 2005 publication by the Transnational Institute and Corporate Europe Observatory, entitled

---

8 The four phases identified by Swyngedouw are the period from the first inception of piped water in medieval Rome up to the second half of the nineteenth century when water was provided by small private companies which supplied only parts of cities. The second phase was the *municipalisation* of the water services which occurred between the second half of the nineteenth century and the First World War – prompted by sanitary and environmental concerns in cities. The third phase was the management of water services by national bodies or public utilities, which occurred after the First World War. The fourth phase started during the 1980s when the third wave of privatisation initiated by the Thatcher government took centre stage (see Swyngedouw 2005: 83–4).

Reclaiming Public Water, documents these anti-privatisation struggles all over the world (Balanya *et al.* 2005).[9] Through these struggles we witness what Polanyi (1944: 130) calls a "double movement": the expansion of the market evokes a counter-force that opposes its further expansion. Many of these anti-commodification movements and protests use the rights discourse to build and sustain their struggle for water, as shown in chapter 8.

At the global level there are fears that the commodification of water may trigger unscrupulous exploitation of water resources, with obvious environmental consequences. The basic argument is that water is one of the *commons* and it is therefore not right to embark on a policy of enclosing it (Dinar *et al* n.d.). On the other side of the debate it is argued that recognising the economic value of water promotes its efficient use, which in turn encourages conservation and sustainability. This debate is inconclusive, but from a human rights perspective – and regardless of whether the service provider is a private or a public entity – states should ensure that the activities of these actors do not hinder or interfere with access to water, especially for the poor (*General Comment 15*: para. 24).

The Right to Water[10] in International Human Rights Law

Although water is acknowledged to be central to the existence and sustenance of all forms of life, including human life, it is only recently that it has begun to receive noticeable attention – both at the national and international level – in terms of explicitly recognising access to water as a human right. Unlike the right to food, which has been explicitly recognised in a number of international human rights instruments, the right to water is in most cases only implicitly recognised – and mostly at the international level. Some of the major public international law instruments which have implicitly or explicitly recognised the access to water as a human right, are briefly reviewed below.

9 The Cochabamba "Water Wars" which occurred in Bolivia since 2001 are an example of strong resistance to the commodification of water services.

10 There is a significant difference between the "right to water" and "water rights". The right to water is often used to signify the entitlement to access and use of water for domestic purposes, while water rights encompass a wider range of entitlements which include the right to divert water out its natural environment. For an elaboration on the distinction between the "right to water" and "water rights", see Hodgson (2004).

Implicit Recognition of the Right to Water

United Nations Charter Article 55

Article 55 of the United Nations Charter – which provides for "a higher standard of living, full employment, and conditions of economic and social progress and development" as necessary conditions for global peace and security – is often cited as the foundation for most ESCRs, including the right to development (Bedjaoui 1994b) and the right to water. Although water is not explicitly mentioned, the argument has been that a purposive interpretation of the phrases "higher standards of living", and "social progress", clearly includes water as an essential constituent. Similarly, it has been observed that respect for human rights and fundamental freedoms would be impossible to contemplate without access to safe and clean water. Although the *UN Charter* is legally binding on all parties, it is sometimes argued that this implicit recognition of access to clean water as a human right weakens its public appeal and influence.

Article 25 of the Universal Declaration of Human Rights (UDHR)

Like the *UN Charter*, Article 25 of the *Universal Declaration of Human Rights* also provides for everyone to have the

> right to a standard of living adequate for the health and well-being of himself and of his family, including food, clothing, housing and medical care and necessary social services, and the right to security in the event of unemployment, sickness, disability, widowhood, old age or other lack of livelihood in circumstances beyond his control.
> (para. 1)

Again, there is an implicit argument here that a standard of living adequate for one's health and well-being cannot be realised in circumstances where one has no access to clean water. Gleick, for instance, argues (1998: 5) that

> [s]atisfying the standards of *Article 25* cannot be done without water of a sufficient quantity and quality to maintain human health and well-being. Meeting a standard of living adequate for the health and well-being of individuals requires the availability of a minimum amount of clean water.

Articles 11 and 12 of the International Covenant on Economic, Social and Cultural Rights (ICESCR)

Article 11 of the *ICESCR* contains a provision that has similar wording to Article 25 of the *UDHR* – except that it adds the phrase "and to the continuous improvement of living conditions". Like Article 25 of the *UDHR*, Article 11 of the ICESCR explicitly mentions food, housing and clothing – but not water. Health is provided for separately in Article 12, which stipulates that "States Parties to the present Covenant recognize the right of everyone to the enjoyment of the highest attainable standard of physical and mental health".

Here again, although water is not explicitly mentioned it is assumed that realising the highest standard of physical and mental health is both conceptually and practically unachievable without access to clean water. A purposeful interpretation of this provision is one that is expected to include water to ensure that people – especially those who cannot provide for themselves – have access to essential needs such as clean water, sanitation, food and medical care, all of which make the attainment of physical and mental health possible. The OHCHR *Guidelines on Human Rights and Poverty Reduction Strategies* (2002: para. 116) adopts a similar interpretation, arguing that,

> [t]he right to health is not to be understood as the right to be healthy: the state cannot provide protection against every possible cause of ill health. It is the right to the enjoyment of a variety of facilities, goods, services and conditions necessary for the realisation of the highest attainable standard of health. The right includes both health care and the underlying determinants of health, including access to potable water, adequate and safe food, adequate sanitation and housing, healthy occupational and environmental conditions, and access to health-related information and education.

General Comment 14, which elaborates on the right to health, offers a similar interpretation – arguing that the right to health is not to be interpreted as the *right to be healthy*, but rather as a right to a "system of protection and opportunities that enable people to enjoy the highest attainable level of health" (para. 14). This interpretation, which seems to be a comment on Article 12 of the *ICESCR*, can be read as an extension of the right to health to include access to water, food and housing. *General Comment 14* states that the right to health should not be understood in a narrow sense, but in a wider and comprehensive sense. The Committee on Economic, Social and Cultural Rights (CESCR), in *General Comment 12*, has taken a similar view when elaborating on the right to food – pointing out that this right is not to be interpreted narrowly, i.e. merely equating it to a package of calories, but should be seen in the overall objective and purpose of the Covenant (see *General Comment 12*: para. 6). A similar view is expressed in the right to health when the CESCR defines the right to health "as an inclusive right extending not only to timely and appropriate health care but also to the underlying determinants of health, such as access to safe and potable water and adequate sanitation" (*General Comment 14*: para. 11).

If one takes a purposive approach to these provisions, it is possible to argue that access to basic clean water is implicitly secured by *Article 12* of the *ICESCR*. This approach has, however, been questioned – with some analysts arguing that this "derivation of a separate right to water is virtually without precedent" (Dennis and Stewart 2004: 494). But critics argue that a narrow interpretation of the provisions in these instruments would make most of them meaningless.

Clearly, Article 11 of the *ICESCR* – which also provides for many ESCRs including the right to food – if broadly interpreted would also include access to water as a constitutive element of the right. This is the position taken by the CESCR in *General Comment 4*, where it is argued that the right to housing should not be interpreted in a narrow sense to mean a roof between four walls; rather, this right should be "interpreted so as to take account of a variety of other considerations…" (para. 7). The CESCR, which is the official body[11] tasked with interpreting, providing guidance and assisting states to comply with the *ICESCR*, has adopted a definition of housing that includes access to clean basic water as an indispensable component.

Article 6 of the International Covenant on Civil and Political Rights (ICCPR)

Article 6 (1) of the *ICCPR* provides for the right to life: "Every human being has the inherent right to life." While this provision does not mention access to clean water explicitly, it has been argued that a purposive interpretation of the principle of an inherent right to life would include anything essential to preserving life (Scanlon *et al.* 2004; Gleick 1998). Many commentators have agreed that a generous or purposive interpretation of the right to life is most likely to embrace, at least, access to water as one of the key components that fall within its ambit. Unfortunately, as *General Comment 6* explains: "[T]he Committee has noted that the right to life has been too often narrowly interpreted. The expression 'inherent right to life' cannot properly be understood in a restrictive manner" (para. 5).

Adopting a generous interpretation creates room for the argument that even if water is "not explicitly mentioned in the final document of the

11 The Committee does not have the adjudicating rights; its major tasks include elaborating on and interpreting various articles of the covenant (like the general comments), receiving States parties' reports and commenting on the progress that countries make towards realizing the Covenant rights.

Covenant, the right to life implies the right to the fundamental conditions necessary to support life" (Gleick 1998: 6) – of which access to clean water is one of the most obvious. In this sense, failure to access clean water, to the extent that it results in people losing their lives, does impinge on the right to life under this article. Based on this understanding the CESCR has argued that the "right to water should be seen in conjunction with other rights enshrined in the International Bill of Rights, foremost among them the right to life and human dignity" (*General Comment 15*: para. 3).

However, Article 6 (1) of the *ICCPR* is sometimes understood as specifically addressing situations related to *arbitrary* deprivation of one's life.[12] In view of this, the main question here is whether death resulting from lack of access to clean water can be defined as an arbitrary deprivation. In recent times it has been suggested that failure to access water does often lead to the deprivation of life in a broader sense:

> Not having access to water and sanitation is a polite euphemism for a form of deprivation that threatens life, destroys opportunity and undermines human dignity. Being without access to water means that people resort to ditches, rivers and lakes polluted with human or animal excrement or used by animals.
>
> UNDP 2006: 5, See also WHO 2003

Article 8 (1) of the Declaration on the Right to Development (DRD)

The *Declaration on the Right to Development*, like many other international human rights instruments, does not explicitly mention access to water. Arguments in support of water as a human right are derived from the broader context in which the declaration was made, based on a purposive interpretation of its provisions. Article 8 (1), in particular, provides for states to take "all necessary measures for the realization of the right to development", ensuring "equality of opportunity for all in their access to basic resources, education, health services, food, housing [and] employment". Again, note how food, health, housing and employment are explicitly mentioned, while water is not. But although water is not specifically mentioned it can be argued that a full list of "basic resources" – that the article alludes to – is likely to include water given its fundamental role in sustaining human life, well-being and development in general (see WHO/UNICEF 2012).

12 This is probably true given the anti-capital punishment campaign during the 1960s – when the two covenants on civil and political rights, and economic, social and cultural rights were negotiated and finalised.

Articles 16 and 24 of the African Charter on Human and People's Rights (ACHPR)

Article 16 of the *ACHPR*, like Article 25 of the *UDHR* and Article 11 of the *ICESCR*, provides that every individual shall have the right to the "best attainable state of physical and mental health", and that the states parties to the Charter "shall take the necessary measures to protect the health of their people". While this does not explicitly mention access to water, a right to the "best attainable physical and mental state" is inconceivable in a situation where access to water is not secured. Similarly, while Article 24 of the *ACHPR* does not provide overtly for access to water, it can be argued that the "right to a general satisfactory environment" – which the article does provides for – cannot be realised under conditions where there is no access to clean water or adequate sanitation.

Derived from Other Explicitly Recognised Rights

A common argument often advanced in support of the right to water is that it is absurd to talk about a person having a right to food, for instance, without basic water for drinking, cooking and washing (Ziegler 2003). As noted above, the CESCR argues convincingly that the right to food should not be interpreted in a narrow sense; instead it should serve to "underline a number of factors which must be taken into account" (ibid.: para. 7). Therefore, the conclusion reached is that even if water is not *explicitly* mentioned on the list of basic human rights that are protected in major international human rights instruments, it is *implied* through the explicit protection given to other rights such as food, housing, environment and health. Proponents of this view argue that it is generally impossible to give meaningful protection to many rights under conditions where access to clean water is not safeguarded (OHCHR 2004).

At this point one might ask why water has not been explicitly mentioned in the human rights instruments in the same way that other ESCRs such as food, health and social security, employment and housing have? One of the answers given is that the list in Article 25 of the *UDHR* or Articles 11 and 12 of the *ICESCR* is not meant to be all-inclusive; rather it should be viewed as representative or indicative of the "component elements of an adequate standard of living" (Gleick 1998: 5). The CESCR (*General Comment 15*: para. 3) has expanded this point, arguing that the

> use of the word 'including' indicates that this catalogue of rights was not intended to be exhaustive. The right to water clearly falls within the category of guarantees essential for securing an adequate standard of living, particularly since it is one of the most fundamental conditions for survival.

Scanlon *et al.* (2004: 12) make a similar argument, adding that the list in Article 25 of the UDHR was only meant to serve an *indicative purpose*, highlighting some of the factors essential to meeting an "adequate standard of living".

Without underplaying the merits of these arguments, it should be submitted that an explicit recognition of water would have generated a more forceful argument for, and influence of, the right to water. However, as argued in the next chapter, human rights as social, political norms, evolve with the changing society; and they are not at any time exhaustive of the values that society deems valuable to protect. The fact that some value was not explicitly mentioned does not mean that it should never be included. Such an argument would only be valid if one follows MacIntyre's (1985) view that since there were no human rights in earlier generations, no new human rights should be expected to emerge today (see Chapter 1).

Explicit Provisions for the Right to Water

Other than the above instruments, which have implicitly provided for the right to water, there have been a few human rights instruments (including some national constitutions) which have explicitly mentioned clean water as a basic human entitlement – although most of them have provided for specific categories of people such as children, women, prisoners, etc. Major human rights instruments that have explicitly provided for water are discussed below.

The Geneva Conventions and Protocols

One of the earliest human rights instruments to refer to water as a right are the Geneva Conventions (II, III and IV) and Additional Protocols I and II. But, as noted above, these are provisions for people in special circumstances – like prisoners of war. For instance, the Geneva Convention III of 1949 (para. 29), provides that,

> apart from the baths and showers with which the camps shall be furnished, prisoners of war shall be provided with sufficient water and soap for their personal toilet and for washing their personal laundry; the necessary installations, facilities and time shall be granted them for that purpose.

Similarly, the Additional Protocol II to the Geneva Conventions, adopted in 1977, provides that "sufficient drinking water shall be supplied to prisoners of war" (para. 26). But still the question of whether the provisions protecting people in specific circumstances can be extended to cover everyone remains to be answered. It is highly unlikely that a household in an informal settlement that has no access to water can rely on these provisions to claim the right to water. Very few judges would see residents of shanty towns as beneficiaries contemplated by the drafters of these conventions and protocols.

Legal analysts have been at pains to explain why this provision was restricted to a special category of people – prisoners of war. One explanation is that the provision was made under the assumption that people who are *not* prisoners of war would have guaranteed access to clean basic water; it was therefore never contemplated that they should be named as beneficiaries of this right. This may well have been the thinking that influenced the drafting of the earlier human rights instruments – including the *UDHR* – which took it for granted that access to water was so basic that it would be absurd to assume that someone might be deprived of it. Following this line of argument it can be submitted that providing for the right to water, explicitly, would be as absurd as providing for the right to air as separate from the right to a clean environment or the right to life. But it has now become apparent that circumstances have changed such that it is now essential to explicitly protect the right to water rather than derive it from other rights (Scanlon *et al.* 2004).

Article 14.2 (h) *Convention on the Elimination of All Forms of Discrimination Against Women* (*CEDAW*)

Among the major international human rights instruments, the *CEDAW* is one that explicitly provides for access to water as a basic right. Article 14.2 (h) provides for the right "to enjoy adequate living conditions, particularly in relation to housing, sanitation, electricity and water supply". Although this provision is made with reference to women, in particular, given the strong emphasis on equality[13] that human rights principles entail it is would probably correct to give this provision a non-discriminatory interpretation and consequently give it a universal application. If the *CEDAW*'s objective is to address discrimination that women have been subjected to, these provisions should be understood to stand true for *any* form of discrimination – not just that perpetuated against women but that perpetuated against *all* people so that the beneficiaries of this provision might not be restricted to women alone. An important point to note here is that this article creates a legally binding obligation on all states parties

13 Even *CEDAW* itself, in the *Preamble*, acknowledges that discrimination of any sort violates the principle of equality – which is one of the fundamental values of the international human rights system.

to ensure that the rights protected therein are realised for all people and not just women.

Article 24.2 (*c*) Convention on the Rights of the Child (CRC)

The other explicit provision in major international human rights instruments concerning the right to water can be found in Article 24.2 (c) of the *CRC*, which provides, *inter alia*, for the right of every child to "the provision of adequate nutritious foods and clean drinking water". Again, and for the reason cited above, this right may not be interpreted as restricted to children only. In the case of children, many rights afforded to them often become reality in a context where adults play a key role. Children have been brought to centre stage to emphasise the vulnerability of their rights. Thus, it might also be appropriate to give this article a universal application.

Article 14.2 (*c*) African Charter on the Rights and Welfare of the Child (ACRWC)

At the regional level, the *ACRWC*, Article 14, explicitly provides for the right to water. It stipulates that states parties to this Charter shall take measures "to ensure the provision of adequate nutrition and safe drinking water". Unlike the *CRC* – where the right to access clean water is provided for independently – the provision under the *ACRWC* is made within the health clause. Article 14, under which water is mentioned, actually has the heading "Health and Health Services". But although water is provided for under the umbrella of health, it is explicitly mentioned as an entitlement for the beneficiaries envisioned in this clause.

The Consequences of Implicit and Explicit Recognition

Looking at both the explicit and implicit provisions concerning the right to water, there are three major points that need to be highlighted.

Interdependence of Human Rights

First, it is clear that the right to water is intricately linked to other human rights. In the many documents where water is explicitly mentioned, it is not mentioned in isolation. This is not only a feature associated with the right to water, but other human rights as well. In both the explicit and implicit provisions, water is inextricably linked to other human rights such that the right to food or adequate housing or health (Ahluwalia 2004). This interrelationship between human rights is captured in *General Comment 14* (para. 3), where it is argued that

> The right to health is closely related to and dependent upon the realization of other human rights, as contained in the International Bill of Rights, including the rights to food, housing, work, education, human dignity, life, non-discrimination, equality, the prohibition against torture, privacy, access to information, and the freedoms of association, assembly and movement.

A similar position is expressed in the *Vienna Declaration and Programme of Action* (1993: para. 5), which states that "[a]ll human rights are universal, indivisible and interdependent and interrelated".

Arguably, if human rights are a set of values that a community gives to itself (Sengupta 2000) based on its commitment to the fundamental values of human dignity and well-being, then all elements that enhance and sustain human dignity must be considered in unison. If one element is considered in isolation or separate from others, human dignity may be compromised given that a human being is an integral whole.

Often the principles of the indivisibility, interdependence and interrelatedness of human rights are invoked against the popular approach of fragmenting human rights into *first*, *second* and *third* generations – as proposed by Karel Vasak (1975) and Maurice Cranston (1973). In a fundamental way, the principle of the indivisibility of human rights also applies to the different rights within the civil and political rights. The important implication of this principle is that all human rights should be given appropriate attention and consideration (*Limburg Principles* 1987: para. 3). This does not, however, imply that all human rights should be given the same weighting in every circumstance since not all human rights have the same risk of being violated at all times. At certain times it is appropriate to focus on or prioritise those rights that are most at risk of being violated, or rights that have severe impact on human well-being and dignity. Similarly, not everyone's right has the same risk of not being fulfilled; thus it is only sensible to draw attention to those whose rights are *most* at risk.

Relying on the principles of the interdependency and interrelatedness of human rights, it has been argued that emphasising one human right, such as the right to water, over others, militates against these principles. Obviously, the real world – where human rights are realised or violated – is often constrained by resources such that it is not possible to give the same attention to all human rights at all times. At times it is practically appropriate to focus on certain rights, though not to the extent of ignoring others (Sengupta 2000; 2004). Further, as alluded to earlier, not all human rights are exposed to the same risk of being violated. In principle, all violations of human rights constitute an affront to human dignity and fundamental freedoms – but not all violations have the same impact on human dignity and freedom. Given these two factors it is not only logical, but also practical, to focus attention on those rights that are at the greatest risk, though without undermining or ignoring others.

Taken for Granted

The second observation that can be made from the various international human rights instruments discussed above is that in the past it was taken for granted that all people always have access to water.[14] At the time when most of these international human rights instruments were being drafted, there might not have been any need for explicit protection – as was felt to be the case for other rights such as food, housing, health, employment, and so on. Currently, these assumptions have been undermined by various factors including the processes of commodifying and commercialising water services, growing poverty and hunger, and increasing competition between the various sectors that use water – all of which have led to the widespread denial of access to water for many people. This, in turn, has undermined the realisation of other human rights such as the right to health, food, equality of opportunity, and a clean environment. Furthermore, the water crisis that may arise from commercial exploitation of water resources calls for clear protection of access to basic water supplies, especially in the Global South.

The Force Behind the Language of Rights

The third observation one can make is that on the basis of the various international human rights instruments reviewed above, it is clear there is an underlying assumption that taking a rights-based approach to water is one of the effective ways of addressing the problems surrounding access to it. In these documents it seems almost beyond doubt that by locating access to water in a human rights framework, a certain moral and political force is created. There is an implicit assumption that clothing access to water in the language of rights makes the appeal more forceful than in any other way. However, the created moral and political force needs to be complemented by what Sen (2004) calls the "agitation route" in order to translate these rights into reality.

14 The former UN Secretary General, Kofi Annan, in his special contribution to the *Human Development Report 2006*, points out one way in which water is taken for granted: "[P]eople open taps and sometimes leave the taps running; people go to supermarkets and just pick from the many brands of water" (UNDP 2006: 78). There are other ways in which water can be said to have been taken for granted; for example, treating water like an inexhaustible resource that should be exploited with little concern – policy-makers have had this attitude for years. People in agriculture and industry have also used water as though it is something that does not matter much.

Undoubtedly the language of rights, though often dismissed by some activists as mere rhetoric, as noted earlier, can create the grounds for collective action, and provide the foundation for making claims against the general public, particularly the state, thus creating the opportunity to engage in democratic politics. For many people there is something politically and morally appealing about the language of rights. For instance, former UN Secretary General, Kofi Annan, argues that water is an essential human need and therefore a human right (see *HDR 2007*). This reflects the assumption that, when expressed in terms of rights, there is some stronger emphasis added – some stronger moral appeal. Similarly, former Brazilian president, Lula da Silva, in a special contribution to the *HDR 2006*, also asserts that "[c]lean, accessible and affordable water is a human right" (UNDP 2007: 79). In the same vein, former Mexican president, Vicente Fox, during the 4th World Water Forum (2006), declared that "water is above all a human right which no one can renounce" and that "it is our moral and political obligation to ensure that nobody is denied his right to this vital liquid" (cited in Dubreuil 2006: 4). The former Bolivian minister of water, Abel Mamani, also affirms that "water must be treated as a human right not another tradable commodity for profit". The mayor of Mexico City also affirmed these assertions when he declared that "[w]ater is a public good and a public right" (ibid.).

For many human rights activists and practitioners, the advantage of framing access to water in the language of rights is that this makes it possible for the law to play an important role "to ensure access to water for all". Furthermore, "a rights-based approach would lead to acceleration in achieving basic and improved levels of access to safe water" (ibid.: 6). Other analysts deploy the language of rights because rights "generate reasons for action", as well as obligations – both "perfect" and "imperfect" ones (Sen 2004: 8).[15]

Does the Language of Rights Make a Difference?

But what difference does clothing human needs in the language of rights make, in reality? While the language of rights is commonly acknowledged to carry moral and political force, we are reminded that in practice the language of rights can be used to disempower people, especially the poor, in circumstances

15 Sen borrows the notion of "perfect" and "imperfect" obligation from Immanuel Kant. Perfect obligation, as used by Sen, signify situations where a duty is coupled or correlated with the legal responsibility to perform or not perform a certain action; while imperfect obligations may not necessarily be ones that are correlated with legally binding duty. However, Sen argues that imperfect obligations go beyond mere charity and voluntarism. They generate some kind of moral responsibility that requires the underlying duty or action to be performed (see Sen 2004).

where there are widespread violations. With particular reference to the access to water, it has been noted that while there has been wide international recognition of access to water as a basic human right, for many people around the world actually accessing it is far from being a basic entitlement that they can claim. In this way "the language of human rights serves as a smokescreen behind which the rights of poor people are violated" (UNDP 2006: 78).

The Right to Water: Content, Scope and Obligations

While the arguments to have water proclaimed as a human right are clear, widely acknowledged, and generally convincing, the question that needs to be discussed is this: what exactly is the nature, scope and content of this right? Although this is slowly being clarified through the work of the CESCR, particularly *General Comment 15*, there is still some work needed to carve out space for water within the broader discourse of rights and development (de Albuquerque 2012). When compared to other ESCRs such as the rights to employment, education and health, work on elaborating the content and scope of the rights to water and food only began relatively recently (Courtis 2007).[16] Because of this, more debate on the scope and practical implications of these rights is essential.

In the case of the right to water, because it is largely derived from other rights its nature, content and scope require more specific elaboration. Questions as to what obligations the right imposes upon duty-bearers, who the beneficiaries of the right are, and what the beneficiaries are entitled to are yet to be refined. This is also the case regarding the nature of remedies or redress that rights beneficiaries can seek in situations where their right is not fulfilled. These matters have been discussed (particularly in *General Comment 15*), but their practical implications have not yet been refined through practice.

Regarding the nature of the right to water, it has been affirmed that it is a fundamental human right.[17] The *Limburg Principles* (1987: para. 1), for instance, assert that

16 For the right to food, formal elaboration started with the formulation of *General Comment 12* in 1999; while *General Comment 15* – which elaborates on the right to water – was only adopted in 2003.

17 Here the arguments in the *Limburg Principles*, the *Vienna Declaration* and the *Maastricht Guidelines on the Violation of Economic, Social and Cultural Rights* are meant to dispel the Cold War mentality that only civil and political rights should be accorded the full status of human rights; while the second and third generation rights are meant to be mere aspirational statements for public policy. A clear affirmation of this position is stated in all three documents listed above, but most strongly in the *Maastricht Guidelines* (para. 4),

> Economic, social and cultural rights [to which the right to water belongs] are an integral part of international human rights law. They are the subjects of specific treaty obligations in various international instruments, notably the *International Covenant on Economic, Social and Cultural Rights.*

Though there are specific differences regarding how the different rights under the Covenant should be implemented, the general principles under the *ICESCR* applies to all rights – including the right to water. When elaborating on the nature of these rights the CESCR is in no doubt that the right to water is subject to a judicial decision-making process just as many other rights are. But the question of justiciability is only mentioned in passing (*General Comment 3*: para. 5). Some analysts have criticised this approach, arguing that the imprecise nature and the "difficulty of developing workable criteria by which to measure states' compliance with, or violation of the rights" under the Covenant, makes it extremely difficult to subject these rights to an independent judicial review process (Dennis and Stewart 2004: 489).

Content of the Right to Water

For the right to water to be meaningful and applicable on the ground, its content must be clearly stated. While the scope of the right addresses the two main questions about the beneficiaries and and duty-bearers, the content of the right outlines the substantive elements of a right (de Wall *et al.* 2001). When addressing the question of content, one is concerned with what exactly the beneficiaries of the right are entitled to under different circumstances. Elements of content elaborate the constituent aspects of the rights. Elaborating on the content of the right to water, the CESCR (*General Comment 15*: para. 10) observes that

> The right to water contains both freedoms and entitlements. The freedoms include the right to maintain access to existing water supplies necessary for the right to water, and the right to be free from interference, such as the right to be free from arbitrary disconnections or contaminations of water supply. By contrast, the entitlements include the right to a system of water supply and management that provides equality of opportunity for people to enjoy the right to water.

---

which declare: "It is now undisputed that all human rights are indivisible, interdependent, interrelated and of equal importance for human dignity. Therefore, states are as responsible for violations of economic, social and cultural rights as they are for violations of civil and political rights."

Given the different situations in which people find themselves, even in the same country, it becomes difficult to formulate a universal content that is applicable in all situations. However, it is possible to formulate general guidelines and norms which act as the "minimum standard of achievement". While a practical problem with regard to a uniform content of the right to water must be acknowledged due to the diversity of circumstances between countries (and indeed within them), there are basic requirements that could be identified to constitute a basic normative content.[18] In this regard *General Comment 15* has provided the scaffolding on which local specifics can be anchored. As noted above, the normative content of the right to water has two aspects: *freedoms* and *entitlements*. The freedom aspect of the right generates the negative obligation not to interfere with anyone's access to water either by public or private entities, or by individuals. Thus, in order to fulfil this obligation, an individual should not be subjected to unwarranted obstructions when accessing water, including arbitrary disconnections. Any arbitrary barriers to accessing water – including cutting off the water supply, contamination of water sources, offering inadequate service hours, or indeed any unnecessary obstructions – infringe on people's freedom to have access to water, and are likely to violate the freedom aspect of the right to water.

Freedom to access water constitutes both the substantive freedom of opportunity to access water, as well as the procedural freedom pertaining to the process of accessing water. The substantive freedom of opportunity to access water implies that no one should be obstructed from accessing water. For instance, people living in an area that is not serviced with water have their freedom of opportunity to access water impaired, in that their chances of getting access to water are less. Similarly, people's freedom of process of accessing water is undermined if, in the process of accessing water, they are exposed to various dangers such as rape, violence, intimidation, abuse, physical and

18 The use of the term "normative content" is adopted by the CESCR to emphasise the point that the Covenant rights need not be legal rights in the Hohfeldian sense of the term (see Chapter 2). This position seems to be a direct reaction to the prolonged argument that economic, social and cultural rights are not jusiticiable, i.e. that they are of a different nature to civil and political rights. Often it is argued that although most countries have ratified the *ICESCR* (156 countries had done so by 2013), most of them have not incorporated the provisions into their domestic legal systems such that they cannot be effectively enforced given that these norms are not self-executing (*General Comment 9*, para. 11). But as Sen (2004) has pointed out, legal enforcement must not be the only way of enforcing these rights, and neither should it be conceived as the most effective means of enforcement (see also Courtis 2007; Cohen and Brown 2008).

mental stress, or other risks. Table 5.5 summarises the content of the right to water and the corresponding obligations based on *General Comment 15*.

While freedom of access requires the opportunity and process of accessing water not be interfered with, the entitlement component requires that sufficient *quantities* of water be available continuously and of a *quality* appropriate for safeguarding human dignity. The entitlement component also requires that water be *physically* and *economically* accessible to all. Here, emphasis is placed on economic accessibility – which includes people's ability to pay for water, its pricing, and its distribution. More concretely, an entitlement to economic accessibility generates a duty to ensure that the bulk pricing of water, and tariffs for water, do not "compromise or threaten the realization of other Covenant Rights" (*General Comment 15*: para. 12 (c) (ii)).[19]

In terms of accessibility, the right to water includes access not just for drinking, but also for other domestic uses – including water for the preparation and production of food (for those households that use water to produce their own food). Although the CESCR (*General Comment 15*: para. 6) has stated clearly that when considering the allocation of water for various uses, priority must be given to water for personal and domestic use, it acknowledges that the right to water includes water for a wide range of uses – including water used in producing food.

> Water is required for a range of different purposes, besides personal and domestic use, to realize many of the Covenant rights. For instance, water is necessary to produce food (right to adequate food) and ensure environmental hygiene (right to health). Water is essential for securing livelihoods (right to gain a living by work) and enjoying certain cultural practices (right to cultural life).

For individuals and groups that depend on water for producing food, the right to water is extended to include water used for food production; and any interference with access to water for such groups by state or non-state actors can lead to violation of the right to water. In this sense the right to water is inextricably linked to the right to food (Ziegler 2003: 13). The CESCR links the right to water with many other rights, including the right not to be deprived of the

---

19 *General Comment 15* has, for one reason or another, avoided using the term "basic water"; instead it uses the term "sufficient", which turns out to be more vague and difficult to quantify in real terms. Sufficiency or adequacy carries with it a high degree of subjectivity that may make it difficult to provide general guidelines and standards. The concept of "basic water", on the other hand, makes it easier to provides a conceptual basis for defining a minimum standard that could guide the quantity needed (See Gleick 1996).

TABLE 5.5 *Normative content of the right to water*

Normative content	State obligations	Violation
Availability: Sufficient and continuous services	To Respect: *Refrain from activities that interfere with the right*, or *limit access*	(a) Absence of measures or steps taken
Quality: Safe and free from harmful substances	To Protect: Prevent third parties from interfering with access	(b) Unequal distribution and access to opportunities
Accessibility: Physical: (within safe and physical reach)	To Fulfil: Facilitate, promote, provide. For those who cannot fulfil the right for themselves	(c) Non-compliance with core obligations
Economic: (affordable for all)	(a) Progressively realise the right – more people gaining access	(d) Arbitrary disconnections
Non-discrimination: (accessible to all,including vulnerable and marginalised)	(b) Guarantee equality of opportunity	(e) Polluting water sources
Information: (Seek, receive and impart)	(c) Take measures (legislative and otherwise) (d) Adopt comprehensive programmes (e) Non-discrimination and equality	(f) Failure to regulate or control water services (g) Failure to enact laws (h) Failure to implement policy (i) Misallocation of funds (j) Failure to take into account international obligations

SOURCE: COMPILED BY AUTHOR FROM VARIOUS SOURCES.

means of existence. In safeguarding the right to water the CESCR (*General Comment 15*: para. 7) argues that

> Attention should be given to ensuring that disadvantaged and marginalised farmers, including women farmers, have equitable access to water and water management systems, including sustainable rain harvesting

> and irrigation technology. Taking note of the duty in article 1, paragraph 2, of the Covenant, which provides that a people may not 'be deprived of its means of subsistence', States parties should ensure that there is adequate access to water for subsistence farming and for securing the livelihoods of indigenous people.

The *Voluntary Guidelines* on the right to food also urge states to facilitate access to productive resources such as land, water, seeds and other services – especially for vulnerable groups and individuals – in an effort to create an environment in which access to adequate food can become a reality for all (FAO 2006). In line with the purposive approach adopted by the CESCR when interpreting the *ICESCR*, the content of the right to water cannot be restricted to drinking water; the right should encapsulate all elements of access to water which in a particular circumstance facilitate the realisation of human dignity and well-being. Thus, the content of the right to water should not be "narrowly interpreted, by mere reference to volumetric quantities and technologies" (*General Comment 15*: para. 11).

Scope of the Right to Water

Regarding the scope of the right to water, the CESCR maintains that the right has a universal reach – meaning that the right envisages "everyone" as a beneficiary, without discrimination on any of the prohibited grounds such as race, gender, social status, country of origin, and so on.[20] This principle of universal application of human rights instruments flows from the *UN Charter* Article 55 (c) which prohibits discrimination on the basis of "race, sex, language, or religion". Article 2 of the *UDHR* reasserted and extended this position to include among the prohibited grounds: political opinion, national or social origin, property ownership, or birth – indeed any other socially constructed and assigned characteristics.

With particular reference to the right to water, *General Comment 15* (para. 12 (c) iii) has recognised the principle of universal application by stating that "water and water facilities must be accessible to all, including the most vulnerable or marginalized sections of the population, in law and in fact, without discrimination on any of the prohibited grounds". Thus, there is overwhelming evidence and clarity on the scope of the right to water; the right applies to *everyone* whether they can afford to pay for it or not. However, although the right is given universal reach, there is strong emphasis placed on paying particular attention to individuals and groups who find it difficult to realize this right:

---

20 I will expand on this in connection with the right to food in the next chapter.

"Whereas the right to water applies to everyone, states parties should give special attention to those individuals and groups who have traditionally faced difficulties in exercising this right" (*General Comment 15*: para. 16).

Contrary to the commonly held opinion that rights such as the right to water apply only to those who cannot afford to pay, the right should be understood to protect *everyone*. What is often confused with having a right to water is the eligibility for free basic water (in countries that have such policies) for those who cannot afford to meet their basic water requirements. But providing free basic water to people who are not able to provide for themselves does not imply that those who are ineligible do not have a right to it; or that their right to water is somehow ignored. Having a right to water is not synonymous with entitlement to *free* water.

What the right to water (as explained in *General Comment 15*) provides for is that everyone should have access to water – including those who are unable to pay for water services. So, in order to translate the right to water into tangible entitlements for those who cannot meet their basic water needs, there must be a way to make sure that such people are given access. Often it is the state that should ensure this through a deliberate and targeted policy or strategy. Existence of such a policy, however, does not imply that those who can afford to pay for water do not have the right to it.

Similarly, providing free basic water to those who cannot afford to pay for it does not amount to discrimination on the basis of income or social status; it only fulfils the principle of fairness and equity in ensuring that everyone has access. *General Comment 15* justifies this bias towards vulnerable groups, as noted above. This approach is in line with the famous Rawlsian Difference Principle, as well as Gewirth's Principle of Deprivation Focus, discussed in Chapter 1. John Rawls, (1972: 68) in *A Theory of Justice*, argues that inequality in the "basic structure" dealing with the distribution of society's resources[21] is justifiable "only if the difference in expectation is to the advantage of the representative man who is worse off". Arguing in defence of the equity principle in human rights, Gewirth (1996), too, is ready to let the scale tilt in favour of those who are unable to acquire a basic minimum of goods – as a way of enhancing their "purposive agency" and thereby increasing their potential for free action. Responding to the objection that a deliberate focus on the poor is

21 Although Rawls is, in principle, prepared to let the scale tilt in favour of the poor rather than keep it in balance, it is difficult to see how this could be effected in practice. Rawls himself demonstrates a strong reliance on the "Zero-Sum Game", arguing that as much as we might want to improve the lot of the poor, we should not make wealthy and highly motivated entrepreneurs worse off in the process – since this would dampen their innovative spirit (Rawls 1972: 68–71).

incompatible with the principle of non-discrimination and equality, Gewirth (1996: 110) argues that

> [t]he most direct reply to this objection is that because human rights impose requirements that equally protect the fundamental agency-related interests of all persons, those deprived persons whose interests are protected inadequately or not at all must become the focus of the rights so far as concerns their effectuation. I shall call this the *deprivation focus*.
>
> (emphasis in original)

In the case of the right to water, the moral strength of focusing on providing basic water services to those who find it difficult to access water lies in the fact that failure to draw attention to such people leads to various social and health problems that can affect the entire society (WHO 2003). And the state bears primary responsibility for ensuring that those who fail to secure basic conditions for human well-being are given the means of achieving them.

Obligations and Violations of the Right to Water

General Comment 3, which has elaborated on the "Nature of States parties' Obligations", stipulates that the nature of the obligation includes both the obligation of *conduct* as well as the obligation of *result* (1990: para. 1). In other words, the states parties to the *ICESCR* have both an obligation to conduct themselves in compliance with the requirements of the Covenant, and to produce outcomes that do not conflict with the Covenant values and spirit.[22] A common feature of the rights under the *ICESCR* is that they are supposed to be realised progressively. As noted in Chapter 3, this does *not* mean that no immediate attention is required. On the contrary, the duty-bearers are expected to take *immediate, concrete, deliberate* and *targeted* steps towards the realisation of the rights (*General Comment 3*: para. 2). In terms of access to water, this requirement is met when specific measures, programmes and steps are devised and implemented. Another indication of compliance with the obligation of progressive realisation is when the number of people accessing basic water increases over time. Instances where access to water is static, or regressing (for example when the proportion of people accessing safe water is declining, as illustrated in Table 5.2), amount to a clear case of failure to comply with the obligation of progressive realisation of the right.

22 More on this in the next chapter.

Violation can result from action of the state (*by commission*) as well as from the state's failure to act (*by omission*). Examples of violation by commission include policies or strategies that are discriminatory, programmes or policies that create barriers to accessing clean water, diversion of public funds which lead to rights not being fulfilled, or drastic reductions of public expenditure which affect the provision of water services (*Maastricht Guidelines* 1997: para. 14). Examples of violation of Covenant rights by omission include the inability or failure to adopt appropriate, immediate and concrete measures; failure to sufficiently regulate third parties such as private service providers; failure by the state to take into account international obligations in its policies and programmes; failure to enforce laws and regulations that secure the rights under the Covenant; and failure to utilise the available resources towards the realisation of the Covenant rights (ibid.: para. 15).

The *Maastricht Guidelines* (1997) summarise the nature and scope of the obligations that the rights under the Covenant, in general, generate; and possible situations when violations might occur:

> [E]conomic, social and cultural rights impose three different types of obligations on States: the obligations to *respect, protect* and *fulfil*. Failure to perform any one of these three obligations constitutes a violation of such rights. The obligation to respect requires States to refrain from interfering with the enjoyment of economic, social and cultural rights. Thus, the right to housing is violated if the State engages in arbitrary forced evictions. The obligation to protect requires States to prevent violations of such rights by third parties. Thus, the failure to ensure that private employers comply with basic labour standards may amount to a violation of the right to work or the right to just and favourable conditions of work. The obligation to fulfil requires States to take appropriate legislative, administrative, budgetary, judicial and other measures towards the full realization of such rights. Thus, the failure of States to provide essential primary health care to those in need may amount to a violation.

Availability of Resources is Not an Excuse

The popular tactic of tying compliance with Covenant obligations to the availability of resources has been countered by the CESCR, the *Limburg Principles*, the *Vienna Declaration and Programme of Action*, as well as the *Maastricht Guidelines* – all of which have strongly rejected the notion that the realisation of ESCRs is solely contingent upon the availability of resources. As pointed out in Chapter 3, resource availability is a necessary, but not a *sufficient* condition for realising ESCRs. Resources will always be scarce (and sometimes unavailable) such that if this criterion were to be set as a condition for realising rights then many of them could never be realised at all. To comply with their Covenant obligations, states parties need to demonstrate serious commitment towards the responsibilities that they assume under it. One of the ways through which this commitment to provide "clean and safe water" to all can be demonstrated, is by putting in place policies and programme that reflect the commitment towards meeting this obligation.

The Obligation to Take Steps/Measures

The obligation to take steps is expected to be met immediately by states parties to the Covenant (*General Comment 3*: para. 2). Failure to "take appropriate steps", or a failure to take "all appropriate measures, including particularly the adoption of legislative measures" (*ICESCR*: para. 2 (1)), may indicate non-compliance with Covenant obligations. Determination of the appropriateness of steps/measures taken is left to the CESCR. In cases where appropriate measures are not taken there are strong indications that Covenant obligations have not been fulfilled.

Unfortunately, when it comes to the right to water, most states do not elaborate what people are entitled to, or what responsibilities in this respect it has committed itself to. The practical impact of the failure to state clearly what the rights of the people are, and what the duties of the state are, can be many. One of the most visible effects is that people have no guidance as to what they are entitled to. The other effect is that public discussions – often seen as a way of clarifying national objectives (Sen 2004) – are often isolated and held at the informal/individual level. Further, it is difficult to create political space when the right in question is not clearly recognised and defined. This is evident in the Zambian example discussed in Chapter 7. Interviews with both water service providers and community members in Zambia show that there is a general sense that the public has been unable to create space in which it can engage in the debate on the right to water. Focus group discussions highlight this point:

> "We have raised the issue that water should be recognized as a basic human right, but there is no one listening to what people are saying."
>
> "It is us the people who are feeling the pain of living without water who should be able to decide whether water should be a human right or not – those guys in government have water and they won't bother recognizing water as a human right; it doesn't affect them."
>
> "People should declare water as a human right because the government doesn't care about what people are going through – they don't even know how we are suffering."
>
> CHITONGE, *Focus Group Discussion, 2007*

Clearly outlining the content and scope of a right is crucial to its realisation. Without elaborate content that describes the right, it would be difficult, first of all, for the duty-bearers to know what their obligations are; and second, for the beneficiaries to know what they are entitled to. For instance, one of the key prerequisites to improving access to water is stating clearly what constitutes "basic water" and who qualifies to receive it. Even if what constitutes basic water varies from place to place (Gleick 1996),[23] it is helpful to establish the minimum standard to which every state party should be striving. However, when setting such a basic minimum care must be taken not to set it too close to the survival threshold.

Identifying Duty-Bearers

In terms of obligations that the right to water generates under the Covenant, it is clear that the state has the primary responsibility to ensure that the Covenant obligations are fulfilled. Like many other rights, Covenant rights generate the obligation to *promote*, *respect* and *protect* rights. With particular reference to water, even in situations where the violation does not directly result from state action, the state is held responsible for the action of a third party. The obligation to protect is envisioned to create a duty on the state to ensure that third parties do not interfere with the individual's enjoyment of the right to water: "Third parties include individuals, groups, corporations and other entities as well as agents acting under the state's authority" (*General Comment 15*: para. 23). Furthermore, in cases where "water services (such as piped water networks, water tankers, access to rivers and wells) are operated or controlled by third parties, States parties must prevent them from compromising equal, affordable, and physical access to sufficient, safe and acceptable water" (ibid.: para. 24).

Of particular and practical importance here is the obligation to *fulfil*. This requires that the state takes positive measures not only to facilitate and assist individuals to access basic water, but also to *actually* provide water to individuals or groups "when they are unable to provide for themselves for reasons beyond their control" (ibid.: para. 25). Focus here is on those who are unable to provide for themselves. The obligation does not oblige the state to provide for *everyone*, but it does require the state to make sure, by various means, that even those who cannot provide for themselves – such as the elderly, orphans, the unemployed, the terminally ill, the disabled or widows – have access to water.

23 Gleick has provided estimates of average water needs per capita. Of course, real circumstances vary widely, but such minimum measures can help in estimating what resources are needed to meet the basic water needs of poor communities (see Gleick 1996: 88).

The Challenge of Realizing the Right to Water

While there are clear guidelines and standards concerning the nature and content of the right to water, implementation of these norms faces a significant number of challenges in many countries, especially low income ones. One of the major challenges pertains to the nature of international law from which human rights are derived. While human rights instruments and other international treaties are quickly ratified by many nations, very few have translated these instruments into domestic legal or policy systems. Related to this is the controversial relationship between international and municipal law. And this is particularly a problem in countries with common law traditions.[24] Unfortunately, even in countries where international human rights instruments are incorporated into domestic law (mostly in civil law traditions), there is no guarantee that these rights will be enforced in a way that will give them effect, particularly for the poor. These issues are further discussed in Chapter 7.

In the case of the right to water, lessons learned from the challenges of giving effect to it to the poor of South Africa are instructive (see Mehta 2006). Despite the existence of a clear constitutional protection of the right to water, plus a comprehensive free basic water policy, many people have still not been able to access clean water (Mehta and Ntshona 2004; Booysen 2004; Bond 2006; South African Human Rights Commission 2009, 2013). Although the free basic water policy has been lauded by many commentators – including the UNDP's *Human Development Report 2006*[25] – "[s]till, its implementation has been difficult. In part, many of its highly laudable aims [have] been negated due to lack of financing and institutional capacity" (Mehta and Ntshona, 2004: 3).

---

24 Most countries that were once colonies or territories of England, or the British Empire, are said to have adopted a common law tradition – with the exception of Malta, Scotland and Quebec which use the civil law tradition. The principal difference between the two systems is the weight given to precedent. In common law tradition, precedents are just as binding as the statutes and jurisprudence that play a critical role in the function of the legal system; while in civil law tradition it is legislation or statutes and ministerial regulations that are seen as the important sources of the legally binding nature of law (See Fletcher 1982). Judicial precedent in the civil law tradition is not widely recognised as legally binding. Civil law developed mainly in continental Europe from Roman Law, which influenced the Napoleonic and Germanic Codes (see Wikipedia for details).

25 According to the *HDR 2006*, "South Africa has demonstrated how the human right to water can serve as a mechanism for empowerment and a guide to policy. Rights-based water reform has enabled it to expand, access and overcome the legacy of racial inequality inherited from apartheid, partly through rights-based entitlements" (2007: 63).

From a study conducted by the Children's Rights Institute, Mosdell and Leatt (2005) also concluded that the many civil protests over water "are an indication that all is not well at local government and service delivery levels". Furthermore, the *6th Economic and Social Rights Report* of the South African Human Rights Commission reported cases where implementation of free basic water has encountered problems. For example, in the Ilembe District Municipality it was discovered that instead of the six kilolitres stipulated by the free basic water policy, all five local municipalities in the district provided only three kilolitres (see SAHRC 2006: 111).

Thus, the challenge of giving effect to rights for the poor is not just about having rights encoded in constitutions and statutes; rather, it is more about finding concrete ways in which such rights can become a reality in their lives. Translating the various claims and rights provided for in legal documents, into concrete rights, requires an integrated strategy that draws from collective action, solidarity, advocacy at a community level, awareness campaigns, skill, capacity-building, and the building of adequate and responsive institutions (ODI 2002: 4); it also requires going beyond parliament and the courts.

What the South African situation seems to highlight is that having these rights enshrined in the constitution is not a waste of time; rather it illustrates quite well that encoding rights in a constitution is a *necessary* but not *sufficient* condition for realising them.

CHAPTER 6

The Right to Food

Origin, Content and Scope

To appreciate the enduring challenges and emerging opportunities surrounding the right to food, it is essential to locate access to food in the current global food production and distribution context. In this context, it is important to note that the right to food, just like the right to water, is not just about securing a bundle of calories for everyone; it involves a complex set of relations which influence the production, distribution, marketing, accessing and utilisation of food. In order to give meaning to the right to food, it is essential to move beyond the narrow focus on legislative and courtroom battles and into the broader spaces of "democratic politics". Democratic politics, in the context of the right to food, simply refers to the exchange (social and political) between people at various levels and the formal public structures of the state. In the case of the right to food these exchanges relate to the processes and policies connected to the production, distribution, allocation, marketing and consumption of food. In this particular sense, then, the right to food constitutes one practical way of "bringing democratic politics to bear on issues of hunger and nutrition" (Drèze 2005: 63). Before discussing the nature and content of the right to food, the global and national food and undernourishment conditions are briefly discussed below. This analysis of global food production sets the background for a discussion of the challenges and opportunities that surround the right to food.

Analysis of the current global food situation suggests that the main challenges surrounding the right to food in many parts of the world today is not so much the shortfall in food production, but more about how the food produced in the world is distributed, accessed and utilised. As Sen (2003) has observed, starvation, famine and undernourishment do not occur because of an inadequate food supply, but primarily because of a neglect for those social issues to ensure that the poor and vulnerable have access to the *available* food. Often, it is this disregard for vulnerable groups which results in the violation of the right to food for millions of people around the globe; indeed most of the time it is the rights of the poor and vulnerable which are often most at risk of being violated (Ziegler 2003). This being the case, there should be a bias towards the poor in any society that is built on the values of respect for human life: "The test of our progress is not whether we add more to the abundance of those who have much; it is whether we provide enough for those who have little" (Franklin Delano Roosevelt 1941).

 | DOI 10.1163/9789004299559_007

However, the presence of hundreds of millions of hungry, undernourished and starving people in the world creates an opportunity for radical change to the food production and distribution system. This requires going beyond the various manifestations of weak political commitment to the right to food, to engaging with the processes that have led to this weak commitment. As has been suggested (Drèze 2005):

> The neglect of social issues in general, and of chronic hunger in particular, is often attributed to 'lack of political will'. This diagnosis is plausible enough, but it does not take us very far since it begs the question as to why there is no political will in the first place. In a democracy, political will is an outcome of democratic politics.

Food in Global Context

Globally, there are close to one billion people (or a seventh of the world's population) who experience hunger, undernourishment and insecure access to food; and it is possible that this figure is underestimated. According to the FAO, in 2010 there were 925 million people who were undernourished, representing 16 per cent of the world's population. While this figure declined to 805 million people in 2014 (about 12 per cent of the global population), the actual number of undernourished people in many parts of the Global South has actually increased (FAO/IFAD 2014). Although the global proportion of the undernourished has significantly decreased from more than a third of the total population in 1970 to about 12 per cent in 2014, the actual number of people facing undernourishment has been rising steadily over the last two decades (except over the last five years) (see Table 6.1). This has coincided with a steady growth in food production, which has been growing at a faster rate than the growth in population. According to the FAO's *Food Outlook Report* of 2011, cereal production increased at an average annual rate of 2.2 per cent between 2000 and 2009 – well above the annual world population growth rate of just 1.16 per cent between 2005 and 2010 (UNDESA 2011). In the period between 2010 and 2014, cereal production increased significantly to an annual growth rate of 3 per cent per year (FAO 2014). Higher average rates of cereal production growth (2.4 per cent per annum) were recorded in Low Income Food Deficit Countries (LIFDCs) between 2000 and 2010 (FAO 2011b: 27).

In terms of crop production, the average annual growth rate, over the same period, is reported to be around 2.6 per cent, with the per capita crop production estimated at 1.5 per cent (FAO 2012). Agricultural production grew much more quickly in Latin America between 2000 and 2010, where a growth rate of

TABLE 6.1 *Trends in Global Levels of Undernourishment (1969–2010)*

Year	Number (millions)	%	Region	Number (millions, 2010)	Share of total (%)[a]	Undernourishment 2010 (%)[b]	Undernourishment 2014 (%)[b]
1969–71	880	34	Sub-Saharan Africa	239.0	26.0	30.0	23.8
1979–81	850	25	Asia and the Pacific	578.0	62.0	16.0	12
1990–92	845	20	L. America and Caribbean	53.0	5.7	9.0	9.4
1995–97	790	17	Near-East and North Africa	37.0	4.0	7.0	6
2000–02	840	17.5	Developed World	19.0	2.0	..	<5
2005–07	850	16					
2008	925	17					
2009	1,038	18					
2010	925	16					
2014	805	12					

[a] = percentage share in the global total of undernourishment.
[b] = regional undernourishment prevalence ratio.
SOURCE: AUTHOR, BASED ON DATA FROM FAO/IFAD *STATE OF THE FOOD INSECURITY REPORTS* 2011 AND 2014, AND *STATE OF THE WORLD FOOD AND AGRICULTURE* 2010–11 REPORT.

50 per cent over the ten-year period was recorded; followed by Sub-Saharan Africa with a 40 per cent increase over the same period (FAO 2012: 102). Thus, an increasing population of undernourished people cannot entirely be attributed to supply and availability factors. In terms of global food production there is enough food produced to meet basic needs that are in line with the principles of food security; as well as meeting the requirements of the right to food. Table 6.2 below gives a summary of the current global food production, consumption, trade and stock carry-over trends.

If one looks at the total amount of food produced, and the quantity of food utilised for various purposes, it is evident that the world produces enough food

TABLE 6.2 *Global Food Production and Consumption Profile (2008–13)*

Production (millions of tons)[a]						**Trade (millions of tons)**[c]					
	2008–09	**2009–10**	**2010–11**	**2011–12**	**2012–13**		**2008–09**	**2009–10**	**2010–11**	**2011–12**	**2012–13**
World	2,286	2,263.2	2,258.8	2,348	2,284	*World*	282.3	272.2	272.4	315.2	293.5
Developing	1,240.6	1,239.2	1,299.7	–	–	*Developing*	72.8	74.4	84.5	–	–
Developed	1,045.3	1,024	937.6	–	–	*Developed*	209.5	197.9	187.5	–	–
Utilisation (millions of tons)[b]						Trade-to-Production Ratio (%)					
World	2,191.7	2,236.3	2,278	2,327	2,313.9	*World*	12.3	12.0	12.1	13.4	12.9
Developing	1,341.4	1,369.1	1,410.9	–	–	*Developing*	5.9	6.0	6.5	–	–
Developed	850.3	867.2	867.1	–	–	*Developed*	20.0	19.3	20.0	–	–
Self-Sufficiency Index						Rollover Stock (millions of tons)[d]					
World	104.3	101.2	99.2	100.9	98.7	*World*	501.2	525.2	479.1	522.6	497.4
Developing	92.5	90.5	92.1	–	–	*Developing*	333.9	344.7	355	–	–
Developed	122.9	118.1	108.1	–	–	*Developed*	167.3	180.5	124.1	–	–
Utilisation Ratio (%)						Stock-to-Utilisation Ratio (%)					
World	95.9	98.8	100.9	99.1	101.3	*World*	22.9	23.5	21.0	21.0	21.0
Developing	108.1	110.5	108.6	–		*Developing*	24.9	25.2	25.2	–	–
Developed	81.3	84.7	92.5	–		*Developed*	19.7	20.8	14.3	–	–

Notes: The 2011–12 and 2012–13 data are for cereal only, and represent estimates and forecast figures respectively.
[a]: includes food used as stock feed, seeds, post-harvest losses, strategic reserves, beer brewing etc. The figures are not restricted to basic human consumption.
[b]: includes wheat, coarse grain, rice, oil seed, vegetable oil, meat and dairy products.
[c]: export figures based on the June/July marketing season for coarse grain; and on the calendar year for the rest.
[d]: aggregate carry-over stocks at the end of the crop season, and as such may not reflect the actual global food stock.
SOURCE: AUTHOR, BASED ON DATA FROM *CROP PROSPECT AND FOOD SITUATION 2011* (FAO 2011B), AND *FOOD OUTLOOK 2012* (FAO 2012).

TABLE 6.3 *Percentage of Food Losses by Region and Food Type* (2010)

	Cereal	Roots & Tubers	Oilseed & Pulses	Fruit & Vegetables	Meat	Fish & Seafood	Milk
Sub-Saharan Africa	20.5	54	31	66	29.7	37.7	27.2
South and East Asia	21.5	49	30	66	21.4	40.2	22.5
Latin America	26	47	21	72	22.4	33.7	23.5
North Africa, West and Central Asia	32.7	38	33	74	24.8	34.6	21.5
Industrialised Asia	34.5	61	19	43	22.5	42	11.2
Europe and Russia	33.5	68	21	56	23.8	29.9	12.7
America and Oceania	33.5	82	22	66	24.5	60.5	20.7
Mean Food Losses[a]	28.9	57.0	25.3	63.3	24.2	39.8	19.9

Note: [a] = simple average. This study was conducted in 125 countries including 41 in Sub-Saharan Africa; 22 in North Africa, West and Central Asia; 16 in South and South East Asia; 24 in Latin America; 42 in Europe and Russia; four in America and Oceania; and three in industrialised Asia. Losses occur at five major stages of the food supply chain: production, post-harvest and storage, processing and packaging, distribution, and consumption.

Looking at food losses by region, it is evident that industrialised countries waste a higher proportion of cereal and roots and tubers, while in developing countries a higher proportion of oilseed and pulses and milk is wasted. These differences can be attributed to differences in the processing and storage facilities, in the technology available, as well as in the cultural practices and social attitudes towards food – all of which is beyond the scope of this discussion.

SOURCE: GUSTAVSSON *ET AL.* (2011).

to meet all requirements – including industrial and other non-food uses – in most years. This is reflected by the self-sufficiency index and the utilisation ratio illustrated in Table 6.2. With the exception of the years 2010–11 and 2012–13, when total food utilisation was slightly more than the total food produced, the world produced sufficient food for all requirements, including strategic reserves. If we take into account the amount of food lost or wasted along the food supply chain (see Table 6.3 below), it becomes more apparent that even at current levels of food production there is enough food to eliminate hunger, undernourishment and starvation, completely.

Although hunger and starvation have been reported in different parts of the world for a long time, available evidence suggest that there has often been enough food to ensure that everyone has enough to lead an active and healthy life. Amartya Sen (1981), for instance, has argued that hunger and starvation are not the result of the world not producing enough food – there has always been enough. Other analysts, writing in the mid-1980s, have also argued that *"Abundance, not scarcity, best describes the supply of food in the world today"* (Lappe and Collins 1986: 7 emphasis in original). During the 1980s a World Bank study (1986: 13) on the status of global food production concluded: "Evidence on food supplies and prices in the 1970s show that there was enough food for all the people on the planet. Projections to 2000 indicate that world food production is likely to keep pace with effective global demand."

Flowing from this conclusion, the World Bank study asks this: why have hunger, undernourishment and starvation persisted when there is plenty of food produced in the world? The report answers by suggesting that "[a]n analysis of the causes of food insecurity concludes that the main cause is not lack of supply or even high prices. The main cause is the weak purchasing power of some households and nations" (ibid.). This diagnosis clearly makes the assumption that everyone should access food through markets, but the question is this: what about those who are unable to access food on the market? This is where democratic politics, in its various forms, can be deployed to create other avenues of making food available, especially to those who have insufficient purchasing power.

The former Special Rapporteur[1] on the right to food makes a similar observation, arguing that Planet Earth "already produces more than enough food to feed the world", adding that "it is clear that reducing hunger does not mean increasing the production of food in rich countries, but rather in finding ways of increasing access to resources for the poor in the poorest countries" (Ziegler 2003: 7). Similarly, a joint UN Human Rights Commission/FAO (2010) report on the right to food argues that "the world produces enough food to feed its entire population. The root cause of hunger and malnutrition is not a lack of food but a lack of *access* to available food" (OHCHR/FAO 2010: 4, emphasis in original).

---

1 The Special Rapporteur on the right to food is an independent expert official appointed by the Commission on Human Rights (now the Human Rights Council) to promote, facilitate, monitor and provide advice on the implementation of the right to food among states parties to the *ICESCR*. There are currently 43 Rapporteurs, independence experts and representatives of the Secretary General of the UN (see http://www.ohchr.org/Documents/Publications/FactSheet27en.pdf). Since 2008, Oliver De Schuster from Belgium has been the Special Rapporteur on the right to food.

It is also interesting to note that only a small percentage (about 12 per cent, see Table 6.2) of the food produced in the world is traded – suggesting that the larger portion of the food that is produced is consumed *where* it is produced. If one looks at the world in terms of developing and developed countries, it is apparent also that the latter produce much more than they consume while the former produce less than what they consume. However, distribution of the food produced globally – either through trade or food aid – has remained highly imbalanced, leading to a situation whereby hundreds of millions of people, globally, remain undernourished; and more than one in seven people are food insecure, living in conditions which disctate they do not know where their next meal is coming from.

It is also apparent from Table 6.2 that developing countries trade lower proportions of their food than the developed ones – which explains the higher stock-rollover ratios in developing countries. This could also be an indication that the majority of people in developing countries are engaged in producing the food they consume, and that they depend less on the market. This is particularly true in regions like Sub-Saharan Africa and South East Asia, where majority of the population lives in rural areas and is engaged in subsistence agriculture. The context outlined above has important implications in the way we understand the challenges in terms of the right to food.

Trends in Global Food Consumption and Waste

While the figures reported in Table 6.2 give an aggregate picture of global food production and consumption, they do not show how the food produced is actually utilised. Existing evidence suggests that an alarmingly large proportion of the food produced in the world is lost or wasted at various stages of the food supply chain. A study conducted by the Swedish Institute for Food and Biotechnology (SIK), in collaboration with the FAO (2011), indicates that more than a quarter of the cereal produced in the world is lost or wasted (see Table 6.3). In the categories "roots and tubers" and "fruit and vegetables", almost 60 per cent of what is produced is lost at different stages of production, processing, packaging, storage, and distribution to the point of consumption.

The Politics of Food Distribution

From the right to food perspective, high levels of wasted food in a world where almost a billion people struggle to find enough to eat raises serious questions about the politics of food production, distribution and consumption. In practical terms, huge food waste raises serious questions about the international community and individual states' commitment to meeting the obligations to respect, promote, protect and fulfil the right to food. Within the rights-based framework, wasting food brings into the spotlight the issue of global social justice. The situation where millions of people are starving while billions of tons of food are wasted or lost in the same country or region, places the burden of proof to account for this on the states parties to the Covenant and the international community. If we consider the figures in Table 6.3 – which indicate that on average 29 per cent of all cereal produced is wasted or lost – this translates to more than 650 million tons of waste each year, or more than half of what is needed to meet global cereal consumption for humans (as Table 6.4 below suggests). What this means is that if only half of the wasted cereal were to be made available for human consumption, more than 2.1 billion people (twice the number of undernourished people) could be provided with adequate cereal (assuming a current per capita consumption rate of 153 kg per year).

In light of this evidence, it becomes even more apparent that the problem of hunger, undernourishment and starvation – and the subsequent failure to fulfil the right to food – is not a problem of inadequate food supply at the global or national level. Hunger is a function of how the food that is produced is distributed globally and nationally, and much less a function of quantity. In a very fundamental sense "the root cause of hunger isn't a scarcity of food or land; *it is a scarcity of*

TABLE 6.4 *Global Cereal Production and Consumption 2010–13 (millions of tons)*

	2010–11	2011–12	2012–13
Total Production	2,258.8	2,348	2,284
Total Consumption	2,278.4	2,327	2,313.9
Food (Human) Consumption	1,058.1	1,071.2	1,082.3
Food-to-Production Ratio (%)	46.8	45.6	47.4
Food-to-Consumption Ratio (%)	46.4	46.0	46.8
Stock Feed	765.1	792.9	787.7
Stock Feed-to-production ratio (%)	33.9	33.8	34.5
Other Uses	455.6	463.0	443.9
Other Uses-to-Production Ratio (%)	20.2	19.7	19.4
Per Capita Consumption (Kg/year)	153.1	153.2	152.9

Note: Total production excludes carry-over stock, which on average is roughly 22 per cent of the total consumption (see Table 6.2, above). Figures for the 2012–13 season are estimates.
SOURCE: AUTHOR, BASED ON DATA FROM THE FAO (2012).

democracy. Democratic structures are those in which people have a say in decisions that most affect their well-being. Leadership can be kept accountable to the needs of the majority" (Lappe and Collins 1986: 3, emphasis in original).[2]

Current global data on cereal production and consumption suggest that less than half (46 per cent for the period 2010–13) of the food produced each year is used for human consumption. If we take into account the food which is lost at the point of consumption, it is apparent that the amount of food needed to satisfy basic human needs constitutes a significantly lower proportion of the amount of food that is actually produced. Food used as stock feed and for other purposes constitutes more than half of the total food produced. This strongly supports the view that there is enough food for everyone.

However, as with the case of water, the aggregate figures on food production and undernourishment presented above mask the different challenges that different regions and countries face. For instance, while the global undernourishment prevalence ratio was only 16 per cent in 2010, the rate for Sub-Saharan Africa (SSA) was almost twice as much – with almost a third of the population there reported to be undernourished (Table 6.1). Although Asia and the Pacific region have the largest number of undernourished people, the *proportion* of undernourished people has remained at its highest in SSA (double that of Asia and Pacific in 2014). When we look at individual countries, similar disparities emerge. In SSA, for instance, while many countries have more than a third of their people undernourished – with Zambia reporting the highest ratio of undernourishment at 47 per cent in in 2010–12 – some countries have an undernourishment ratio of less than 5 per cent (see Table 6.5).

Similarly, while some countries such as Niger, Nigeria, Cameroon, Central African Republic, Chad, Ghana, Malawi, Mozambique, Rwanda, Sierra Leone, Togo and Zimbabwe have recorded a significant drop in the level of undernourished people between 1990 and 2012, undernourishment in countries such as Burkina Faso, Madagascar, Uganda, Tanzania and Zambia increased over the same period of time (see Table 6.5).

In countries such as Namibia and Botswana the undernourishment rates have largely remained unchanged in the reference period. Table 6.5 also suggests that undernourishment is slightly more prevalent among male children than their female counterparts; and significantly more of a problem in rural areas – except in Swaziland, South Africa, Egypt and Botswana where the rural and urban prevalence ratios are almost the same.

---

2 Amartya Sen (1999) makes a similar observation, arguing that famine has never occurred in a democracy – i.e. where people effectively participate in decisions that affect their lives.

TABLE 6.5 *Undernourishment Prevalence in Selected African Countries (1990–2012)*

Undernourishment in total population (%)						Child undernourishment (%)			
						By Sex		By Residence	
	2010–12	2007–09	2004–06	1999–02	1990–92	Male	Female	Urban	Rural
Africa	29.5	29.3	30.3	33.3	36.6	20.6	19.2	14.5	20.8
Sub-Saharan Africa	26.7	26.5	27.2	30	32.8	23.1	21.6	16.8	24
Botswana	27.9	31.9	32.9	34.5	27.4	13	13	12	14
Burkina Faso	25.9	24.4	25.8	26.4	22.9	38	37	26	41
Cameroon	15.7	15.6	19.5	29.1	38.7	21	17	11	26
Central Afr. Rep.	30	32.6	40.6	45.1	49.5	31	26	26	30
Chad	33.4	36.4	37.3	41	61.1	37	37	30	38
Egypt	<5	<5	<5	<5	<5	8	7	7	8
Ethiopia	40.2	43.8	47.7	55.3	68	39	38	23	40
Ghana	<5	5.8	9.5	16.6	40.5	18	17	12	21
Madagascar	33.4	29.1	28.1	32.4	24.8	41	38	35	41
Malawi	23.1	23	24.7	26.8	44.8	20	19	16	20
Mozambique	39.2	39.9	40.3	45.3	57.1	20	15	13	19
Morocco	5.5	5.2	5.2	6.2	7.1	10	10	7	14
Namibia	33.9	32.7	26.8	24.9	37.5	21	21	15	25
Niger	12.6	13.6	20	25.8	36.9	45	44	27	47
Nigeria	8.5	7.3	6.8	10.2	19.3	29	28	22	32
Rwanda	28.9	34.2	42.1	46.5	52.6	23	22	16	24
South Africa	<5	<5	<5	<5	<5	13	11	12	11
Swaziland	18	18	..	18	12	6	5	5	6
Sierra Leone	28.8	33.1	35.5	41.1	41.9	32	29	23	33
Uganda	34.6	31	27.9	26.5	26.6	21	20	14	21
Tanzania	38.8	36.1	35.1	40.4	29.4	22	22	17	23
Togo	16.5	19.8	20.4	25.2	32.8	27	25	16	32
Zambia	47.4	47.5	48.3	43.9	34.3	21	18	17	20
Zimbabwe	32.8	33.9	38.2	43.1	44.1	17	16	11	18

SOURCE: AUTHOR, BASED ON DATA FROM *THE STATE OF FOOD AND AGRICULTURE 2011 & 2012* (FAO 2011C AND FAO 2012)

When compared to other regions of the world, most countries in SSA face huge challenges in terms of fulfilling the right to food. Although undernourishment is not synonymous with the failure to fulfil the right to food, in most cases the inability to meet basic food needs or entitlements, is a direct outcome of violations of the right to food. Existing evidence suggests that the majority of the people

> suffering from hunger and malnutrition are the poor and marginalised, struggling to survive in rural areas. About 50 percent of people suffering from hunger are smallholders and 20 percent rural landless people. Another 10 percent are pastoralists, fisherfolk and forest users. The remaining 20 percent live in urban areas.
>
> OHCHR/FAO 2010: 10

The discussion above forms the context in which the right to food should be situated. The critical questions that arises here are: what does the right to food mean in this context? What are the implications, challenges and opportunities under the current global and national food systems?

These general observations about food production, access, availability and hunger are supported by empirical work based on historical famines in different countries such as Great Bengal, Ethiopia, the Sahel, Bangladesh, India and Ireland – which highlights the fact that famine, in all these cases, occurred at a time when there was surplus food available (see Sen 1981). Although there are some analysts who argue for increasing global food production as a solution to existing challenges of hunger, undernourishment and starvation (Collier 2008: 70), it is apparent from the available evidence that solving the problem is not simply a matter of increasing global food production; food production can treble or quadruple, but that will not solve the problem as long as the challenges of access to food are not addressed. With this in mind it is not surprising that hunger persisted, even in countries such as India at a time when they were experiencing a "green revolution" during the 1980s. In other words, the challenges of undernourishment, hunger and starvation are not merely supply related issues, but largely matters of distribution and access. Thus, the real challenge regarding hunger and undernourishment is finding the means to ensure that everyone has access (both physical and economic) to adequate food on a sustainable basis.

Finding a workable solution requires that those who are unable to access food through the market are provided with the means to access it. To achieve this, sustained engagement in radical democratic politics – which has the potential to shift the entrenched *shared meaning* and *positions* around how food should be distributed and accessed – is indispensable. Supporters of the right to food campaign all over the world see the rights approach as a powerful way of bringing issues of access to food into democratic politics. For these advocates the moral and social force of the language of rights offers the possibility of bringing issues surrounding the allocation, distribution and access to food into the public domain, with the potential to influence public opinion. For example, Drèze (2005: 59) notes that even if the right to food and other ESCRS

> are not enforceable in court, [asserting] economic and social rights can have profound influence on public perception of who is entitled to what. These perceptions, in turn, can make a concrete difference in diverse ways. For instance, in situations where the effectiveness of food security programmes depends on the vigilance of the public, perceptions of rights can matter a great deal.

Before discussing the specific challenges of implementing the right to food it is essential to discuss what the right to food is: its foundations, content, scope and reach.

The Origin and Foundation of the Right to Food

Literature on the right to food traces its origin and foundation to the *Universal Declaration of Human Rights* (*UDHR*) and subsequent international human rights instruments, particularly the international Bill of Rights (which is *ICESCRs* and the *ICCPRs*). Although the *UDHR* was the first international decree to use the language of rights when talking about food and other basic human needs, the notion of food as a basic human entitlement was widely adopted and practised in many communities around the world, centuries before the *UDHR* was proclaimed. For example in many traditional African societies, every person, including strangers, was entitled to basic food, such that a member of a community experienced hunger and starvation only when there was no food in the entire community. Many accounts of social life in the history of settled human communities point to the existence of some rudimentary form of understanding and practice of entitlement to basic food for everyone – especially the weak, the old, the sick, the young, strangers, travellers, orphans and the disabled. For instance, Elman's (1966) review of hunter communities found that generosity to those who lacked basic needs such as food, water or shelter was a common feature.

Food and water were regarded as basic human needs which had to be provided to all, including prisoners of war; and in most cases the central authority had structures in place to ensure that everyone had access to basic needs, especially in times of famine or other crisis. Polanyi (1944: 53) argues that the principle of redistribution was practised by many early and medieval civilisations - including ancient Egypt, China, India, Babylonia, Greece and Rome, and by the Incas of South America – and was central to the political organisation of society. In most of these civilisations

> [w]e find, as a rule, the process of redistribution forming part of the prevailing political regime, whether it be that of tribe, city-state, despotism, or feudalism of cattle or land. The production and distribution of goods is organized in the main through collection, storage, and redistribution, the pattern being focused on the chief, the temple, the despot, or the lord.

In ancient Egypt, for instance, it has been reported that during times when many people were facing starvation, they were fed from the central granaries (John 1951). In ancient China, in times of disaster such as floods, famine or epidemics, the local authorities opened granaries, distributing free grain; while the rich were asked to support the poor, and the monarchy sent gifts to ameliorate the condition of the poor (Lee 1950). In times of trouble the Babylonians distributed food rations from the temple granaries to provide relief to the general population.

There are several examples in history which one can cite to show that access to food was regarded as a basic human entitlement – to be fulfilled, primarily, at family level or through the support of the community. Although accessing food was not regarded as a legal right in the Hohfeldian sense (see Chapter 2), it was largely regarded as a basic need and every human had to have it in appropriate quantities. In most communities, although the primary responsibility to provide food rested with the individual household, family or community, the larger society was always expected to step in whenever the individual family or village was unable to secure basic food through its own production, exchange or purchase mechanisms. Communities in many parts of the world have taken this as a moral obligation, though not necessarily a legal duty.

Over the years, at various international gatherings (see Table 6.6), similar views have been expressed – stressing the point that making food available to all is an important value that global and local communities should support and protect. The first World Food Conference, held in Rome in 1974, explicitly referred to food as a human right. This view was reaffirmed at the World Food Summit in 1996, the World Food Summit +5 in 2002, as well as the Rio +20 Summit in 2012. Thus, at the international level, there is an apparent willingness to give attention to issues of access to food as a basic human entitlement.

TABLE 6.6 *Major International Conferences Affirming the Right to Food*

Conference/ Declaration	Year	Participation	Statement
World Food Conference (Rome)	1974	135 countries 16 UN agencies	"Every man, woman and child has the inalienable right to be free from hunger and malnutrition in order to develop fully and maintain their physical and mental faculties"
International Conference on Nutrition (Rome)	1992	159 countries 15 UN agencies 144 NGOs	"Hunger and malnutrition are unacceptable in a world that has the knowledge and the resources to end this human catastrophe... We recognise that globally there is enough food for all"
Rio Earth Summit (Rio de Janeiro)	1992	180 countries	"Undertake activities aimed at the promotion of food security and, where appropriate, food self-sufficiency"
World Conference on Human Rights *Vienna Declaration*	1993	171 countries 800 NGOs	"...food should not be used as a tool for political pressure..." "...extreme poverty and social exclusion constitute a violation of human dignity..."
World Summit on Social Development *Copenhagen Declaration*	1995	190 states 62 UN agencies and interregional bodies	"...improving access to food by low-income people in developing countries, as a means of alleviating poverty, eliminating malnutrition and raising their standards of living"
World Food Summit *Rome Declaration*	1996	186 countries 19 UN agencies 23 intergovernmental bodies 13 NGO caucuses	"We, the Heads of State and Government, ...reaffirm the right of everyone to have access to safe and nutritious food, consistent with the right to adequate food and the fundamental right of everyone to be free from hunger..."

TABLE 6.6 *Major International Conferences Affirming the Right to Food* (cont.)

Conference/ Declaration	Year	Participation	Statement
Millennium Declaration	2000	188 member states	"We resolve...to halve, by the year 2015, ...the the proportion of people who suffer from hunger..."
World Forum on Food Sovereignty (Havana) *Havana Declaration*	2001	400 delegates from 60 countries (mainly peasants and smallholder farmers and NGOs)	"In defense of the principle of the people's inalienable right to food, we propose the adoption by the United Nations of an International Convention on Food Sovereignty"
World Food Summit +5 (Rome)	2002	182 countries	"We renew our commitments made in the Rome Declaration at the World Food Summit in 1996"
Maputo Declaration	2003	All African Union member states	"We, the heads of states, resolve to ensure the establishment of regional food reserve systems, including food stocks linked to Africa's own production"
Nyeleni Declaration (Mali)	2007	500 peasant and smallholder farmers, pastoralist and fisherfolk from 80 countries	"Food sovereignty includes the right to food – the right of peoples to healthy and culturally appropriate food produced through socially just and ecologically sensitive methods"
Rio +20	2012	192 UN member states and civil society groups	"We reaffirm our commitments regarding the right of everyone to have access to safe, sufficient and nutritious food, consistent with the right to adequate food and the fundamental right of everyone to be free from hunger."

SOURCE: COMPILED BY THE AUTHOR FROM VARIOUS SOURCES.

Several international declarations, including the *UDHR*, have confirmed the idea that food is a basic human right. By making such a declaration, there is something substantively different added to the notion of access to food.

However, despite all the international declarations, conferences and solemn proclamations aimed at ensuring every person has access to adequate food, the number of people suffering from hunger has increased – especially since the mid-1990s (see Table 6.1).

In the same vein, the CESCR also observes that despite numerous affirmations of the right to food "a disturbing gap still exists between the standards set in article 11 of the Covenant [i.e. the *ICESCR*] and the situation prevailing in many parts of the world" (CESCR 1999: para. 2 (1)). It is thus not clear at this stage whether declaring food as a human right makes any difference in the lives of people who suffer from hunger, undernourishment and starvation. What does the right to food mean for those who daily face the pain and anguish of having no food or insufficient food?

What is the Right to Food?

The existing literature on the right to food does not provide a precise, dictionary-type definition of what it is. Such as definition would be extremely difficult to make given the complexity and multiplicity of factors related to access to food. However, many working definitions of this right have been suggested by various analysts and institutions (Ahluwalia 2004: 13). In the literature on the right to food it is common to adopt a normative definition of the right, stipulating the conditions under which the right to food is expected to be fulfilled. For example, the CESCR – the UN body mandated with responsibility for elaborating on ESCRs, including the right to food – states that the "right to adequate food is realised when every man, woman and child, alone or in community with others, has physical and economic access at all times to adequate food or means for its procurement" (*General Comment 12*: para. 6). Analysts have often taken this as the formal definition of the right to food (see Ziegler 2003: 7; OHCHR/FAO 2010: 2; Cohen and Brown 2008: 135; Courtis 2007: 324). However, a much more comprehensive definition has been provided by the former Special Rapporteur, who has defined it as:

> The right to have regular, permanent and free access, either directly or by means of financial purchases, to quantitatively and qualitatively adequate and sufficient food corresponding to cultural traditions of the people to which the consumer belongs, and which ensures a physical and mental, individual and collective, fulfilling and dignified life free of fear.
>
> ZIEGLER 2001: 7

In this definition the responsibility to ensure "regular, permanent and free access...to...adequate and sufficient food" is primarily placed on the individual or the family to which an individual belongs; while the state has the responsibility of ensuring that the right to food is respected, protected and fulfilled by all. This is clear in the 2003 report of the Special Rapporteur on the right to food, which states: "The right to food does not mean handing out free food to everyone. Rather, the right to food means that Governments must respect, protect and fulfil the right to food as clarified in *General Comment No. 12*" (Ziegler 2003: 7).

The view that the right to food is not about providing free food to everyone is widely supported. For instance, Cohen and Brown (2008: 137) argue that the "right to adequate food is not about state obligation to directly provide three meals a day to everyone living within their territory". However, the obligation to respect, protect and fulfil *does* impose the obligation upon the state to directly provide food in cases where individuals or families are unable to acquire adequate food on their own. The CESR (*General Comment 12*: para. 15, emphasis in original) has elaborated on this:

> [W]henever an individual or group is unable, for reasons beyond their control, to enjoy the right to adequate food by the means at their disposal, States have the obligation to *fulfil* (*provide*) that right directly. This obligation also applies for persons who are victims of natural or other disasters.

Understood in this sense, the right to food places primary responsibility on the individual, family or group; but it also generate clear obligations on the state – including the obligation to directly provide food in situations where individuals, families and groups are unable to. It is specifically in situations where the individual, family or village is unable to meet basic food needs that the state is obliged to take serious steps to fulfil the right.

However, while obligations for individuals and the state, in most definitions of the right to food, can be inferred, there is general vagueness in most attempts to formally define it – as is often the case with many other rights. For most human rights – including civil and political rights – it is almost impossible to adequately define them in a single formulation; rights are elaborated by case law, public debate, independent experts, ministerial regulations, public policy, practice and experience. It is often futile to come up with a single formulation that encapsulates all dimensions of a right. A right's content, scope and reach are often illuminated and shaped by real life challenges and experiences. This is why human rights are not static, but are constantly changing to effectively respond to the changing social, political and economic situations (Jones 1994). Thus, a very legalistic and rigid approach to the definition of the right to food – as is often the case among authors with a legal-positivist persuasion – can lead to a narrow understanding of the values that the right seeks to protect. It is for this reason that the CESCR has repeatedly advocated for a broader interpretation of human rights (including the right to food), urging states to avoid narrow and restrictive interpretation of Covenant rights.

With particular reference to the right to food, the CESCR has argued that "the right to adequate food shall…not be interpreted in a restrictive sense which equates it with a minimum package of calories, proteins and other specific nutrients" (*General Comment 12*: para. 6). Defining the right to food broadly makes it possible to pursue other ways of giving effect to the right. Such a definition creates room for both judicial as well as non-judicial avenues of realising the right for the hundreds of millions of people around the globe who suffer hunger, undernourishment and starvation. A purposive approach to the right to food makes it possible "to create a framework that makes governments accountable for carrying out duties vis-à-vis their citizens, and to empower citizens, especially poor and vulnerable people"(Cohen and Brown 2008: 138). This approach also makes it possible to bring issues of access to food into the broader domain of democratic politics.

However, it has been noted that such broad and imprecise formulations of the right makes it difficult to determine whether the right is being violated or not – thereby rendering adjudications on the matter problematic if not impractical (Neier 2006). Some authors have argued that the broadness and vagueness of most ESCRs is the reason why there are two Covenants and not one: "The decision to put the two sets of rights in different treaties with different supervisory mechanisms was well considered, and the underlying reasons for those distinctions and decisions appear to remain valid today"(Dennis and Stewart 2004: 465). This view assumes that adjudication is the only way of giving effect to human rights – but as some analysts have noted, judicial processes may not always be the best way to give effect to human rights, including civil and political rights (Courtis 2007; Cohen and Brown 2008).

Access to Food as a Basic Human Entitlement

Despite the differing views on the right to food, there is wide acknowledgement that access to it should be regarded as a basic human entitlement. What this implies is that issues of access to food should be evaluated from within a rights-based framework that recognises people as the centre of political and social institutions – and not as mere objects of charity. Seen from this angle, the essential part of the right to food is that it "provides a...framework, the concept of rights and obligations, and the relevant mechanism needed to achieve accountability" (FAO 2011a: 7). Not only that, the right to food ushers in a framework that makes it possible to create spaces where various actors – including the state and private sector – can be held to account for their actions or inactions. This framework can empower people through genuine participation in decisions that affect their lives. In a fundamental way, the right to food is essentially a means to create spaces in which the right can be contested. It is therefore essentially a practice of radical democratic politics in the sense that implementing the right to food involves a fundamental shift in the arrangements around the way it is produced and distributed. For example, this would involve undoing any structures or relations that constrain people's – especially poor people's – access to food, land, inputs, water and other elements that contribute to making food production possible; or the denial of any means through which people acquire food.

In this sense the right to food differs markedly from food security, food sovereignty[3] and self-sufficiency (OHCHR/FAO 2010). The key fundamental difference between the right to food and food security is that the right to food creates a coherent framework in which critical issues of governance can be addressed in the fight against hunger, undernourishment and starvation – by engaging in radical democratic politics that puts pressure on all public actors, especially government agencies, to make sure that their actions or failure to act do not lead to some people being unable to acquire adequate food. This is radically different from food security, which is mainly concerned with issues of availability and accessibility without addressing how the state should deal with these issues (see FAO 2011a: 7; Ahluwalia 2004: 13). In this case, food security is a precondition for realising the right to food, but it is not sufficient in itself to give effect to the right to food (Ziegler 2003). Thus, it can be argued that the right to food encompasses all elements of food security – but that it goes beyond the concerns of food security and introduces concepts of obligation, participation, accountability and non-discrimination. If these concepts are put into practice the right to food inevitably leads to the playing out of radical democratic politics where access to food is contested in public, social and political *spaces*.

---

3 Food sovereignty is a concept developed by social movements – mainly peasant and smallholder farmers, and fisher-folk – which argues for the right to be able to produce and sell food autonomously on a sustainable basis. The concept uses the right to food discourse to make its claims, but the two discourses are not the same (see *Nyeleni Declaration* 2007).

Current Status of the Right to Food

Unlike the right to water, there are several international human rights instruments that have explicitly recognised the right to food. Table 6.7 below provides a summary of major international and regional human rights instruments that have either explicitly or implicitly recognised the right to food.

As evident in Table 6.7, access to adequate food has been widely affirmed as a human right. More than 90 per cent of states have ratified human rights instruments such as the *CRC*, *CEDAW*, *ICCPR*, *ICESCR* and the UN Charter – meaning that most of the world has recognised the values contained in such instruments and voluntarily committed to protecting them.[4] It is interesting to note also that no state party has deposited a reservation to Article 11 (1 and 2) of the *ICESCR* – the main instrument protecting the right to food. This might be an indication of the wider acceptance that the right to food enjoys.

At the national level, review of national constitutions and framework law suggests that 23 countries have explicitly provided for the right to food in their constitutions, while 33 have recognised the right to food implicitly through other human rights such as the right to life or the right to an adequate standard of living. Some 15 countries have recognised the right to food in the directive principles for state policy. In total there are about 56 national constitutions around the world that have either explicitly or implicitly recognised[5] the right to food. There are also 51 countries in which the international treaties that explicitly recognise the right to food are directly applicable. A number of countries have already applied these, while some are still developing framework law on the right to food (see Knuth and Vidar 2011).

4 It is important to note here that while many countries have signed and ratified these treaties, a number of countries have deposited reservations not to be bound by particular provisions of a treaty. In the case of the *CEDAW* there are more than 60 states parties that have deposited reservations on various provisions – the most common one being Article 29 (the provision on paid maternity leave).

5 It is essential to note here that there are various ways in which the right to food is recognised. In some countries the right is explicitly and separately recognised in the national constitution (e.g. South Africa, Kenya and Colombia); in other countries the right to food is recognised for a specific section of society, such as children (Colombia, Costa Rica), or prisoners and detainees (South Africa). In many countries the right to food is recognised as part of a broader human rights package such as the right to life (India), the right to an adequate standard of living (Malawi, Ukraine, Brazil, Congo). In other countries the right to food is provided for in the directive principles for state policy (e.g. Nigeria, Ireland, Zambia, Uganda, Sierra Leone). There are countries that have provided for the right to food in more than one way (e.g. Malawi, Eritrea, Guatemala, Pakistan, Brazil, Bolivia and Panama; see also FAO 2006).

TABLE 6.7 *Major International Human Rights Instruments Related to Food Security*

Instrument	Year	Provision	Article	States Parties
Explicit and Direct Provision on the Right to Food				
Universal Declaration of Human Rights (*UDHR*)	1948	"Everyone has the right to a standard of living adequate for the health and well-being of himself and of his family, including **food**, clothing, housing and medical care and necessary social services"	25 (1)	48/8b
International Covenant on Economic, Social & Cultural Rights (*ICESCR*)	1966 [1976]	(1) "The States Parties to the present Covenant recognize the right of everyone to an adequate standard of living for himself and his family, including **adequate food**, clothing and housing" (2) "The States Parties… recognizing the fundamental right of everyone to be free from hunger, shall take…measures: To improve methods of production, conservation and distribution of food"	11 (1 & 2)	160
Convention on the Right of the Child (*CRC*)	1989 [1990]	"States Parties shall…take appropriate measures: To combat disease and malnutrition…through the provision of adequate **nutritious foods** and clean drinking-water"	24 (c)	189
African Charter on the Rights and Welfare of the Child (*ACRWC*)	1990	"States Parties to the present Charter shall undertake…to ensure the provision of **adequate nutrition** and safe drinking water"	14 (2c)	40a
The Right to Development (*RTD*)		"States should undertake…all necessary measures for the realization of…inter alia, equality of opportunity for all in their access to basic resources, education, health services, **food**, housing, employment"	8 (1)	146/8/1d

TABLE 6.7 *Major International Human Rights Instruments Related to Food Security* (cont.)

Instrument	Year	Provision	Article	States Parties
Implicit Provision for the Right to Food				
United Nations Charter (UN Charter)	1945 [1945]	Nations shall promote: (a) "a higher standard of living, full employment, and conditions of economic and social progress and development" (b) "universal respect for, and observance of, human rights and fundamental freedoms for all"	55 (a & b)	193
International Covenant on Civil and Political Rights (*ICCPR*)	1966 [1966]	"Every human being has the inherent right to life"	6 (1)	160
Covenant on the Elimination of all Forms of Discrimination Against Women (*CEDAW*)	1979 [1981]	"To enjoy adequate living conditions, particularly in relation to housing, sanitation, electricity and water supply"	14 (2 h)	186
African Charter on Human and People's Rights (*ACHPR*)	1981	(1) "All peoples shall have the right to their economic, social and cultural development" (2) "States shall have the duty, individually or collectively, to ensure the exercise of the right to development"	22 (1 & 2)	53a

Notes:
[a] refer only to members of the African Union
[b] the UDHR is a non-binding declaration and thus does not create legally binding obligations. But together with the ICESCR and the ICCPR it constitutes the international bill of rights and states parties to the either of the two have recognised the UDHR. In 1948, out of 58 countries represented, 48 voted for, while 8 countries abstained.
[c] the year in brackets refer to the year when the treaty came into force.
[d] This is also a non-binding instrument. 146 members of the general assembly voted for, while 8 abstained and 1 member voted against the right to development.
SOURCE: COMPILED BY THE AUTHOR FROM VARIOUS SOURCES.

Thus, it is apparent that a majority of countries around the world recognise the importance of the values contained in the right to food, and have committed themselves to ensuring that these values are respected, protected and realised. The challenge around the right to food is not so much about the right not being well recognised – as is the case with the right to water. Rather, the challenge revolves around translating the entitlements contained in the various documents and instruments into real entitlements which people without access to food can claim. Taking practical steps at the local and national level to give meaning to the values encapsulated in the right to food has proved to be more challenging for the majority of countries in the Global South. In view of this, it can be submitted that while formal recognition through constitutional, legislative and other legal frameworks is important, realising the right to food takes more than this – it requires sustained contestation by various actors, including social movements, NGOs, civil society groups and state agencies. This will ensure that appropriate decisions and actions are being taken to give *meaning* to the right.

The Right to Food in the International Human Rights System

Research from different parts of the world has shown that there is no clear correlation between the ratification of human right treaties and the protection of human rights. In some cases, ratification or legislation seems to have a negative effect on the protection of human rights (Hathaway 2002: 1940). Thus, "it is not enough to recognise the right to food constitutionally and to enact law on [the] same; such laws needs to be 'owned' by those who are most in need of its enforcement. Legislation needs constant follow up from all sides, in order to be effective" (Knuth and Vidar 2011: 32). This is perhaps where the value added by adopting a rights-based approach to issues of access to water, food, education, healthcare, etc., is more evident. As noted earlier, application of the RBA principles of equity and non-discrimination, accountability and participation, is one way of creating spaces in which pressure to give effect to a particular right can be exerted, and the struggle for a particular right or group of rights can be sustained. As Golay and Ozden (n.d.: 39) have noted, "If history has taught us that rights can be secured only through struggle, it also teaches us that achieving the fulfilment of those rights also requires struggle".

In the struggle for human rights, their interdependence becomes essential – for the simple reason that the struggle for human rights is most effective when certain basic rights are protected. For example, to be able to effectively secure the right to water, food or education, the basic rights to assemble, free expression, participation, protest, and information must first be protected (OHCHR/FAO 2010: 5–6). In situations where these basic rights are not protected it becomes extremely difficult to give effect to other rights such as the right to food.

Thus, in the human rights approach, the struggle should not end with the signing of international treaties or proclamations of national statutes or constitutions; that is just a first step in the process of giving effect to a particular right. The real struggle continues far beyond the specific pieces of law, parliamentary processes and protocols. However, legislation and legal protection of a particular right, at the national or international level, creates a foundation upon which the struggle can be built, and as such forms an important element of the struggle. While many human rights advocates and activists are often sceptical about the usefulness of legislation – since most laws are not implemented or make no difference to the lives of the many people who suffer from hunger and starvation – it is essential to bear in mind that legislation only creates the *foundation* on which the struggle to give meaning to human rights can be built and sustained. Legislation is important in making it possible to begin to talk about rights such as the right to food. However, legislation only creates an opportunity – it is up to the various sectors of society to grab the opportunity presented by legislation. Examples of how this can and has been done are illustrated in Chapter 8.

Normative Content of the Right to Food

The *ICESCR* is the main instrument dealing with the right to food. Its provisions constitute the foundation on which the right to food, its content, scope, reach and obligations have been elaborated and expanded on. Article 11 of the *ICESCR* provides for two components of the right to food: the right to "adequate food" (Section 1) and the right of "everyone to be free from hunger" (Section 2). Although sometimes the two components are referred to as constituting two different rights it is probably more helpful to refer to them as "two components of the right to food" (FAO 2009). Some analysts have referred to Section 1 as the *primary norm*, and Section 2 as the *sub-norm*, noting that the two are inextricably related:

> The practical implications of taking, as primary norm, the right to adequate food rather than the right to be free from hunger are significant. Whereas the former facilitates the adoption of a maximalist approach, the latter, which is more akin to a sub-norm, is able at least in theory to be satisfied by the adoption of policies designed to provide a minimum daily nutritional intake
>
> IN DENNIS AND STEWART 2004: 495

Although this interpretation has been seen by some analysts as an "alteration of the substantive content of the Covenant",[6] it has been conceded that if this interpretation is referring to two components of the same norm, it can be taken as a "plausible proposition" (ibid.). The view of the CESCR is that the right to be free from hunger is the basic minimum of the right to food, a threshold below which a state party to the Covenant should strive to avoid. This is explained more clearly in terms of the obligations of states parties to the Covenant generated by Section 2 of Article 11 of the *ICESCR*: "Every state is obliged to ensure for everyone under its jurisdiction access to the minimum essential food which is sufficient, nutritionally adequate and safe, to ensure their freedom from hunger" (*General Comment 12*: para. 14). However, the focus of *General Comment 12* – and indeed the vast literature on the right to food – is on Section 1, which constitutes the primary norm of the right.

The emphasis placed on adequate food by the CESCR is understandable when one takes a normative approach – which emphasises the maximum rather than the minimum standard. However, the important point is that both the minimum and the maximum standards are protecting the same right, and contribute to realising the object and purpose of Article 11 in particular. Being free from hunger implies having access to adequate food, just as having access to adequate food creates a condition in which one can be said to be free from hunger. In this sense the two provisions, while not exactly the same in effect, are essentially protecting the same value of ensuring that all human beings have sufficient food to secure a life of dignity and self-fulfilment.

The intention to include the two articles was probably meant to emphasise the point that the ultimate aim of the right to food is to ensure that everyone is free from hunger, which implies having access to adequate food. The structure of Article 11 also suggests that the drafters of the *ICESCR* understood that in order to realise the right for everyone to be free from hunger, the starting point should be to ensure that everyone has access to adequate food. In this sense, fulfilment of Section 1 (access to adequate food) logically leads to the realisation of Section 2 (freedom from hunger). Another way of looking at the two components is that Section 2 is fulfilled as a result of realising Section 1, and the two are related to each other in that sense.

While the main basis for the right to food under the international human rights system is Article 11 of the *ICESCR* there are other documents that have

---

6 On this issue the CESCR has been accused of "rewriting Article 11 by resurrecting and adopting alternatives that were considered and rejected by the negotiators" (see Dennis and Stewart 2004: 494).

explicitly provided for access to food as a human right and have elaborated on what this entails in practice. The provisions of Article 11, as may be evident, are formulated in a broad manner that does not provide clear guidance regarding what exactly it means to have the right to food, and what this right includes. To provide some practical guidance on the rights provided for in the *ICESCR*, the Economic and Social Council (ECOSOC) of the United Nations – created in 1985 – established the CESCR, which is formally recognised as the authoritative body entrusted with interpreting and elaborating on matters related to the Covenant. The CESCR is also entrusted with assisting and monitoring the implementation of the rights under *ICESCR* by states parties, and there are several ways in which the CESCR carries out its mandate. In terms of interpreting and elaborating on the rights under *ICESCR*, the CESCR occasionally formulates *General Comments* – which expand and clarify the content of a particular right, outline the obligations for states parties to the Covenant, and elucidate the conditions under which the right is violated. For the right to food the CESCR formulated *General Comment 12*, in 1999, to elaborate on its normative and substantive content, and the obligations for states parties as well as the international community. Table 6.8 below summarises the normative content of the right to food as elaborated in *General Comment 12*.

The seven components of the normative content of the right to food are similar to the elements of the food security framework. However, the right to food goes beyond the food security framework by elaborating on what the obligations of the state are with regard to each of these components; and also indicating when these obligations are not fulfilled. It is in these two aspects that the right to food framework has far-reaching political ramifications when compared to the food security framework. When elaborating on the right to food, the CESCR (*General Comment 12*: para. 4) notes that

> the right to food is indivisibly linked to the inherent dignity of the human person and is indispensable for the fulfilment of other human rights enshrined in the International Bill of Human Rights. It is also inseparable from social justice, requiring the adoption of appropriate economic, environmental and social policies, at both the national and international levels, oriented to the eradication of poverty and the fulfilment of all human rights.

This sums up the core normative values contained in the right to food; namely, advancing human dignity and the fulfilment of other human rights though the promotion of social justice. The social justice element brings the right to food, and indeed many other rights, into the realm of radical democratic politics – where the actual meaning and implication of this is contested by various

TABLE 6.8 *The Normative Content of the Right to Food*

	Adequacy	Availability	Accessibility	Food safety	Dietary need	Cultural acceptability	Sustainability
Specification	Appropriate quantity and nutritional content	Presence of the right food close to where it is needed	Physical: Accessible to everyone via self-acquisition or entitlement. Economic: Sufficient purchasing power; Access to productive resources.	Food is free from harmful substances	Appropriate mix of nutrients corresponding to physical needs	Non-nutritional values attached to food	Steady supply of food for present and future generations
State Obligations	Ensure improved production, efficient transport and distribution	Efficient food distribution and Food Aid programmes	Facilitate access to productive resources (land, water, inputs, seeds etc.)	Prevent contamination of foodstuffs	Promote dietary diversity, nutritional information and awareness	Respect different cultural values on food	Ensure sustainable ways of producing food, preventing food wastage
Violation Indicators	Failure to take necessary measures	Inefficient food distribution system	Absence of food programme for vulnerable groups	Absence of measures, policy and law on food standards	Failure to provide nutritional information	Failure to respect cultural values on food	Failure to ensure sustainable food production

SOURCE: AUTHOR, BASED ON INFORMATION FROM *GENERAL COMMENT 12* (CESCR 1999).

sections of society. Sometimes, public debates – as well as case law – provide some guidance on the content of the right, as well as determining when the right is violated or fulfilled.

As noted earlier, some analysts have argued that the content of the right to food, like many ESCRs, is vague – therefore making it difficult to adjudicate (see Neier 2006; Drèze 2005; Dennis and Stewart 2004). For example – notions of adequacy, maximum resources, acceptable rates of progress made towards realising a particular right, cultural appropriateness and dietary needs are difficult to verify in concrete terms, thereby making it problematic to determine whether a right has indeed been violated or not. It has been reported that during the discussions of the Open-ended Working Group tasked with considering the feasibility of an *Optional Protocol to ICESCR* in 2004, some of the delegates argued that rights under the *ICESCR* are largely imprecise and therefore difficult to enforce (Dennis and Stewart 2004: 473). From a different angle, Drèze (2005) has argued that the right to food is more complex, with more imprecise responsibilities and entitlements than many other rights such as the right to education or information; because of this the right to food is more difficult to implement.

> The right to food is, in some ways, a more complex right than the right to education or the right to information. To start with, the entitlements and responsibilities associated with the right to food are far from obvious. In the case of, say, the right to information, some basic entitlements and responsibilities are easy to identify: every citizen has a right of access to public records (subject to specific exceptions, pertaining for instance to 'national security'), and conversely, every civil servant has a duty to part with the relevant records under pre-specified terms.
>
> DRÈZE, 2005: 54–5

While such criticisms have merit, the difficulty of precisely demarcating where the responsibilities and entitlements start and end does not only apply to the right to food; other rights such as the right to information – under certain circumstances – have responsibilities and entitlements that are equally complicated and just as difficult to disentangle. All rights are potentially complex, and reaching clarity on matters of duties and benefits is not always straightforward; if it was, there would be no need for jurisprudence and adjudication.

For the right to food, the purpose of elaborating the content of the right is not primarily to make it justiciable through legal processes and means, but to provide some guidance to both duty-bearers and right-holders concerning what the right includes and protects. This is often achieved through complex processes of interpreting and applying a wide range of issues related to the right. For duty-bearers, meeting the obligations under Article 11 does not necessarily entail a judicial process reaching a determination on whether the obligations in question have been fulfilled or not; obligations can be met through enacting legislation, by administrative means, or through a political process whereby the state directly engages with sections of society to find a common solution to the challenges of accessing adequate food.

The Special Rapporteur and Independent Experts on the Right to Food

Apart from the *General Comments*, the CESCR also elaborates on the content and implementation of the rights under the Covenant through the work of the independent experts and Special Rapporteurs for specific rights. As noted earlier, the Special Rapporteur on the right to food has been reporting on its status, as well as some of the challenges surrounding its implementation. In one of the reports the former Special Rapporteur on the right to food asserts that

> [t]he right to food is a human right that entails Governments' obligations to guarantee the food security of their population. In a world richer than ever before, it is unacceptable that people can be left to die of starvation. Nor should anyone be condemned to the misery of stunted mental and physical development that results from chronic hunger and malnutrition. All human beings have a right to live in dignity, free from hunger.
>
> ZIEGLER 2006: 8

Most of the reports by the Special Rapporteur on the right to food are based on the country missions. These missions are undertaken to examine the status of the right to food in a particular country, via an investigation of the practical measures taken by that state to respond, in particular, to challenges surrounding the right to food. In one report, the Special Rapporteur observed that

> [t]he right to food implies that action is taken progressively by the government to ensure that hunger and malnutrition are, progressively, eradicated. The human rights approach mean that progress should be monitored and Governments held accountable if they do not take adequate action.
>
> ZIEGLER 2003: 8

Since 1999 – when *General Comment 12* was adopted – the CESCR, the Special Rapporteur, as well as independent researchers and analysts, have debated the merits and the challenges of the right to food, elaborating on the practical implications for duty-bearers and right-holders and also the technical issues surrounding the application and implementation of the right. Although the CESCR is recognised as the authoritative interpreter of the rights under the *ICESCR*, several commentators and analysts have contributed to the debate and elaborated on various aspects of the right to food – including its nature, content and scope. In addition, several courts have adjudicated in the matter (see Chapter 8).

Although there have been robust debates on various aspects of the right to food, it has been observed that while the right has been provided for under the *ICESCR* for more than 40 years, "efforts to develop and clarify its content are relatively recent, especially in comparison with other rights recognised by the same covenant – i.e., labour rights" (Courtis 2007: 321).[7] Like the right to water, it has been observed that there has been little movement in giving effect to these rights in many countries – largely because there has not been a process of wider contestation. The existing evidence does not attribute the failure of individual countries to fulfil these rights to a failure to provide for them in their national constitutions or in their failure to ratify the Covenant. Even in countries that have recognised the right to water or food in their Bill of Rights, these rights have gone unmet for millions of people (see Hathaway 2002). Thus, the crux of the matter goes beyond constitutional recognition of the right.

Giving effect to the rights recognised under a national constitution is not an obvious function of having a constitutional provision or ratification of an international human rights convention or treaty. The right to food, like many other ESCRs, is not given freely – its realisation requires the creation of spaces where it can be effected and given meaning; and the process of giving effect to the right goes beyond constitutional provision. Real rights are always the product of a protracted struggle, not just by a few individuals but by the broader society. Essentially, for the right to food to be given substantive meaning and effect, democratic political engagement is indispensable. In situations where the right to food is removed from real politics, it loses its essence.

7 In comparison with the right to water – which was only recognised officially in 2003 through *General Comment 15* – the right to food has a much longer lifespan and a more direct legal basis.

Scope of the Right to Food

For the right to food to be meaningful it has to be specific in terms of what it entails. Although issues of scope are crucial for the judicial route, clarification of the scope of a right is also important when considering other ways of ensuring that a particular right is respected, protected and fulfilled. Three critical aspects of the scope of a right include: (1) what the right encompasses (2) who the intended beneficiaries of the right – the right-holders – are, and (3) who the duty-bearers are?

In terms of the right to food, the question of what exactly the right covers has already been discussed in the section that discussed the content of the right to food (see Table 6.8). However, the right to food is, in fact, a much more widely scoped right which goes beyond the right to mere access to adequate food. It covers issues surrounding nutritional information, secure food distribution systems, functioning of food markets, food safety, and, in some cases, sustainable access to productive resources such as land, water and other inputs. The wider scope of the right to food is confirmed by the CESCR (*General Comment*, 12: para. 12), which argues that

> availability refers to the possibilities of either feeding oneself directly from productive land or other natural resources, or for well-functioning distribution, processing and market systems that can move food from the site of production to where it is needed in accordance with demand.

Again, this reflects a complex set of factors that need to be taken into account when analysing the scope of the right to food. These factors are clearly dependent on the particular circumstances in which the right is being assessed. For example, in order to guarantee adequate food for people living in rural areas, access to land, water and other productive assets has to be considered (OCHR/FAO 2010: 3). Thus, the right to food is

> a multidimensional right, the realisation of which depends on many factors. In a normal situation, for the majority of persons, the right to food is realised primarily through their own efforts, by producing or procuring the food they need. This depends on access to land and other productive resources.
>
> FAO 2011: 117

Regarding the beneficiaries of the right to food, Article 11 (1) of the *ICESCR* is very clear – the right is for everyone: "the Covenant recognises the right of *everyone* to an adequate standard of living...including adequate food" Similarly, Article 11 (2) of the *ICESCR* affirms the "fundamental right of *everyone* to be free from hunger". This is further reaffirmed by the CESCR (*General Comment 12*: para. 1), which states that the

> human right to adequate food is of crucial importance for the enjoyment of all rights. It applies to *everyone*; thus the reference in Article 11 (1) to 'himself and his family' does not imply any limitation upon the applicability of this right to individuals or to female-headed households.

In view of the principle of non-discrimination, which the human rights approach embraces, the right to food cannot be restricted to a certain section of society on the basis of gender, race, age, sexual orientation, origin, social status, etc. The right is accorded to *everyone*, citizen or non-citizen. In this context, even foreign nationals residing in a state that is party to the Covenant have the right to food extended to them. In this regard it has been observed that the "*ICESCR* does not mention territorial or jurisdiction as delimiting criteria for the scope and application of the treaty" (Coomans 2007: 326). The obligation here is to everyone under a state party's jurisdiction. The CESCR (*General Comment 12*: para. 14) has made this clear: "Every State is obliged to ensure for everyone under its jurisdiction access to the minimum essential food." What this implies is that everyone, including foreign nationals, can claim the right to food under Article 11 (1 and 2). A good example of this is the Swiss Federal Court's decision in 1996 (though not relying on the Right to Food Provisions under the *ICESCR*), that undocumented foreign nationals residing in Switzerland had the right to "all basic human needs, such as food, clothing and housing" (cited in Courtis 2007: 330). The wider scope provided by Article 11 can be justified on the grounds that food is the foundation on which life itself, and other human rights, largely depend. The basicness of the right to food can be used as a justification to universalise its scope so as to avoid excluding anyone from its ambit. If one accepts this position then claims to the right to food – whether by judicial, administrative, legislative, political or policy means – can be made by anyone residing in a state party to the Covenant. However, the primary obligation to fulfil the right lies with the individual or family; it is only in situations where the individual or family is unable to fulfil the right for themselves that the state should be called in as a matter of duty to respond. So, while everyone is a beneficiary of the right, this does not mean that everyone has a claim against the state to be provided with adequate food or to be freed from hunger.

The Nature of Obligations for States Parties to the Covenant

Under the *ICESCR*, the obligations for states parties to the Covenant are provided for, generally, in Article 2 (1–3). However, the nature, scope, interpretation, application and implication of these obligations are the subject of intense debate. One dominant view on this is that the Covenant imposes only the obligation of *conduct* and not the obligation of *results*. This is a minimalist argument which asserts that the Covenant only imposes the obligation to *take measures*, *steps*, or act in a way that creates an environment in which the rights can be realised progressively. The main argument for the minimalist view has been that the "rights set forth in the *ICESCR*...are not described as obligations to be performed by the states parties in full and at once. Rather, they represent goals to be achieved progressively" (Dennis and Stewart 2004: 476). This is the position that was adopted by the US government during the negotiation and drafting stages of the Covenant, and it has remained the official US policy on ESCRs, as noted in Chapter 3. Unfortunately, this argument has been commonly used to defend the position that these rights, unlike civil and political rights, are aspirational goals and not to be confused with "real" human rights.

However, there are other analysts who take a hybrid interpretation of Article 2 (1) of the Covenant; they argue that states under the *ICESCR* have the obligation of *results* (outcome) as well as the obligation of *conduct*. Proponents of the hybrid view argue that in cases where

> the various rights are silent on the concrete steps to be taken by states in fulfilment of their obligations with regard to rights 'recognized', the relevant obligations can best be understood as hybrids between obligations of result and obligations of conduct. They are obligations of result in the sense that states must match their performance with their objective capabilities. They are loose obligations of conduct in the sense that states are obliged to take active, though largely unspecified, steps towards their satisfaction.
>
> ALSTON AND QUINN 1987: 185

While Article 2 of the Covenant stipulates that states parties "undertake to take steps" (Section 1), and that they "undertake to guarantee " (Section 2), such provisions are open to interpretation and it is always contentious to determine which interpretation is correct. The CESCR in *General Comment 3*, which elaborates on the nature of the obligations generated under the *ICESCR*, affirms that Article 2 (1) "include[s] both what may be termed (following the work of the International Law Commission) obligations of conduct and obligation of result" (*General Comment 3*: para 1). However, it is acknowledged that because of the principle of "progressive realisation" which the *ICESCR* envisions, the nature of obligations under the *ICESCR* differs "significantly from that contained in Article 2" of the *ICCPR* – which embodies an immediate obligation to respect and ensure that all of the relevant rights are fulfilled. But the CESCR (*General Comment* 3: para. 9) contends this view, arguing that

> realisation over time, or in other words progressively, as foreseen under the Covenant should not be misinterpreted as depriving the obligation of all meaningful content. It is on the one hand a necessary flexibility device, reflecting the realities of the real world and the difficulties involved for any country in ensuring full realisation of economic, social and cultural rights.

The CESCR encourages interpretation of the obligations "in the light of the overall objective, indeed the raison d'être of the Covenant which is to establish clear obligations for States parties in respect of the full realisation of the rights in question" (ibid.).

Despite these guidelines on how to interpret the state's obligations under the Covenant, there are intense debates – especially among international law experts – on whether the Covenant should be interpreted as generating obligations of *conduct*, of *result*, or of both. The substantive difference between these two types of obligation is often not made clear in the debates, given that any "deliberate, concrete and targeted" steps, as elaborated in *General Comment 3* (para. 2), are anticipated to produce some outcome. Thus, even if one were to restrict the obligation under Article 2 (1) to the obligation of conduct only, the taking of steps is only justifiable if it is aimed at achieving something; steps or measures are not under-taken for the sake of just taking steps. Arguably, it would be absurd to infer that taking steps is an end in itself. The main objective and purpose for taking "concrete, deliberate and targeted steps" is to achieve certain outcomes – even if these outcomes are not precisely formulated. Thus, while the *ICESCR* does not require that all people whose right to food is violated should be fulfilled by the state immediately, it does generate the obligation of outcome – in the sense that the impact or results of steps taken or not taken should be considered when determining a state party's compliance.

In the case of the right to food, there is some clarity as to what the obligations are for states parties – and Article 11 of the Covenant has listed a number of actual steps that should be taken. In this sense the obligations concerning the right to food are clearer than the general obligations provided in Article 2. Among the steps that states parties to the Covenant should take are measures to "improve methods of production, conservation and distribution of food...

dissemination of knowledge of the principles of nutrition and by developing or reforming the agrarian system...to achieve the most efficient development and utilisation of natural resources" (Article 11 (2a)).

Notably, the Covenant does specify the actual actions that states must take in order to fulfil their obligation under the Covenant – except for Article 9, which does not elaborate. The clarification of obligations is critical at the implementation and monitoring phases of a particular right because this provides guidance to duty-bearers regarding what they are expected to do. Such clarification measures are also important for civil society groups who are involved in monitoring compliance with Covenant obligations and national laws. Without clearly outlined obligations it is difficult to determine whether the failure to give effect to a particular right has occurred or not.

In practical terms, unclear obligations and unclear content of a right can be disempowering to ordinary citizens in that they may not be able to ascertain what the right has granted them and whether violations of rights have occurred or not. If the obligations and duties are not clear, it is difficult, for instance, for a farmer to argue that because the state failed to provide input support and his/her crops could not grow, the state violated his/her right to food. Unfortunately, determination of such obligations is always a complex process that involves gathering huge amounts of evidence and extended argument and counter-argument about what the specific obligations and benefits are. This is not unique to the right to food. As with other ESCRs, the CESCR has made a general observation that the Covenant generates obligations at three levels: the obligation to *respect*, *protect* and *fulfil*.

> The obligation to respect means that Government must not violate the right to food (e.g. evict people from their land, destroy crops). The obligation to protect means that Governments must protect their citizens against violations by other actors (e.g. by instituting regulation on food safety). The third obligation to fulfil the right to food means that the Government must facilitate the right to food by providing an enabling environment for people to feed themselves (e.g. engage in land reform, stimulating employment) and secondly the Government must be the provider of last resort in cases where people are unable to feed themselves for reasons beyond their control.
>
> ZIEGLER 2003: 7

The conceptualisation of these different obligations as degrees or levels, and not categories of obligations, highlights the nature of the specific duties expected. There is, however, a general view that the obligation to "respect" carries a much lighter duty for the state, and only requires it to refrain from actions that can lead to the violation of a particular right (see Alston and Quinn 1987). In the case of the right to food, as noted above, the state should refrain from actions such as displacing local people so as to deprive them of the means to secure their own food via food production or another form of livelihood. While the obligation to respect is primarily directed at the state and its various organs, the obligation to "protect" requires the state not simply to refrain from certain actions, but to take legislative, administrative and policy steps to actively ensure that its agencies and private actors are not interfering with access to adequate food. To fulfil this obligation, states parties are required to demonstrate that they have taken appropriate measures that should at least include setting up quasi-state bodies to monitor non-state actors' activities that may be impacting on access to food. Such measures could also include regulating proper and honest labelling of food by producers and retailers, as well as setting up specific standards for various foods. As for the obligation to fulfil, the CESCR has divided this obligation into two parts: the obligation to *fulfil* (*facilitate*) and the obligation to *fulfil* (*provide*). "The obligation to fulfil (facilitate) means the State must proactively engage in activities intended to strengthen people's access to and utilisation of resources and means to ensure their livelihood, including food security." The obligation to fulfil (provide) means that "whenever an individual or group is unable, for reasons beyond their control, to enjoy the right to adequate food by the means at their disposal, States have the obligation to *fulfil* (*provide*) that right directly" (*General Comment 12*: para. 15, emphasis in original).

Clearly, the obligation to fulfil (provide) is the more onerous one, and it applies only in situations where an individual or group is unable to access adequate food on their own. In this sense, while the obligation to respect imposes a negative duty on the state, the obligation to protect and fulfil generates positive and more demanding duties that require it to take some form of action. Furthermore, while the right to fulfil (facilitate) requires the state to create an environment that enhances people's abilities to realise their right to adequate food, the obligation to fulfil (provide) is more onerous in that it requires the state to go beyond a facilitatative role and actually deliver the right in cases where the individual or group has been unable to secure adequate food for itself.

Obligation of the International Community

The other important issue that arises in connection with state obligations under the *ICESCR* is the level of obligation on third parties. Here the bone of contention is not so much whether other states have a duty to ensure that the rights under the Covenant are realised; the formulation of general obligations under Article 2, especially Section 2, clearly envisions the obligations under the Covenant be undertaken by states parties collectively. As has been noted by several analysts and commentators, while the primary obligation under Article 2 (1) rests with the individual state (FAO 2011a; Ziegler 2003), there is a collective obligation on the international community under Article 2 (2) – which requires all states parties to undertaken the duty to guarantee the rights in the Covenant (Ziegler 2006). Some analysts have gone further to suggest that the "obligation to fulfil means that (rich) states have a duty to provide some form of bilateral or multilateral assistance to needy people living in poor countries in order to realise their ESC [economic, social and cultural] rights" (Coomans 2007: 79). The basis for this interpretation is Articles 3 and 4 of the *ICESCR*, but also Articles 55 and 56 of the UN Charter – although some analysts have argued that the obligations generated by these provisions are to be understood as negative duties to refrain from actions that might lead to the denial of these rights in other countries, and not a positive obligation to fulfil these rights (Dennis and Stewart 2004). Nonetheless, it is important to note here that even though the provisions for international cooperation in many international treaties are clear, "the detailed legal implications of [these] obligations remain notoriously imprecise" (Alston and Quinn 1987: 187). Further, while it is clear that there are explicit provisions for international support to be provided to advance the realisation of human rights within the UN system, in practice it is doubtful that richer countries regard these provisions as generating legal obligations to provide support. Bilateral and development assistance provided by richer countries is often carried out on a philanthropic basis and not as a fulfilment of the obligation to assist or cooperate.

At a multilateral level there has been a culture of self-expunction on the part of the powerful multilateral institutions (World Bank, IMF and WTO) – which have repeatedly distanced themselves (especially during the 1980s and 1990s) from human rights obligations, including the rights to water and food. In view of this, some analysts have argued that although the World Bank and the IMF are not specialised agencies of the UN, they fall indirectly within the UN mandate by virtue of their having been constituted by UN member states, i.e. fundamental human rights obligations apply to them also (Ghazi 2005).[8] In the case of the WTO, the relations between various WTO rules – in particular the Trade Related Intellectual Property Rights (TRIPS) and the CESCR provisions –

8 There have been suggestions that due to pressure from civil society groups, as well as some changes within these institutions, there is slow progress towards acknowledging human rights responsibilities. For instance, former World Bank president, James Wolfenson observed that even if the Bank does not use the language of rights, its work on poverty and other programmes is directly related to and influenced by human rights outcomes (see Ghazi 2005: 95).

often lead to conflicts between the two. It has thus been pointed out that while TRIPS may not restrict food production in any discernible way, strict implementation of them can result in cases where food production and access are restricted (Haugen 2007). Thus, the obligations generated by the *ICESCR* for these institutions are, at best, unclear.

Immediate Obligations and Progressive Realisation

Although it has been noted that the obligation under the Covenant constitutes an obligation of *conduct* as well as of *results*, there is wide agreement that some obligations are subject to progressive realisation while others require immediate implementation and fulfilment. For instance, the obligation to *take steps* is not subjected to progressive realisation; while the obligation to *fulfil* (*provide*), in most cases, would be subject to progressive realisation. A closer look at the Covenant itself suggests that there are some obligations that require immediate fulfilment, while others can only be realised over a period of time. For instance, under Article 2 (2a) of the Covenant, the list of measures to be undertaken to give effect to rights such as improving the method of food production and reforming the agrarian system cannot be realised immediately. However, taking steps has been widely recognised as part of the obligation that should be fulfilled immediately. Taking steps or measures, mentioned in Article 11 (2.1) of the Covenant, has been interpreted widely to generate immediate obligation of conduct which requires the state to enact legislation, formulate and implement policy and programmes, set up monitoring bodies, etc. The steps or measures taken should address all critical issues relating to "the food system, including...production, processing, distribution, marketing and consumption" (*General Comment 12*: para. 25). Taking steps to prevent discrimination in access to food on any of the prohibited grounds is also seen as an immediate obligation that the state assumes. With particular reference to the right to food, CESCR (*General Comment 12*: para. 18) has observed that

> any discrimination in access to food, as well as to means and entitlements for its procurement, on the grounds of race, colour, sex, language, age, religion, political or other opinion, national or social origin, property, birth or other status with the purpose or effect of nullifying or impairing the equal enjoyment or exercise of economic, social and cultural rights constitutes a violation of the Covenant.

In this case, failure to take steps to address issues of discrimination in accessing food, failure to regulate, monitor and correct the activities of non-state actors which impinge on access to food, and inhibition of access to humanitarian food aid, are just some examples of non-compliance with Covenant obligations under Article 11 (see *General Comment 12*: para. 19).

Many critics have argued that all these provisions and obligations are meaningless in situations where a country has no resources to realise the right to food; that it makes no sense to pile up obligations on states that have no capacity to fulfil these rights. In cases where the state uses lack of resources as an excuse for not fulfilling its obligations, the CESCR (*General Comment 3*: para. 10–11) has stipulated that the state party

> must demonstrate that every effort has been made to use resources that are at its disposition in an effort to satisfy, as a matter of priority, those minimum obligations... [E]ven where the available resources are demonstrably inadequate, the obligation remains for a State party to strive to ensure the widest possible enjoyment of the relevant rights.

For this reason, the CESCR has been reluctant to accept pleas of inadequate resources as an excuse for not fulfilling Covenant obligations. In most instances the failure to comply with these obligations has nothing to do with availability of resources, but rather a lack of commitment towards giving effect to these basic rights. It is in situations where the state and other actors are not showing commitment to the right to food that sustained engagement in democratic politics can be a force for change.

What Do All These Provisions Mean at the End of the Day?

Many critics, especially activists and civil society groups, are sceptical about all these provisions. As Drèze has noted, these elaborate concepts and duties often come to nothing in many countries; most states ignore the provisions and that is why there are still almost one billion people who suffer from hunger, undernourishment and starvation. As noted earlier, the debate about duties and obligations is an important aspect of the struggle for human rights in general, and ESCRs in particular. But this debate should not just be about the technical issues of interpreting the articles of a particular treaty – it should also include the views of the wider community. If human rights are cherished values that a society gives itself, then members of that society should have an important contribution to make in deciding what those values mean, how they should be implemented, and what their implications are. Thus, the debate about the scope, nature, degree and type of obligations should not just be an academic exercise by the legal fraternity – it should be an important building block in the struggle for human rights.

At the practical level, clarifying these issues creates a base on which claims can be made against the state and other actors. Whether the claim made is legal, political or moral, the success of such claims depends on the validity of the arguments on which the claim is based. Even if one is making a political claim that the state needs to provide food to starving people, for this claim to be successful requires a solid foundation on which it can be rooted. Some of these provisions, in treaties and constitutions, provide a strong foundational base on which the claims can be constructed.

In a fundamental way, the most effective way of giving effect to rights such as the right to water or food is by making a political claim. Such a claim, properly supported, is most likely to generate political will and commitment. A political claim to the right to food means forwarding the various elements of the right into the political arena through avenues such as the mobilisation of social forces, parliamentary representation, protest and lobbying. For politicians to give serious attention to the right to food there has to be a strong enough incentive for them to act. That incentive, in a democratic society, can be provided through various strategies – including demanding and participating in the democratic processes. Relatively successful examples of such strategies include the Zero Hunger Programme in Brazil (da Silva *et al.* 2011) and the Right to Food Campaign in many parts of the world – especially India – as we shall see in Chapter 8.

CHAPTER 7

The Rights to Water and Food in International Politics

Many human rights activists and people struggling to secure basic needs such as clean water and food on a daily basis, question the relevance of international human rights treaties, declarations, constitutions and other pieces of legislation. They wonder if human rights – such as the rights to water and food – make a difference in the lives of millions of people who live in situations in which they are not sure about the next meal. They are sceptical about whether international pronouncements on the right to water and food have any influence on the way water and food are produced, distributed and accessed. Many ask, what does having the rights to water and food protected in the Bill Rights do for a person whose water is disconnected, or for a person who goes to bed hungry because there is nothing to eat? For activists and human rights campaigners it is often frustrating when it becomes apparent that these instruments have little or no influence on the way water and food are accessed. Because of the apparent lack of "teeth" of many human rights instruments, several activists and scholars have dismissed these proclamations – at the national and international levels – as mere rhetoric meant to soothe the masses who continue to suffer from hunger, undernourishment and starvation.

The Role of International Human Rights in Promoting Social Change

Studies that have examined the role of international human rights instruments in prompting social and political change have concluded that these instruments often have insignificant effects (see Hathaway 2002; Hafner-Burton and Ron 2007). Similarly, O'Neill (2000) in *Towards Justice and Virtue*, for instance, argues that the international treaties and declarations make lofty proclamations and promises but fail to ensure that such promises become part of the institutional structure of society. In a case study that examined the impact of constitutional protection of the right to water on the poor in South Africa, it has been noted that while the language of rights initiated reform of policies and programmes such as the free basic water policy, many poor people are unable to benefit from such reforms (Mehta 2006). Thus, activists and analysts alike have questioned

 | DOI 10.1163/9789004299559_008

the usefulness of these provisions, arguing that they only exist on paper and do not translate into anything tangible on the ground for most of the poor. Certainly, citing a clause from a constitution or international covenant that provides for the right to water or food, gives little consolation to someone who has no food or is unable to access clean water. Some analysts have argued that while there is wide agreement on the need to reform structures, institutions and relations around water and food, there has been a lack of effective instruments to effect these changes; that the use of human rights has proved to be equally as blunt in effecting the much needed radical social, political and economic institutional reforms which can change the way we deal with access to water and food. Some have argued that in our daily interactions surrounding water and food, human rights are trampled upon by the market (Bond 2006; Bakker 2007).

These debates raise a critical question about the practical implications of human rights in both international and national contexts. This chapter looks at the role of these proclamations, focusing on the rights to water and food, in shaping international and local politics regarding access to water and food. It examines whether having human rights explicitly recognised in international or municipal law makes any difference in the lives of the millions of people who suffer hunger, undernourishment, starvation and face severe constraints in accessing clean water for domestic use as well as water for productive purposes. It is argued here that in addition to raising concerns about the daily life effects of human rights, it is also important to analyse the role of human rights instruments and debates in promoting the sort of institutional and policy reforms which might make it possible for the poor to access basic necessities easily. Unfortunately, these debates are often framed narrowly, especially among human rights activists – focusing on the immediate material effect of the rights while overlooking the wider influence of effecting change in policy and the political structures of power and social relations. Framing the debates and strategies widely opens up new spaces for possible engagement in the broader process of institutional and policy change at both international and domestic levels.

Thus, it is essential in the struggle to give effect to human rights to realise that engaging in the struggle to change institutional and power structures is equally as important as engaging the struggle to bring about immediate material results by lobbying the state to provide food relief to starving populations. Such victories would not be possible if there were no strategies to bring issues of hunger into the political spaces of public policy. Going beyond the obvious material victories in the struggle for human rights makes it apparent that the widespread failure to fulfil the rights to water and food is a consequence of inadequate institutional and policy reform – a failure to radically transform the way people relate and interact around water and food. Thus, engagements need not be limited to the material condition of providing water to people who find it difficult to access clean water or adequate food, but rather should include institutional and policy reforms. For this reason, giving effect to the rights to water and food cannot avoid engaging in radical democratic politics at both national and international levels, with the specific aim of altering the configuration of power and social relations around access to clean water and food.

The strategy of engaging in broader democratic politics becomes more necessary if one accepts the view that human rights are never given freely, and rather that they are the product of sustained collective struggle. In this sense, the rights to water and food are at the heart of radical democratic politics that seeks to transform institutions and policies so as to create conditions where access to water and food become basic human entitlements for all. Achieving this transformation is not something that should be expected to be an outcome of a "benevolent state" (even where such states exist), parliamentary action or a court of law. No, creating conditions where all people have access to clean water and food can only be a product of protracted struggles which produce the spaces in which access to water and food for all become a reality. Critics often argue that achieving this is not possible; that there will always be people who are unable to access clean water or adequate food. But it is important to realise that adopting this defeatist position can be one way of protecting the status quo – a way of depoliticising issues of access to water and food. Furthermore, such views are subtle ways of exercising power through a shared meaning which precludes radical change, and which removes issues of access to water and food from the arena of democratic politics.

The International Dimensions of Rights to Water and Food

Up to this point it is apparent that the rights to water and food, like many other rights, rely heavily on international human rights instruments; few countries have explicitly recognised access to clean water and adequate food in their national constitutions and framework laws. Yet giving effect to these rights is something that takes place in the specific national and local contexts. Consequently, it is important to look closely at how the international treaties and laws relate to national laws, and what the influence of these instruments is on municipal legal systems, national institutions and policies. If the rights to water and food are largely recognised in international human rights instruments, then an analysis of whether these instruments contribute to giving effect to these rights in the specific national and local contexts should shed light on the efficacy of international human rights instruments.

Before looking at what, exactly, the international human rights treaties are, and how they function in the domestic arena, it is essential to discuss some of the motivations behind the decision to ratify treaties that recognise access to water and adequate food as human rights. Human rights critics have often argued that since most fundamental human needs which have been explicitly proclaimed as human rights remain far from being "real" ones for most people – especially the poor – should we even be fighting for access to clean water and adequate food to be recognised as human rights? There are several grounds on which the argument for recognising access to water and adequate food as human rights can be defended. First, proponents of these rights argue that declaring access to water and adequate food as human rights helps to identify the right-holders as well as the duty-bearers, thereby creating space in which these rights can be contested. In this regard, formal explicit recognition of a right is often seen as a way to emphasise the point that states, in their actions, have to pay attention to the obligations that they have committed themselves to. As Jolly argues, formal recognition of access to water and adequate food as human rights helps to "ground the priority on the bedrock of social and economic rights, it emphasizes the obligations of states parties to ensure access, and it identifies the obligations of states parties to provide support internationally as well as nationally" (cited in Gleick 1998: 3).

In this sense, proclaiming access to water and adequate food as human rights is a statement about a human value that deserves the attention of the international community. The actual realisation of a particular right, while it should be an essential consideration, should not be the only condition for determining whether a particular value should be protected or not. However, critics have maintained that such proclamations can be made without resorting to the language of rights; that recognising everyone's entitlement to have access to clean water and adequate food can be a national objective rather than a right (see Dennis and Stewart 2004; Cohen and Brown, 2008). It is important here to elaborate on the difference between national aspirational goals and human rights.

The biggest difference is, perhaps, that in the case of a human right, failure or violation triggers clear duties on the part of the duty-bearer to *do* something; while in the case of an aspirational goal, failure to achieve the goal may not lead to a clear identification of the exact duties and necessary remedial actions. It is precisely this clear allocation of responsibilities under human rights which creates the fertile ground on which to deploy democratic politics. As we shall see later in this chapter, on situations where there is no clear recognition of a particular right, it is extremely difficult to deploy democratic politics – there are simply no spaces for such engagements. Thus, the value added in proclaiming basic human needs as human rights is that it clearly identifies responsibilities as well as expected actions, and by so doing creates space for engaging with key actors – especially the state.

Second, proclaiming access to water and adequate food as human rights moves these basic needs from being entirely local or national issues into the global domain. As human rights, access to water and adequate food become part of the international human rights system and this can be an avenue through which international pressure can be generated to ensure that appropriate attention is paid to these issues at the international level, particularly for those who have no (or inadequate) access.

Third, as Scanlon *et al.* (2004) have noted, formal recognition of the rights to water and food makes implementation more practical and more possible – and therefore more likely to lead to the development of guidelines and jurisprudence that would, in turn, provide assistance to the practical questions of forming institutions and policies that might be appropriate for their implementation.

Fourth, explicit acknowledgement of access to water and adequate food as human rights can help focus national and international policy on issues of the environment, water resource management, food production, distribution and marketing, etc. With particular reference to water – when formulated as a human right – access to basic water should take precedence over other concerns (Gleick 1998). When access to water and adequate food are explicitly recognised as human rights they also entail a general respect for the environment – for the simple reason that it would be difficult to realise the rights to water and food in situations where there is no such respect.

Fifth, recognising access to water and adequate food as human rights provides tools for analysis and the basis for demanding accountability and participation. Such proclamations enable civil society groups to anchor their claims for the need to give effect to these rights, especially in instances where a large number of people have no access, or constrained access, to these basic needs. Simply put, once these basic needs are proclaimed as basic human rights it becomes possible for members of civil society to begin to demand that states fulfil the minimum obligations that these rights generate. In other words, recognition of these basic needs as rights makes it possible to deploy democratic politics in the struggle to secure these basic essentials for all. As Gleick (1998: 29) has observed, "explicit recognition of water as a human right could ... present a tool for civil society to hold government accountable for ensuring access to sufficient, good-quality water". In this sense, proclamation of a right creates space where the struggle for the proclaimed rights can be waged. With regard to the right to food, it has been suggested that proclaiming the right "contributes to strengthening relevant institutions and coordination of mechanisms with regard to implementation. It integrates partners such as civil society organisations, human rights commissions, parliamentarians and government sectors" (FAO 2011a: 7).

Sixth, when access to water and adequate food are proclaimed as human rights, they cease to be treated as matters of charity and become, instead, entitlements that should not be taken away arbitrarily; with the state recognised as a duty-bearer to respect, promote, protect and fulfil these rights (*General Comment 3*: para. 9). Most fundamentally, framing these basic needs in terms of basic human rights creates the potential to challenge existing unequal power relations to the extent that human rights affirm equality, non-discrimination and respect for all peoples. It is this "symbolic rhetorical force" that gives human rights the power to unify these otherwise very different and diverse constituencies (Donald and Mottershaw 2009).

In this sense, power and social relations are critical to understanding ESCRs. People go hungry or without water not because there is not enough of them in the world, but "because they are marginalised economically and powerless politically" (de Schutter 2012: 3). Thus, the struggle for human rights, in general, is a struggle to reconfigure the way power is distributed and exercised, and this is what makes human rights contentious at every level. This observation has been made by many human rights activists and practitioners who assert that proclaiming access to water and adequate food as human rights creates spaces for making those who exercise public power (including civil society organisations and NGOs) accountable, as well as linking the exercise of power to the *responsibility* which should accompany its exercise (Donald and Mottershaw 2009: 13). This implies a radical challenge to the status quo.

However, as noted earlier, it has been contested that the formal recognition of these rights makes very little difference in reality, especially for the poor. For instance, Bond (2004), when commenting on the right to water, cites the example of South Africa – where the right to water is clearly recognised and yet this has not translated into significant impact in terms of improved access to it for the poor. In the case of the right to food, it has been observed that despite various commitments by states parties to the Covenant, around one in seven people go to bed each night without having eaten (de Schutter 2012). In Africa, it has been observed that

> [t]he enjoyment of social, economic and cultural rights – the right to health, education, a clean environment, food, water and development – is still a distant dream for most Africans, the majority of whom remain under the poverty line despite the universal endorsement of the Millennium Development Goals and other development plans such as New Partnership for Africa's Development (NEPAD).
>
> UNECA, 2009:90

While these are valid concerns, it can be argued that there exists a fundamental misconception that mere proclamation of these rights will automatically translate into the right to water and food for everyone, everywhere. But the meaning of the right to water or food is not that everyone should be provided with water or fed by the state. These rights are meant to facilitate the creation of conditions in which people can realise these rights with dignity and not simply through charity (see OHCHR/FAO 2010: 3). Furthermore, these rights are meant to create spaces in which people can struggle to reconfigure those existing unequal power relations that result in so many people failing to access clean water or adequate food in the first place. Most fundamentally, as noted earlier, recognising access to water and adequate food as human rights creates the *potential* for a genuine reconfiguration of the power relations, the *potential* to transform institutions and policies such that access to water and food is mediated by different structures and sets of interactions. Giving *effect* to these rights, therefore, requires more than just an explicit statement of the existence of such rights – though this is, of course, is essential. It requires a fundamental realignment of the unequal distribution and exercise of power which results in some people going to bed without food, while others throw away tons of food every day. This realignment of power cannot be achieved without sustained collective political engagement and social action (Chapman *et al.* 2005).

The Challenges of Giving Effect to Economic, Social and Cultural Rights

While there are clear guidelines and pronouncements on the nature and content of these rights, as we have seen in the preceding two chapters, mainly at the international and, in some cases, at the domestic level, implementation of these norms face many challenges (Donald and Mottershaw 2009). One of the challenges pertains to the nature of international law in general, and international human rights law in particular. The main challenge in this regard is that while human rights instruments and other international treaties are quickly ratified by many nations, very few of them have translated these instruments into domestic legal or policy systems. In practice, there is a big gap between the national and international arena – there are different types of politics at play.

With particular reference to African countries, it has been observed that enthusiastic ratification of international treaties has often not been followed by compliance with the requirements of such treaties. In most cases, even the basic requirement to submit periodic reports to relevant UN bodies is not met. An assessment of reports submitted by African states suggests that in some cases reports are ten years overdue; by 2007 "only 14 states had actually complied with all their reporting responsibilities" (see Horn 2009: 59). However, concerns around reports submitted by states parties are raised not just in relation to African states; there are also concerns about the quality of the reports that most states parties to the Covenant submit. In the case of the right to food, the CESCR reports that "while reporting guidelines are available relating to the right to food, only few States parties have provided information sufficient and precise enough to enable the committee to determine the prevailing situation in the countries concerned" (*General Comment 12*: para. 2).

With specific reference to the *ICESCR*, while 49 African states had ratified the Covenant by 2010, in most of these states ESCRs are not explicitly recognised (UNECA 2009: 90). In the case of the right to adequate food only seven African states have explicitly provided for the right to food and of these only three[1] have included the right to food in the Bill of Rights. As for the right to water, seven countries have mentioned it explicitly, and only two have included it in the Bill of Rights in their constitution.[2] While constitutional provision does not automatically guarantee a right, constitutional protection of a right does does at least provide the basis for building collective action aimed at giving effect to the right. Such recognition often forms the starting point for policy and legislative reform (FAO 2011a).

Related to the issue of domestic protection of Covenant rights is the tricky relationship between international and municipal law. This is particularly problematic in countries with common law traditions.[3] However, even countries where international human rights instruments are directly applicable in domestic law, there is no guarantee that these rights are implemented in a way that gives them effect. Case studies carried out by the Overseas Development Institute (Conway *et al.*, 2002) reveal that even rights provided for in national constitutions have problems being implemented. Experience from human rights activists, practitioners and researchers shows that even in countries where ESCRs are justiciable, realisation of these rights is not an automatic matter – people have to fight for these rights through the courts, as well as on the streets (Donald and Mottershaw 2009).

1 These are South Africa (para. 27b), Kenya (para. 43c) and Malawi (para. 13b). The other four states that have explicitly mentioned the right to food – Namibia (para. 16), Nigeria (para. 16.2d), Ethiopia (para. 90) and Uganda (para. 14b) – have done so under directive principles of state policy.

2 The right to water is mentioned explicitly in Uganda (para. 14b), South Africa (para. 27b), Gambia (para 216.4), Kenya (para. 43d) and Zambia (para. 112c) – but only South Africa and Kenya have included the right to water in their Bill of Rights. The 2012 Zambian Draft Constitution has included both water and food in its Bill of Rights.

3 See Note 25 of Chapter 5.

Generally, there has so far been very little empirical work completed that systematically examines the impact of explicit recognition of human rights, particularly ESCRs, on state parties' conduct, institutional and policy reforms. Many human rights activists and practitioners often assume that codification of a right will lead to, or enhance, its realisation. Some human rights lawyers believe in the slow process of adopting and giving effect to these rights and often argue that the world is still cultivating the culture of human rights (Vincent 1986); many in this camp are willing to wait. Human rights activists, on the other hand, are often impatient with the slow progress being made in giving effect to ESCRs, especially in the Global South.

While the Special Rapporteur on the right to food commended the South African government for adopting a diverse set of programmes and policies directed at addressing issues of food security, it was observed that a large section of the population still remained vulnerable, with many still chronically food insecure (de Schutter 2011: 4). His report further noted that large-scale inequality in accessing assets such as land and water was hindering the realisation of the right to food for many people; and that such a situation was unlikely to lead to the state satisfying its human rights obligations under the rights-based approach (ibid.: 11).[4] The *Seventh Report on Economic and Social Rights* by the South African Human Rights Commission (SAHRC) has noted that while there have been improvements, there are still huge challenges in giving effect to the rights protected by the constitution. On the right to water, the SAHRC notes that there has been no evidence of progressive improvement, largely because free basic water is provided only to a few registered indigents, but also because of serious capacity problems in many municipalities – making it difficult to progressively improve access to water for many people (SAHRC 2009). In the case of the right to food, the SAHRC concludes that the state is not moving expeditiously or effectively to give effect to the right – mainly because of a lack of coordination between the different strategies adopted by different government departments, but also because most of the programmes have no clear objectives.

Thus, the issue of realising human rights is not just about having them encoded in constitutions and statutes – it is more about finding ways in which these rights can become a reality in the lives of the poor. And that is a major challenge. Translating the various claims and rights provided for in legal documents into concrete rights requires an integrated strategy that relies on collective action, agitation at community level, building awareness and skill in the application of rights, and the construction of adequate and responsive institutions.

4 South Africa has not yet ratified the *ICESCR*, and, as such, it is not yet a state party to the Covenant – however, the South African constitution has provided for the right to food.

However, if we compare the situation in South Africa – where these rights are explicitly recognised – to the situation in other countries where they are not,[5] the difference this makes in the struggle for these rights becomes evident. For example, in the case of Zambia – where both the right to water and food are only mentioned as aspirational goals – there has been little action from the state to give effect to these rights (see RAPDA 2010). Because most of the ESCRs are implicitly recognised, it is difficult even to have public debates about these rights, not to mention litigation or collective action (Chitonge 2007). At the official level there has been little in the form of acknowledging or proclaiming the right to water or access to adequate food, and this has made it extremely difficult to engage the state on these issues. Some senior state officials hold the view that the country is not yet ready for such rights (ibid.). Like many other ESCRs, the rights to water and food are not something that politicians and bureaucrats are at ease talking about. In Zambia, and many other countries in the Global South, debates about these rights only occur in a few academic papers and reports. Often the resource card is played, such as in the argument that since South Africa has more resources this is why it can afford to protect the right to water and food in its Bill of Rights. But as noted in Chapter 3, there is no clear correlation between protection of human rights and resources available to the state.

What a comparison between the South African and Zambian situation highlights is not that having these rights enshrined in the constitution automatically translates into tangible rights; rather that formal recognition of them is a *necessary* (but not in itself *sufficient*) condition for realising them. As Mehta and Ntshona (2004: 3) have observed in the case of the right to water in South Africa, critics should not overlook the fact that its inclusion in the Bill of Rights is in itself a remarkable achievement, and one unique to South Africa. The challenge, however, lies in creating a condition where these formally recognised rights are given meaning and effect, especially for the poor.

Nonetheless, despite the depressing public silence about the rights to water and food in Zambia, there is a strong basis for engaging in the debate and in the

5 ESCRs in Zambia's 1996 Constitution are recognised in Article 112, which falls under the Directive Principles of State Policy and the Duties of a Citizen. But Article 111, immediately before, states that "[t]he Directive Principles of State Policy set out in this part shall not be justiciable and shall not thereby, themselves, despite being referred to as rights in certain instances, be legally enforceable in any court of law, tribunal or administrative institution or entity." However, some authors have taken this as the official recognition of the right to water. For example, Scanlona *et al.* (2004) in their list of countries that have legal provision on the right to water have included Zambia.

struggles to give effect to these rights. The two most obvious bases for asserting these rights in Zambia are: (1) the Constitution (currently the 1996 amended Constitution), and (2) the international human rights treaties that the Zambian government has ratified. Relevant to the rights to water and food is the *ICESCR*, which is often cited among the major international human rights instruments which have protected these rights – as noted in Chapters 5 and 6 above. All the commitments made by the Zambian government at the international level create grounds for engaging with it to ensure that the obligations specified are respected and fulfilled.[6] However, most of the instruments upon which the obligations are based amount to little more than a weak foundation for building human rights struggles upon at the national level.

Application of International Human Rights Instruments in Municipal Law

The general question that has been raised in the context of public international law in general is whether international treaties and laws affect the behaviour of states in ways which improve the realisation of human rights (Hathaway 2002). Partly, this question relates to the debates articulated by legal positivists, who argue that international human rights law, in particular, lacks an enforcement mechanism that gives force and coercive power or the threat of sanctions (punishment) – which are fundamental characteristics of municipal law according to this school of thought (see Chapter 2). While this debate has been extended to various treaties, here we focus on issues related to the *ICESCR*, and in particular the rights to water and food. In this regard, the question of whether the international and municipal Bill of Rights contribute to improving the conditions of people who cannot access clean water or adequate food is indeed a critical one, and has raised both empirical – as well as theoretical – dimensions.

Although very little empirical work has been carried out to date to assess the influence of ratification of the *ICESCR* on the fulfilment of various ESCR obligations, existing empirical work on the impact of international human rights treaties, in general, suggests that the influence is mixed at best. This is true not just for international human rights instruments, but also with regard to national institutions and policies that mediate human rights. For instance, Hafner-Burton and Tsutsui (2005), focusing on the rights under the *ICCPR* as well as rights under the Convention Against Torture (CAT), find that while in a few countries these treaties contribute to significant improvements in the respect

6 Zambia ratified the *ICESCR* and *ICCPR* in 1984, the *CEDAW* in 1985, and the *CRC* in 1991.

for human rights (in democratic countries with an active civil society), in an overwhelming number of countries these treaties do not seem to have any effect. However, studies that have adopted a qualitative case-by-case approach have often concluded that the ratification of these treaties *does* contribute to change in the behaviour of the state, especially in democracies[7] (Neumayer 2005). Nonetheless, the general conclusion drawn from several studies on this topic is that "while 'human rights' have become a popular way of discussing social justice, its effects are often difficult to pin down, or require more nuances and disaggregation" (Hafner-Burton and Ron 2007: 381). Regarding the effects of ratifying the *ICESCR*, and the rights to water and food in particular, little work has so far been done to assess what the actual impact regarding fulfilling these rights are, despite many countries having ratified the Covenant as indicated in the previous chapters. One of the explanations offered for the absence of an empirical assessment of the effects of the *ICESCR* on the lives of poor people, in particular, and the respect for human rights in general, is the "disinclination of international lawyers to confront the efficacy of international law" (Hathaway 2002: 938).

Of course, assessing the efficacy of international human rights law is a complex exercise that would require some understanding of how states operate, and the motives at play in choosing to ratify a particular treaty. However, some form of evaluation of the effects of these rights can enhance the understanding of the rights themselves, and also the challenges that their realisation involves. Just as some activists are reluctant to spend time understanding the basis of the rights they advocate or lobby for, many human rights enthusiasts and international lawyers and analysts sometimes convey the sense that ratification or codification is all that is needed, and pay little attention to the impact of ratifying a treaty. As noted earlier, ratification or codification is only the first step on the long road to giving effect to the rights protected in the treaty or framework law. Giving effect to rights that are protected in this way is not something that can be achieved simply by recounting and chronicling articles from a treaty or a constitution. Giving effect to them is more likely to be realised by engaging in democratic politics to create pressure through various means to ensure that treaty and constitutional provisions are not just rights on paper, but actual entitlements.

The approach of seeing ratification or codification as the point of arrival, rather than departure, often leads to a demobilisation of civil society as a result of the exaggerated faith that has been placed in the power (moral or legal) of

---

7 In both cases (Hafner-Burton and Tsutsui 2005; and Neumayer 2005) the definition of "democracy" is contentious, and assumes more than it defines.

these provisions to alter the priorities and agendas in the state spaces. But experience from around the world has shown that without sustained public pressure to push certain issues into the state space as a priority, the business-as-usual mode is adopted by everyone – including civil society groups themselves. Consequently, no genuine changes are effected. In the business-as-usual mode, most rights – whether civil and political, or ESCRs – are used to fight narrow battles for the wealthy and powerful among the key actors.

International Law in Municipal Law: An Overview

Why do States Ratify International Treaties?

Relying on international human rights instruments in the struggle for human rights is, in practice, quite complex. As noted above, while many countries have ratified the *ICESCR* and other legally binding international human rights treaties, these instruments seem to have little influence beyond serving as mere political statements. There are practical challenges which arise when someone is relying on these provisions as the basis for claiming the rights to water and food, regardless of whether the struggle is taken to the courts or takes the form of protests on the streets. In view of this, it is probably appropriate to ask if these treaties really make any difference – whether treaties are "effective in changing states' behaviour for the better" (Hathaway 2002). A crucial question surrounds the motive behind states' choosing to be bound by these international treaties when in practice such treaties seem to have little influence over the way a state conducts itself.

There are several explanations advanced that elaborate further on the issue of why states ratify human rights instruments, including the idea that states do so to take up a position within the international community and to associate themselves with a code of conduct widely accepted among the "civilised" community of nations. Thus, the incentive to ratify treaties may not be purely a rational decision, or a choice from many alternatives – it could simply be a result of peer pressure. Dugard (2000), for instance, argues that among the reasons why states ratify international treaties is the need to move with the times, to be part of the "club", to respond to public opinion, and out of fear of being the "odd man out".

From a legal point of view, one of the challenges that emerge when it comes to implementing international human rights norms revolves around the relationship between international and domestic law. Just how these international human rights instruments apply in states parties to a particular treaty is a more complex matter than is usually portrayed. In theory, it has been widely accepted that when interpreting and applying domestic law, judges should, at least, consider international law and strive to avoid interpretations of domestic law that are inconsistent with international law (ibid.). Applying this principle, many countries have included clauses in their constitutions that address this matter,[8] and there are many countries (particularly countries with a civil law tradition) in which certain international treaties apply directly. With regard to the *ICESCR*, it has been observed that of the 156 states that are party to the Covenant, the *ICESCR* applies without the need to adopt special domestic legislation in 77 of them (FAO 2006).[9] In these countries the *ICESCR* is self-executing; it does not require special legislation to be incorporated into domestic law. Technically, this means that civil society groups or individuals in any of these countries can rely on Article 11 of the *ICESCR* to claim the rights to water and food – through litigation or non-judicial avenues – even though these rights are not provided for as justiciable rights under municipal law. In practice, however, this is more difficult than it sounds.

The CESCR has adopted the position that "[i]n general, legally binding international human rights standards should operate directly and immediately within the domestic legal system of each State party, thereby enabling individuals to seek enforcement of their rights before national courts and tribunals" (*General Comment 9*: para. 4). Similarly, the *Vienna Convention on the Law of Treaties* provides that "[a] party may not invoke the provisions of its internal law as justification for its failure to perform a treaty" (Article 27) – implying that when domestic law is in conflict with the provisions of these international treaties, the spirit and purpose of the treaty should be upheld. Many countries have, in fact, adopted this position.[10] But despite such clearly stated guidelines and principles, the practical application of these norms is not as simple as assumed in many official documents. In terms of the rights to water and food, relying on these provisions only is a challenge – whether one takes the legal or other routes. One of the major challenges, regardless of the route that one takes, is that judges and most civil society and human rights activists are often unaware, or reluctant, to rely on these provisions.

---

8 For instance, Article 39.1 (b and c) of the South African Constitution provides that "[w]hen interpreting the Bill of Rights, a court, tribunal or forum ... *must* consider international law, and *may* consider foreign law (emphasis added).

9 This applies to most non-Commonwealth countries in Africa – except Ghana and Malawi, where the *ICESCR* and other ratified international treaties apply directly.

10 For example, the Mali Constitution provides that "[t]reaties and accords that are properly ratified or approved have, from the time of their publication, superior authority over laws of the state" (Article 116). In most countries the courts are required to take into account international law when interpreting domestic law.

Approaches to the Relationship Between International and Municipal Law

Broadly speaking, there are three common approaches to the relationship between domestic and international law. One is the *monist* approach promoted by Kelsen, Verdross and Scelle; the other is the *dualist* approach developed by Triepel and Anzilotti (see Cheng 1991: 25). The third is the *hybridisation* approach advanced by various UN bodies and other international human rights organisations, as well as by progressive international relations scholars. In essence, the monists argue that public international law and municipal law are essentially manifestations of the same legal order and should not be regarded as two separate genres of law. According to this view, international law should directly apply in municipal law "without any act of adoption by the courts or transformation by the legislature" (see Dugard 2000: 43). On the other hand, the dualists argue that international law and municipal law are two separate legal realms, and as such the latter should be applied to a domestic legal system "only if adopted by such courts or transformed into local law by legislation" (ibid.). Commenting on this view, Lauterpacht makes the observation that

> [a]ccording to the dualist view, international law and municipal law differ so radically in the matter of subjects of the law, its sources and its substance, that a rule of international law can never per se become part of the law of the land; it must be made so by the express or implied authority of the state.
>
> CITED IN DUGARD, 2000: 43

The harmonisation (hybrid) theory advances a middle way between these two extremes, arguing that parts of international law are the same as most municipal laws, such that international law can be partially applicable, directly, in domestic law. Proponents of the harmonisation theory argue that the monist-dualist controversy is actually not necessary because although international and municipal laws may have different sources, content and subjects, they both regulate social, political and economic relations (Cheng 1991).

In the context of the current discussion on the rights to water and food, adopting a monist position would require that the courts enforce the Covenant rights – and in particular the contents of the rights to water and food – just as they would enforce the domestic Bill of Rights or other statutes. In this sense, the Covenant rights can be relied on directly by individuals, just as they rely on the various relevant provisions of domestic law. Similarly, the monist position would imply that human rights activists can invoke the rights under the *ICESCR* to demand that the state fulfil its Covenant obligations regarding access to water and food. On the other hand, adopting the dualist position means that either the courts can apply Covenant rights when adjudicating on matters relating to the rights to water and food, or the legislature should make provisions which make Covenant rights applicable to municipal law. In this case then, the rights to water and food, as provided for in the *ICESCR*, would remain inapplicable in most countries with common law traditions in those situations where the courts have not taken the initiative to adopt an inclusive interpretive approach, or in cases where the legislature chooses not to directly incorporate into domestic law the rights to water and food as specified under the *ICESCR*.

However, empirical evidence from human rights litigation shows that the hybridisation approach is common in most countries, even those with common law traditions (Dugard 2002; Cheng 1991; Hansungule 2004). In the case of human rights law, it is apparent that the dualist approach fails to take note of the fact that most of the human rights protected by international law are, in fact, protected in domestic law – to the extent that in certain cases there is no need even to incorporate certain elements of international law into domestic law. Furthermore, a close look at most of the national constitutions, particularly the Bill of Rights, provides evidence of the intersection between international and municipal law. This is especially true for civil and political rights, which are protected using similar wording in both international and domestic law. For instance, the right to life, and the freedoms of speech, assembly, association and movement, as provided for in many domestic Bill of Rights, have the same content and wording as in the *ICCPR*. Thus it can be argued that the domestic legal system can also protect the rights protected in the two international Covenants, and that there is actually no need to shift the goal posts to accommodate international law (Dugard 2002; Bedjaoui 1991a).

However, there are points of divergence between the two systems which often surface when dealing with real life situations, especially with regard to ESCRs – which are adequately provided for in international human rights law, but often either implicitly acknowledged or not even mentioned at all in municipal law. In such cases, a problem arises concerning how to apply these international principles in a given national situation in which they are not explicitly recognised as human rights. For instance, in countries where the right to water or food is not even mentioned, how should the right be given effect? With regard to the non-legal route, while relying on international human rights law such as the *ICESCR* may be a rallying point behind which to win international support, it is much more challenging to create support that relies on something that is not widely recognised locally. It is much harder to win support in the campaign for the rights to water and food in a country where public debate on such rights is non-existent. Generally speaking, in countries that have formally recognised these rights there is a higher degree of collective action taken by civil society groups and social movements than there is in countries where such rights are not explicitly recognised. In situations like this, international law alone is probably of limited practical help. One of the main reasons for this limitation is the nature of international law itself.

The Nature of International Law

Traditionally, international law has been entirely concerned with the regulation of relationships between states. From the time of Groitus,[11] international law has concerned itself purely with regulating the conduct of states and not of individuals (Bedjaoui 1991a; Gathii 1999). Conduct between individuals or between individuals and the state fell outside the ambit of public international law. It is for this reason that up to the present, individuals have no legal standing in most international law instruments and therefore are not subjects of international law (Cheng 1991). In the past, partly because of the positivist influence that emphasised the principle of state sovereignty, and partly because of the concerns about promoting the peaceful coexistence of states, the way a state dealt with its citizens was not seen as a matter that international law needed to address. Prior to the Second World War a sovereign state was free to treat its citizens in any way it saw fit. But the dangers of a legal positivist approach, as witnessed in the Holocaust and from the human suffering that resulted from the atrocities carried out by autocratic fascist regimes in Europe before and during the Second World War, became all too clear. And so, the way states interact with their citizens is increasingly becoming a concern of the international community (Dugard 2000). Slowly, the character of international law is shifting to embrace the social aspirations of individuals in certain states. As Gathii (1999: 113) observes:

> This new social character of international law can be seen through the debates, during the post-World War II era, on the reformulation of international law from a state-centered agenda, focused on the classical doctrines of state sovereignty and territoriality, and the regulation of relations between states, to an individual-centered concept, that is more concerned with the identification and protection of the social, political, and economic rights of the individual.

11 Groitus is widely acclaimed as the father of public international law.

Nevertheless, "in spite of an interesting evolution, due, in particular, to the entry of human rights into the sphere of international law, the day when we shall see individuals accepted as *direct* subjects of the norms of international law is still a long way off" (Cheng 1991:13, emphasis in original).[12]

The Doctrine of Consent

The other challenge that arises from the nature of international law which makes it difficult to enforce human rights provided for in international instruments, is that, traditionally, international law has largely relied on the doctrine of consent (Dugard 2000). As such, enforcement of international law relies largely on the *goodwill* of the state in question (Vincent 1986). A state violating international law may decide, with impunity, to repudiate the decision of the international community or court. For example, in the *Nicaragua v. United States of America* case, the US government did not only refuse to appear before the International Court of Justice, it also refused to accept and be bound by the findings and ruling of the court (Dugard 2002: 5). In this case, even when human rights are being violated, it becomes difficult for international law to offer refuge for victims. Use of political and economic sanctions is one of the ways in which compliance can be promoted, but this route has proved to be ineffective in correcting human rights wrongs, especially if the human rights violator is a superpower. Although there are some analysts who talk about "smart sanctions", it is not clear if there is such a thing, let alone whether they are effective in securing the protection of ESCRs like the rights to water and food (Tostensen 2002).

12 Even today, there are few international human rights instruments which have a mandatory individual complaint mechanism (these include the *Civil and Political Rights Covenant*, the *Convention Against Torture*, the *Convention Against Racial Discrimination* and the *Convention Against Discrimination of Women*. An optional protocol for the *ICESCR* was adopted by the UN General Assembly in Resolution A/RES/63/117 on 10 December 2008. But even this is only an option for the state. Even if the state ratifies the optional protocol there is no guarantee that this will lead to more effective protection of human rights given the weak commitment that states often make with regard to international agreements, on the one hand, and the weak enforcement mechanism characteristics of international law, on the other. As for socioeconomic rights, an optional protocol for individual complaint exists, but it has been ratified by only a handful of states. The importance of the individual complaint mechanism is that it enables an individual who has exhausted all internal remedies to approach the Human Rights Council to seek redress for his or her grievances. Although the absence of an individual complaint mechanism does not take away the substance of the rights (*Maastricht Guidelines* 1997), such measures may, however, open different avenues that can be pursued by victims of human rights violations, particularly civil society groups.

Non-Self-Executing Norms

The other difficulty associated with enforcing international human rights law is that most of the human rights norms are not self-executing; that is to say, they would need accompanying legislation and ministerial regulation in order to be practically implemented. This is mainly due to the broad form that international legal instruments such as the *ICESCR* take. In most cases, even constitutional provisions require subsequent legislation for them to become operational, i.e. specification of exactly what the content, scope and reach of a particular right is, including obligations, remedies and benefits. For example, stating that everyone has the right of access to basic water, begs the questions: what is "basic water"? Who should be responsible for providing this water? Under what circumstances is someone entitled to basic water? And most importantly, what recourse does one have if this right is not fulfilled?

Put differently, the broad nature of treaties, as well as constitutional rights, implies that they inevitably require accompanying legislation and ministerial regulation before they can be relied on by people who face deprivations of various kinds. Addressing this problem, *General Comment 9* (para. 11) leaves the matter open to the discretion of the implementing officer.

> [I]n most States, the determination of whether or not a treaty provision is self-executing will be a matter for the courts, not the executive or the legislature. In order to perform that function effectively, the relevant courts and tribunals must be made aware of the nature and implications of the Covenant and of the important role of judicial remedies in its implementation.

Leaving the application of internal human rights instruments to the discretion of the judiciary does not address the challenge which the implementation of Covenant rights poses. However, the CESCR has contributed significantly to elaborating upon the content of the *ICESCR* through the *General Comments*, though these still may not provide appropriate guidance in very specific contexts.

Generally, the widely accepted practice in most countries now is that the courts are required to give due regard to international law when interpreting municipal law, where applicable (Dugard 2000). For example, the South African Constitution provides that when interpreting the law, the courts *must* consider relevant international law and adopt an interpretation of domestic law which is consistent with international law. The position of international law in the South African judicial system is stated more strongly in Section 233 of the

Constitution, which requires that, "[w]hen interpreting any legislation, every court must prefer any reasonable interpretation of the legislation that is consistent with international law over any alternative interpretation that is inconsistent with international law."

Such constitutional norms confer a procedural obligation upon the judiciary: first to refer to relevant international law; and second, in the process of interpreting domestic law, judges are required to ensure that they adopt an interpretation which is not in conflict with international law. Nonetheless, this assumes that the judicial officer in question is aware of the relevant international law. In most instances that is not the case; judgements are finalised without reference to international law for many reasons – including lack of awareness and or willingness.

International Financial Institutions and Human Rights

Related to the role of international human rights instruments is the issue of the role of international financial institutions (IFIs) with regard to human rights. Although it has been argued that organisations such as the World Bank and the the IMF "are bound by international law with regard to the right to food" (Ziegler 2006: 15), these institutions have repeatedly argued that international treaties are agreements between states and do not extend to them. For instance, the IMF's General Counsel, referring to the *ICESCR*, argued that

> [f]or its part, the Covenant is a treaty among States which contains obligations addressed to states. Neither by its terms nor by the terms of the Fund's agreement with the United Nations is it possible to conclude that the Covenant is applicable to the Fund.
>
> CITED IN COOMANS 2007: 368

Using these kinds of arguments, the IMF and the World Bank have often exempted themselves from the obligations of international human rights law. Because of this, the effect of their actions on ESCRs has often not been subjected to the scrutiny specified by the two Covenants. Yet it is clear that the actions and policies of both these institutions have had a serious negative impact on Covenant rights, including the rights to water and food – especially in the Global South (Ahluwalia 2004; Coomans 2007). In a number of developing countries, governments are pushed into privatising water and other public services as conditions for accessing debt relief and aid packages from bilateral donor agencies. To cite just one example among many,

> in Tanzania, ... privatisation of the poorly performing Dar es Salaam Water Supply and Sewerage Authority (DAWASA) was one of the preconditions given for Tanzania to qualify for the Highly Indebted Poor Countries (HIPC) initiative of the World Bank and the IMF.
>
> BAYLISS 2003: 6

A question that arises is whether these IFIs should be held responsible for the actions and policies that they carry out and which result in the violation of human rights. In recent years the general view has been that it is time that the Bank and the Fund, especially, to account for human rights violations resulting from their operations (Ghazi 2005).

Both the Bank and the Fund have conveniently escaped being held responsible for violations of human rights on the pretext that their mandate is not political, but economic (Wolfenson 2005). For a long time the Bank has relied on Article IV[13] of its articles of agreement to argue that issues of human rights are of a political nature and therefore fall outside of the its mandate (Gathii 1999). However, as Bleicher has observed, "political neutrality may have been essential for the Bank in its early years", but in the current global structure it is deceptive to maintain that the Bank and the Fund have no business in political issues such as human rights" (cited in Dias 1989: 60).

Apart from this, there are four reasons that support the view that the Bank and the Fund need to take into account human rights obligations in their work. First, the Bank and the Fund are considered to have "international legal personality" – which makes them *subjects* of international law and therefore responsible for human rights violations (Skogly 1999: 243). Second, although they are not specialised agencies of the UN, the two Bretton Woods institutions are under obligation to respect human rights by ensuring that their activities do not result in the violation of such rights (Dias 1989). These obligations are implied by their relationship with the UN Charter (Coomans 2007: 369). Third, and especially with regard to the *ICESCR*, the Bank and the Fund have been given a special role in implementing the rights elucidated in the Covenants. Article 16 (2) (b) of the *ICESCR* clearly envisions the participation of specialised institutions in the implementation of these rights. Fourth, the Bank and the Fund are constituted by the UN member states, most of which have ratified these treaties. The

---

13 Article IV (10) of the Bank's articles of agreement stipulates: "The Bank and its officers shall not interfere in the political affairs of any member; nor shall they be influenced in their decisions by the political character of the member or members concerned. Only economic considerations shall be relevant to their decisions, and these considerations shall be weighed impartially in order to achieve the purposes stated in Article I."

former World Bank president acknowledged this, stating: "We're an institution which is owned and, to an extent, dominated by the very same people who wrote the *Universal Declaration of Human Rights* and the subsequent Human Rights instruments" (Wolfenson 2005: 21).

In recent years there have been indications that the Bank is showing some signs of change when it comes to taking human rights into account in its operations (Ghazi 2005; Coomans 2007).

Directive Principles and the Rights to Water and Food

Other than in the international treaties, most countries – particularly in the global South – have provided for the rights to food and water under the non-justiciable sections of their constitutions. Without going into the debates about whether access to water and food are actually human rights or not, it is important to note that the provisions for the rights to water and food in international treaties and national constitutions are there for a number of reasons; they are not stated in various national constitutions without reason. In this context it becomes necessary to examine the role of directive principles[14] in a constitution. First, the role of directive principles of state policy has to be seen in context. Traditionally, the Commonwealth constitutional system avoided including directive principles on the basis that a constitution is a "prescriptive" rather than a "programmatic" statement. If programmatic statements *are* included they are usually in the form of preamble statements (Kabudi 1995: 275). The main reason for programmatic principles not being seen as appropriate in a constitution, so the argument goes, surrounds the notion that a constitution is enacted

> for the sole purpose of establishing structures of government and its institutions and prescribing judicially enforceable rules of law. Statement of national goals and directive principles are not part of the traditional Anglo-American view of constitutions because they are programmatic in nature, in the sense that they provide for a programme of political, socio-economical and cultural development and ethical principles to be pursued by the government and other organs and they are normally non-justiciable, that is, they cannot be enforced in a court of law.
>
> KABUDI 1995: 275

14 Directive principles are a non-justiciable part of the constitution meant to provide guidance in the formulation and implementation of state policy, and also to set goals for social policy (see Kabudi 1995).

This is the tradition that was adhered to by the British when they negotiated the draft constitutions of the newly independent countries in most parts of the world. However, the tradition has been gradually abandoned by a number of states who have subsequently decided to *include* directive principles.

First introduced by the Irish Free State in 1922, directive principles have been incorporated in many developing countries' constitutions – including the Indian Constitution (1947); the Pakistani Constitution (1962); the Sri Lankan and Bangladeshi Constitution (1972), the Nigerian Constitution (1979); and the Zambian Constitution (1996). Reasons for including directive principles in these constitutions included ideological commitment to a set of social and economic goals to which the nation aspired. In some countries these principles are expected to play a transformative role. This view was affirmed by the Indian Supreme Court, when it stated that

> [t]he purpose of the directive principles is to fix certain social and economic goals for immediate attainment ... Through such [principles] the constitution seeks to fulfil the basic needs of the common man and change the structure of society. It aims at making the Indian masses free in the positive sense.
>
> CITED IN KABUDI 1995: 277

Based on this understanding of directive principles, Indian courts have played an active role in ensuring that the state pays attention to the values that were contemplated in them, as we shall see in the next chapter. Many Indian judges have progressively interpreted this part of the constitution, together with justiciable clauses such as the right to life, to give meaning to broader social economic objectives espoused in the constitution.[15]

A more definitive statement on the role of the directive principles is stated in the Nigerian Constitution Drafting Committee Report, which argues that

> [a] Constitution should not be simply a code of legally enforceable rules and regulations; it is a charter of government, and government involves relations and concepts that are not amenable to the test of justiciability or capable of enforcement only in courts of law. The objectives may be in the nature of immediate specific policy goals or of the long-term ideals ...

15 For an example of how the Indian courts have made use of justiciable parts of the Indian Constitution to give effect to non-justiciable social objectives such as those contained in the directive principles, see *Per Olgla Tellis vs. Bomaby Municipal Corporation* [*1986*] A.I.R. (*Sup. Ct.*) *180*.

> Unless these goals and the fundamental attitudes and values that should inform the behaviour of its members and institutions are clearly stated and accepted, a new state is likely to find itself rudderless, with no sense of purpose and direction. By defining the goals of society prescribing the institutional forms and procedures for pursuing them, a statement of fundamental objectives and directive principles in our constitution seeks to direct and concert the efforts and actions of the people towards the achievement of these goals.
>
> CITED IN KABUDI, 1995: 277

Often the argument against including programmatic statements or principles in the constitution is that it may lead to judicial activism, a situation that undermines the fundamental democratic principle of the separation of powers (Corder 2002). At the heart of this debate is the concept that the judiciary has no mandate to meddle in matters pertaining to policy – which is reserved as the prerogative of members of the executive, who have a mandate to formulate and implement policy. In the case of the courts, judges are not elected (they are appointed) and therefore lack a legitimate mandate to interfere with matters of policy formulation, in which the directive principles fall.

The courts, however, have jurisdiction over matters related to *how* the policy is implemented (the mandate to review policy and programme procedures) so as to ensure that government policies are in line with constitutional values and objectives. In this view, the widely endorsed notion of the non-justiciability of directive principles – which include most of the ESCRs – is often supported on the basis that making such principles justiciable would lead the courts down the unintended avenue of deciding upon matters of policy *formulation* rather than matters of policy *implementation*. In this regard, the South African courts have been at pains to decide whether an act by the executive amounts to policy formulation or implementation. If an act by the executive falls within the former category the courts are expected to be guided by the principle of judicial deference; if it falls within the latter, the courts are expected to intervene.[16] But

16 *Pharmaceutical Manufacturers Association of South Africa: in Re: Ex Parte President of the Republic of South Africa & Others* 2000 (2) SA 674 (CC). This a case in which the president of the Republic of South Africa appealed to the Constitutional Court against the Supreme Court of Appeal's decision that presidential Proclamation R49 of 1999 was null and void – thus rendering the South African Medicines and Medical Devices Regulatory Act 132 of 1998, that the Proclamation was supposed to bring into force, ineffective. The question raised in the Constitutional Court was to consider "whether a court has the power to review and set aside a decision by the President" of the RSA to bring an Act of Parliament into force.

this task (of distinguishing between policy formulation and policy implementation) is often a matter of predisposition of a particular judge, and the arguments are often not convincing.

So the relevance of directive principles in a constitution should not be based on whether the directive principles are justiciable or not. The fundamental point is that the directive principles constitute a set of goals to which various organs of the state should orient their efforts and actions, and their activities should be measured against these set goals. As one Indian lawmaker noted, directive principles, are a way of entrenching "economic democracy" (cited in Drèze 2005: 50).

Seen from this angle, the directive principles create norms against which policy and legislation should be assessed by all stakeholders, especially civil society groups. Unfortunately these provisions have not been utilised, partly because of the widespread belief that only a legally enforceable clause can be relied upon. We can see here the influence of legal positivism, i.e. only what is codified in statutes and regulations, and capable of being enforced, should be regarded as human rights. The influence of this view has tended to minimalise not only many states' sense of expediency when it comes to paying attention to the rights to water and food for the poor; but also limiting the extent of public debate that can create alternative routes[17] for giving effect to these rights.

So What Difference Do Human Rights Make?

There have been heated debates about whether recognition of ESCRs such as the rights to water and food – in international or even municipal law – makes any difference in the lives of the poor and marginalised. Critics often argue that legislation only works to serve the interests of the elite and those in power, not those of the poor and marginalised. Some question the relevance of the relevant pieces of legislation at both international and domestic level. With specific reference to international law, it has been argued that the relevant laws have failed to make a difference where they are needed most (Hafner-Burton and Tsutsui 2005); and most critics question the efficacy of using human rights to bring about social and economic change, empowerment and social justice.

While one can sympathise with the sceptics – given the widespread and open disregard for human rights, and laws, by individuals as well as institutions that exercise power – it is important to note that human rights create opportunities

17 Sen (2004: 26–8) distinguishes the legislative from the recognition and agitation routes in the effectualisation of human rights.

for practising the sort of democratic politics that can challenge the status quo, including the way that power is distributed and exercised in society. Many activists who have been using human rights tools to fight for various causes have often acknowledged the open-endedness of the human rights strategy. For example, Felix Morka in Nigeria (working with SERAC),[18] has observed that "human rights is a language of possibilities ... which gives people a sense of self in relation to the state" (cited in Donald and Mottershaw 2009: 20).

For ESCRs such as the rights to water and food, the language of rights creates opportunities for ensuring that more attention in society is directed towards the needs of the vulnerable and the marginalised. Human rights tools make it possible to engage in struggles which have the potential to transform institutions and policies and make them more responsive to the basic human needs of everyone.

A huge misconception among human rights sceptics and enthusiasts alike is the unwarranted expectation that the constitutional recognition of rights should automatically translate into tangible entitlements for everyone. It is perhaps more constructive to think about human rights as basic tools that create space for democratic politics; as tools that create possibilities for social change. But these possibilities have to be converted into something real. This can be achieved through various means including: litigation, collective action, public campaigns, social mobilisation, electoral processes, etc. – that is, by engaging in democratic politics. Otherwise the possibilities will remain just that: possibilities. A first step in creating these opportunities is the recognition of these rights at the domestic as well as the international level. Formal and explicit protection of these rights makes it possible to challenge not just the state's failure to live by these norms, but also to challenge the laws, institutions and policies that hinder their realisation (de Schutter 2012: 5). Without formal recognition and protection of these rights it becomes difficult to create the spaces where genuine attention can be drawn to the plight of those who are vulnerable and disempowered.

This is not to argue that constitutional protection is the only basis for collective action – social mobilisation and collective action can be (and have been) organised even in the absence of constitutional protection. However, where human rights are recognised it becomes easier to mobilise social action around a particular issue. In a situation where a clear proclamation about the status of a right has not been made, it is difficult to create public discourse around it. Nonetheless, even where constitutional protection of these rights is afforded,

18 SERAC stands for Social and Economic Rights Action Centre, an organisation that mobilises communities against forced evictions, displacements and demolitions.

"sustained mobilisation may be required to ensure they are realised" (Donald and Mottershaw 2009: 20). Experience from many countries where the right to water or food has been recognised explicitly or implicitly shows that little has been done beyond recognition alone. Sustained collective action in support of these rights is essential for building public opinion, drawing public attention, and, most importantly, creating the political will and the public support necessary to actualize these rights into something tangible. As the HDR 2007 (p. 61) observes:

> The obvious starting point for a drive towards universal access to water and sanitation is political will, broadly defined as the resolve to put the issue at the centre of the national agenda. It is not difficult to identify the financial, technological and institutional obstacles to progress, but these obstacles are often symptoms of a deeper malaise – a deficit in political leadership.

One of the reasons explaining the lack of political will and commitment to promoting wider access to water and food is the view that if access were to be recognised as a human right, it would heap pressure on government resources. Much of this thinking has been promoted by international financial institutions and donor agencies, which have adopted a hostile attitude towards ESCRs,[19] arguing that recognising these rights would result in huge budget deficits and a destabilisation of the macroeconomic environment in poor countries. Given the role these institutions have played in the formulation and implementation of policy in the Global South since the early years of the SAPs, it is not surprising that policies and legislation at the national level have shied away from the language of rights when it comes to important services such as water, education and healthcare. But if there is sustained and broad-based collective action in support of these rights at both international and domestic level, it will be possible to create the required political will and commitment, as well as the necessary legislative framework and institutions which can support this. The challenge is to ensure that there is sustained society-wide momentum in support of these rights – political will is always created where there is sufficient support.

19 In earlier debates both the World Bank and the IMF argued that their mandate did not allow them to engage in matters of a political nature, like human rights. The Bank, in particular, defended this position on the basis of Article IV of the its articles of agreement. But as Ghazi (2005: 95) has observed, both the Bank and the Fund have been involving themselves in activities that have a direct connection with human rights. In recent years, the Bank has come to realise that this position is not practical, and has been accommodating human rights values in its work.

CHAPTER 8

The Rights to Water and Food

Strategies and Lessons from Global South

Human rights philosophy, language and strategies are used by many people in different circumstances in the struggle for different things: ranging from access to land, political liberation, gender equity and recognition; to the struggle for democracy, genuine participation, livelihoods and dignity. These struggles, some of which have been going on for centuries, offer valuable lessons about how human rights have contributed to social change. Using human rights as instruments for social change requires that attention be paid to the role human rights have played in past struggles. Not only this: effective use of human rights as a tool for social change requires that lessons be learned from the struggles that are happening today, struggles in which human rights are playing a central role in articulating and framing the fight (Slim 2002).

The main purpose of such a learning exercise is not necessarily to replicate the strategies that worked either in the past or in some other context, but rather to use this experience as a starting point for devising a particular strategy in a specific context. This process of learning from the past and from current struggles should not just focus on the successes and victories, but also on learning from past mistakes and failures and, most importantly, learning from the risks of deploying a human rights strategy in the struggle for justice in the field of drinking and eating. Learning from past and present human rights struggles and strategies also requires that the warning that human rights can be deployed by people who seek merely to "benefit from the moral authority and political appeal of the human rights discourse" – with no serious commitment to the politics of social change – be taken seriously; and the warning that human rights can be negatively deployed for the purpose of "regaining the high moral ground in order to fend off criticism and mobilize resources" (Univ 2002: 4). Often, there is a strong inclination to ignore, dismiss and disparage past and present experiences on the pretext that "our" circumstances or struggles are very different. However, learning from past and present struggles can be a source of inspiration.

A crucial lesson is that a lack of flexibility in using human rights, and a narrow approach to the fight for basic human needs like the right to water and food, often lead to frustration. Many human rights activists and members of radical social movements get frustrated when their expectations are not met and when laws seem not produce the results they anticipated: when laws seem unable

 | DOI 10.1163/9789004299559_009

to bring about the desperately needed social change. But experience of the struggle for human rights from different parts of the world has shown that giving effect to most of them requires flexibility and a broader approach that allows one to go beyond merely listing clauses in the constitution, or identifying duty-bearers and benefits; rather, it requires the deployment of different strategies and tools as circumstances allow. This is not to say that laws are less important – in fact they provide the grounds for struggle and collective action – but "collective action and public attention potentially foster greater implementation of laws, particularly in democratic regimes" (Srinivasan and Narayanan 2007: 9).

This chapter provides some examples of the various ways in which human rights instruments and policy frameworks are being used by different civil society groups to promote the advancement of the rights to water and food, specifically. The discussion here focuses on civil society groups' experiences in their deployment of human rights in the struggle for access to water and food – the experiences of governments, multilateral and bilateral organisations, and donor and development agencies are not discussed here mainly because much of the work of these bodies is well-publicised and does not need repeating here. In addition, most of these organisations articulate and deploy a view of human rights that is often different from groups which "straddle the middle hill country between the moral highlands and the muddy lowlands" (Slim 2002: 4). In all these examples it is apparent that giving effect to a particular right is not something that happens automatically; it is often the outcome of a long (and sometimes frustrating) struggle. Most importantly, these examples also highlight the fact that effective struggles for human rights are those for which people believe that change is possible; that it is possible to do things differently; that it is possible to change the arrangements around access to clean water and adequate food such that all people can secure these basic needs.

Lessons from Experience

For any strategy to be effective in the struggle to give effect to human rights in general, and ESCRs in particular, a thorough analysis of the context in which the right is intended to be given effect is essential. In view of this, it follows that attempts to replicate strategies that have proved effective in one context may prove to be less successful in realising a particular right in another – even if there are similarities between the contexts. However, although strategies aimed at giving effect to the rights to water and food have to be devised by considering the local context, general lessons can be drawn based on strategies and programmes which have worked before. For example, a local organisation committed to the fight for the rights to water or food in South Africa or Mali can learn a lot from work and strategies adopted by the People's Union for Civil Liberties movement in India, the National Right to Food Network in Malawi, Action for Nutrition and Human Rights (ABRANDH) in Brazil, SERAC in Nigeria, or the National Human Rights Commission in Kenya. In other words, while strategies have to be rooted in the specific context, broader lessons can be drawn from other strategies that have worked elsewhere, whether the strategy was legal, administrative, policy-oriented or one of social action.

At this point it is important to acknowledge the huge and varied challenges which have to be faced in *any* struggle that is dedicated to giving effect to human rights in general, and ESCRs in particular. Like it is for any other struggle, facing and dealing with challenges lies at the heart of the matter; this cannot be avoided if the strategy is to yield any positive results. Despite the challenges involved in giving effect to the rights to water and food there are encouraging examples of how different people in different parts of the world are devising struggles which create spaces where it becomes possible to give effect to these rights. Broad lessons on strategies which have proved to be effective in different parts of the world can be drawn from these experiences. In doing so it is important to bear in mind that the ultimate goal of the struggle for the rights to water and food is to bring about changes to the way we think about access to water and food by through changing the social, economic and political structures surrounding their production and distribution. But achieving meaningful change to the way we think about all this is not possible without first engaging in radical democratic politics (which has both local and global dimensions) – the process that can bring about these changes cannot be apolitical.

Identifying and Navigating the Challenges

Experience from different human rights analysts, practitioners, activists and lobbyists alike, reveals that there are numerous challenges in the process of giving effect to human rights. For the rights to water and food, many activists and experts are aware that these rights are not given effect by simply including a clause in the national constitution or some other piece of legislation, or by simply mounting protests in the streets, or through prolonged courtroom battles. Giving effect to human rights in general is a process that requires sustained effort and contestation, combining and changing strategies at different levels of the struggle. At the core of the fight for human rights is the need to bring about a fundamental change in the way power is exercised, and because change is not easily or "cheaply" achieved (since change within the human rights framework can make certain people uncomfortable), there is always the challenge of overcoming the resistance to change that some sections of society may demonstrate. The idea of creating a world where every person has access to basic clean water is quite threatening to some, and so such ideas are often dismissed as a utopian fantasy. As Sen (2003) argues, this defeatism – which often "masquerades as hard-headed realism" – has been so widely accepted that it has become the status quo position: natural and unchangeable:

> [M]assive endemic hunger causes great misery in many parts of the world, debilitating hundreds of millions and killing a sizable proportion of them with statistical regularity. What makes this widespread hunger even more of a tragedy is the way we have come to accept and tolerate it as an integral part of the modern world, as if it is a tragedy that is essentially unpreventable (in the way ancient Greek tragedies were). I shall argue that not only is the problem of world hunger decisively solvable, but that one of the greatest barriers to achieving that solution lies in the widely shared skepticism about such a solution, the defeatist and baseless fear that we shall not succeed against so big a challenge.
>
> SEN, 2003

As was shown in Chapters 5 and 6, it is not that the world does not have enough water to ensure that every person on the planet has access to it, or that the world does not produce enough food to eliminate chronic hunger, undernourishment and starvation. No, this situation is prevalent because societies all over the world operate in such a way that undernourishment and starvation have been widely accepted as part of life. The world has too easily accepted that there is little that can be done to change how water and food are distributed and shared.

Human Rights as Tools for Social Change

Resistance to change the way water and food are distributed can come from governments, members of the legislature, judges, NGOs or elite groups whose interests may be threatened by such change. As has been observed, "governments and legislators are often wary of adopting 'legislation with teeth'; they are more comfortable with laws that do not imply major constraints and obligations" (FAO 2011a: 25). Even if legislation "with teeth" is adopted, one cannot operate on the assumption that the radical challenge that human rights pose to the configuration and exercise of power will not be contested by those in power. By virtue of the radical challenge that human rights pose to power relations, those exercising power are most likely to resist genuine change, even though they may rhetorically adopt, endorse and use the language of rights.

Other than overt objection to the radical change that human rights necessitate, there is also a more subtle challenge that emerges from the experience of deploying human rights in the struggle for justice, equity and basic needs. The challenge here often comes from people who adopt, advocate for and subscribe to human rights, but who have little interest in changing the status quo. Although such individuals and organisations may profess commitment to the rights-based approach and can be very vocal about pushing the agenda of rights in countries in the Global South, their view of human rights may be "to provide a fig leaf for the continuation of the status quo" (Univ 2002: 3); they are, in fact, far removed from the idea of using human rights as a tool for social change. For such people, adopting a rights-based approach is just "a new way of feeling good"; a way of taking the moral high ground; a pious rather than a prophetic way of viewing things (Slim 2002). For this reason it is essential when deploying the human rights strategies to be aware of the fact that human rights talk can be utilised to serve very divergent ends. For example:

> Rights-talk in Washington or Paris might be used piously as new words for the same old liturgy in the cathedral of international trade and development... But from another place (a slum or the scene of a rigged election) and spoken from another voice (that of a poor man or a woman land rights lawyer) the same words of rights-talk could function prophetically as a demand for redress to change and challenge power.
>
> IBID.: 3

Because human rights can be used to serve these diverse and sometimes contradictory interests, voices and agendas, they are inherently political (Gready 2008). Therefore, it is how the divergent interests play out that determines whether real change is realised or not. For genuine change to occur – whether the strategy adopted is the legal route, the non-legal route or a combination of different routes – collective action is indispensable to generate the necessary pressure to breathe life into statutes and laws. The main challenge in this regard is that no matter how well legislation is formulated, it does not automatically translate into real entitlement:

> No agreement or treaty is enforced automatically, regardless of how positive or progressive its content may be. Popular pressure, mobilisation and organisation to demand its enforcement are the elements that give life to these documents and make them work in the search for social change.
>
> MONSALVE AND SEUFERT 2012: 3

Translating the constitutional or Covenant rights into real entitlements is a matter of contestation. In this instance, provisions on the rights to water and food, be they at the national, regional or international level, are not automatically translatable into real entitlements to basic water and adequate food; achieving this requires (sometimes) a protracted contest between the divergent interests around the way access to water and food is structured. To realise genuine entitlements to water and food requires radical reconfiguration of the current structures and the exercise of power around their production and distribution. Such a transformation agenda targets institutions and relations to make them more inclusive and more empowering, especially to those who find it difficult to access these basic needs. While using human rights provides the tools that can contribute towards the reconfiguration of power and social relations, the major challenge in this regard lies in mounting enough pressure to bring about genuine reconfiguration of the structures and institutions through which power is exercised. Given this situation, without a strong coalition of support for the right to food and the right to water, very little change in the current structure and arrangements can be achieved. Without sustained public pressure to decisively bring these issues into public spaces, undernourishment and starvation will continue to be widely accepted as "hard-headed realism" (Sen 1993); as something that we cannot do much about; as something that we should learn to live with.

Choked by Defeatism

Although there have been several conferences and international (as well as national) policy documents highlighting the plight of the starving and water-deprived masses in the Global South, there seems to be a growing defeatist discourse which espouses the idea that it is impossible to eliminate hunger and water deprivation; that some people just have to make do with less food and water, or none at all. At this level the biggest challenge is to overcome the stranglehold of defeatism around water and food. The primary struggle in this regard is to dislodge the strongly entrenched myth that it is impossible to realise a world where undernourishment, hunger and starvation are completely eliminated. When these myths are dislodged it becomes possible to think more creatively about how to achieve the eradication of thirst and hunder, both nationally and globally – and the chances of successfully using human rights as a tool for effecting this change increases.

One of the main reasons why – in the case of access to clean water and adequate food – very little change or improvement happens despite a plethora of conferences, declarations and laws, is precisely because most of the people who face the pangs of hunger, undernourishment and starvation, as well as inadequate access to clean water, have their interests obscured. Genuine change happens when these people's interests become a rallying point for public action that seeks to increase their share and participation in the contest around the production, distribution and consumption of water and food. The main challenge in making this happen revolves around mobilising broad-based and sustained support, since the relatively better-off – who may have the appropriate voice and power – often seem disinterested in pushing such an agenda; they are often aloof to engaging in *realpolitik*. As VaneKlasen *et al.* (2004) observe, it is often the relatively well-off who are successful in claiming and benefiting from these rights, and most of them are only interested in rights that benefit them directly. Reflecting on the Indian experience, Srinivasan and Narayanan (2007) observe that the people most in need of food are the poor and the marginalised, most of whom are unable to effectively engage in the rights contest. Initiating and sustaining wider public action around water and food, so as to build and sustain a critical mass that makes it possible to change the way power is distributed and exercised around water and food, is crucial.

This is not just a matter of having the right mobilisation skills, it also involves a careful analysis of how power is configured and how various groups relate to and benefit from this power. Failure to map out power dynamics in a particular context may lead to adopting strategies that are ineffective and sometimes counter-productive. As noted earlier, the arena where rights are contested and claimed is not always pro-poor. A human rights strategy has to be prepared for this inevitable conflict and has to be aware of the various potential arenas of contestation (VaneKlasen *et al.* 2004). Experience from different parts of the world, and at different times, shows that in any contest over rights, "poor people's rights, such as the right to food, are likely to be considered less important than the rights of more influential groups, such as property rights or the right to set up a business" (FAO 2011a: 25).

A Fragmented Front

Related to the challenges posed by anti-change forces is the fact that human rights, although they are theoretically indivisible and interdependent, in practice do compete with each other. This is a major challenge at the implementation level where different state agencies and some sections of civil society approach rights in a fragmented way, often creating vicious competition for resources. Departments or sectors that are well-organised tend to get the attention and a larger share of the national or donor resources. Generally it is the more organised and well-established sectors – such as education, health and housing – which capture a larger share of public resources. In the case of the right to water, the water sector itself is often fragmented, which makes it difficult to attract public interest and contest successfully for public resources. One of the reasons given for the fragmented nature of the water sector is the fact that water itself has multiple users with very diverse interests – all of which makes it difficult to present a unified front (Chitonge 2007).

With specific reference to countries in the Global South, it has been noted that the water sector is only just beginning to reorganise itself into a well-coordinated sector that can exert political pressure. Slaymaker and Newborne (2004) in a report on the status of water supply and sanitation in the Poverty Reduction Strategy Papers (PRSPs), concluded that the water sector has not been given significant attention in most of them. The reason they give for this is that the "water sector stakeholders have failed to mobilise and engage with PRSP processes as effectively as their counterparts in other sectors" (ibid.: 7).

In the case of the right to adequate food there are many diverse actors and interest groups that directly and indirectly impact upon access to food. This makes it difficult to bring all of them together to bear down on access to food. For instance, access to land and water may have serious consequences for people's access to food, and yet the land sector often operates separately from the water and food sectors such that the different actors may not even see how their interests are connected. In this sense, it becomes a huge challenge to mobilise sustained public support and action from all the different actors who may even see each other as competitors. This has made it difficult for an integrated approach to collective action.

Often civil society groups, especially social movements, act, lobby and agitate on very specific and narrow issues like water for domestic consumption in urban areas only – when in actual fact it is often the same people denied access to water who have no access to land, inputs, services, and eventually food (Ziegler 2006).

While this fragmentation of human rights at the practical level reflects the complexities involved in ensuring that these rights are given effect, creative ways of integrating collective action over a range of closely connected rights can enhance the process of making human entitlement real for all. The main rationale behind the need for an integrated approach is the simple, but widely recognised fact that it is the same people who are denied the right to freedom of assembly, participation and expression whose rights to water and adequate food are denied; it is often the same people whose voices are not heard, whose points of view are not listened to, and who find themselves without access to clean water and adequate food. Thus, looking at these rights in an integrated way creates a common front in the struggle for access to basic necessities for the poor. If the rights to water and food are about changing the way we think about structures around access to water and food, there is a strong case for a holistic collective approach with a broader vision of achieving a society where people's dignity and entitlements are protected.

In theory it might to be possible for human rights activists, advocates and practitioners to include a whole range of rights in their struggle for social and economic change. Practical considerations, however, actually dictate that focus be directed at very specific issues or rights so as to adequately articulate the issues and also to direct public attention and support on issues related to access to water and adequate food. Thus, it may be more effective to adopt an approach that integrates the specific activities surrounding particular rights to create common ground and goals to which all collective actions can be directed. For instance, struggles around the creation of an effective irrigation system, an appropriate land tenure system, or a farm input support, health and education delivery system – and even participatory and decision-making systems – can be linked together to contribute to a "broader vision of practical change" (Chapman *et al.* 2005: 6). Although many organisations using the rights strategy are now beginning to make these linkages within and between organisations (ibid.),[1] forging effective integration of different strategies still remains one of the major challenges for most organisations involved in the fight for human rights (Alston and Robinson 2005).

Galvanising a Critical Mass

The other challenge that the human rights struggle faces, which becomes evident from experiences shared later in this chapter, is that of mobilising and sustaining support. Many human rights activists write and speak as if mobilising public support and action is like switching on lights or opening a tap. Experience with lobbying and mobilising public support – even for things like access to clean water and adequate food which many people would empathise

1 One good example is Action Aid. In Brazil, Guatemala and Bangladesh, the organisation has taken a more holistic approach – which includes a broader approach to human rights within the organisation. It is also making concerted efforts to establish partnerships with other organisations working on issues that are broadly linked, especially with social movements focusing on very particular issues. Experience so far has revealed that the most successful projects are those with wider linkages with other organisations (Chapman 2005).

with – suggests that this is neither an easy nor a one-off task. If we accept the idea that those people affected by the lack of water and conditions of hunger, undernourishment and starvation, should be at the forefront of the struggle for the rights to water and food (Vaneklasen *et al.* 2004: 11), the major challenge that arises is to get them organised and to sustain their interest given that such struggles may not yield immediate and tangible results. In this regard, mobilising and sustaining a critical mass around access to clean water and adequate food is a huge challenge given the fact that the power to effect change that is inherent in human rights struggles is often only realised when there is a critical mass – i.e. when a specific issues attracts sufficient and widespread public support. As we shall see in the Zero Hunger Campaign example from Brazil, it was the wider public support initiated by civil society and faith-based groups that brought the issue of hunger on to the political agenda and generated a social movement which pushed the state to grasp the issue of hunger as one of its priorities (da Silva *et al.* 2011). Similarly, in Bolivia, massive public support for people's access to basic water added significant currency to the famous "Cochabamba water wars" which led to significant concessions around water pricing, water distribution and the broader policy framework surrounding water.

Unfortunately (or fortunately, depending on how one sees this), the fight for human rights is a game of numbers; without the "right" numbers it is difficult to gain attention from the media and, later on, from those who exercise power at different levels. To get the right numbers requires sustained mobilisation and awareness campaigns, and this is not easy. People who have been involved in mobilisation and campaigns for any cause will testify that getting people interested is always an uphill battle at every stage of the struggle for basic essentials such as access to clean water and adequate food. For instance, activists in India acknowledge that "collective action is difficult to initiate and sustain, but when it succeeds it can be extremely empowering for those who are individually marginalised or powerless" (Srinivasan and Narayanan 2007: 9).

The Flexibility Deficit

Another common challenge that has been widely acknowledged among human rights activists and practitioners is that often people working in this area have adopted a rigid approach to the struggle. Some human rights practitioners cannot think outside legal provisions or case law: they are confined rigidly to the legal route as the only way of giving effect to human rights. This rigid and narrow approach to human rights becomes a challenge in the Global South where the judicial system has limited capacity. This has often resulted in huge backlogs, high court costs, inefficiency and corruption (FAO 2011a: 25). Furthermore, a rigid legalistic approach to the human rights struggle limits it to legal professionals and experts (as suppliers of information on which cases are built), with little participation from the public. For those who rely on this approach to human rights, focus is on "what the law says", which often "downplays the dynamic aspect of the political process that shapes the extent to which rights are enforced and realised in people's daily lives" (VaneKlasen *et al.* 2004: 7). Related to this is the view that taking a very legalist approach to human rights works from the

> assumption that the political system is relatively open and democratic and that the policy concerns of the powerless can be met through the work of professional lobbyists backed up by adequate resources, solid information and soundly researched, well-presented arguments. This approach is likely to have little impact on expanding citizen participation, community organisation, leadership development or political awareness – elements that are vital for confronting power and serve as the backbone for ensuring long-term change.
>
> CHAPMAN 2005: 14

As noted above, a more flexible and integrated approach to human rights – one in which different strategies are integrated in a manner that reinforces and contributes to the broader vision of social change – is most likely to be effective in engaging with the complex issues involved. For instance, the right to food may not be successfully given effect in the courts, but the wider public support that draws from a broader constituency can be effective in bringing the issue onto the political agenda in the first place. Even in cases where the legal route ends in a favourable decision with regard to the right to water, for instance, actually fulfilling the order of the court may not occur if there is no public pressure for the state to effectively implement such an order. However, many human rights practitioners only know, and are willing, to try only the legal route – leaving other possible avenues to non-experts and NGOs. In this regard it is always a challenge to convince human rights practitioners to adopt an integrated approach which includes the non-legal routes.

Building Strategic Alliances

Experience from human rights struggles also suggests that there are many activists who view the struggle for human rights as being essentially a battle with the state. Broadly, in terms of social change, it is the state that can actually implement or decide not to effect any changes, and because of this the struggles for human rights are mostly directed at changing the exercise and control of state power. However, it is not always the case that the state is the enemy in the fight for human rights. In some cases, and in order to give effect to the right to water, it will be an unavoidable part of the struggle to build strategic alliances with state institutions and agencies, while at the same time avoiding the dangers of losing sight of the bigger picture of bringing about change in the relations and exercise of power. Activists with long experience in the fight for human rights acknowledge that at times "strategic alliances" have to be built with the state in order to effect the necessary change. Indeed, such "strategic" alliances may be the only effective way to challenge power and bring about change. As some analysts have observed, "redressing injustice, and accessing political and economic resources, requires using the system where possible and challenging and expanding it where necessary" (VaneKlasen *et al.* 2004: 8). Many human rights practitioners and advocates concede that, at times, it is necessary to forge strategic alliances with the state, while at the same time demanding accountability, genuine participation and transparency. In this view the state should be seen as "neither monolithic nor necessarily hostile", but rather as "a shifting surface of openings and closure for external interventions on the right to food, making it crucial that participatory spaces are institutionalised and their powers clearly defined" (Gready 2008: 740).

This view links with the idea adopted in this book that the state is an arena of contestation. As Maunder observes, "neither rights nor justice can be given to a passive and inert group of people. Sustainable justice requires their central and active agency in all processes connected with identifying and securing their rights" (cited in Gready 2008: 742). Thus, a more strategic approach to the struggle for human rights, including the rights to water and food, has to regard the state not as the enemy but as the space where the contest for these rights unfolds. Sometimes the struggle involves contesting against state institutions, policy and practice; while at other times working with the state to bring about the required change may be necessary. Again, experience of human rights struggles supports the view that real changes in power relations occur through serious engagement in the state space, and not by antagonising or ignoring this space. It is through engagement in the state spaces that genuine empowerment can occur by a process of questioning and seeking to "transform deeply embedded power relations from the most intimate to the most public and visible" (VaneKlasen *et al.* 2004: 9). Struggles for the rights to water and food become more meaningful if the contest – whether it be for recognition, or for practical implementation of these rights – occurs within the state space. Programmes that give effect to the rights to water or food are formulated and implemented by the state, and for such programmes to benefit from the value and vision of human rights requires a very strategic participation in the state space – and in so doing contributing to the "production of space" itself.

The Rights to Water and Food Strategies

Despite the challenges noted above, individuals and groups throughout the world – in different circumstances – have found creative ways of contesting for, and reshaping, the state space around the rights to water and food. This contestation has taken various forms, including: legal challenges in the law courts; meeting with policy-makers; documenting and publicising violations of rights; public protest; sensitisation and training of communities; and lobbying for public support through parliamentary caucuses. In real life struggles activists and practitioners have been utilising different strategies and tactics to contest in and reshape the state space. Below are some examples of such strategies, specifically relating to the rights to water and food.

National Right to Food Network: Malawi

In Malawi, a consortium of 25 NGOs calling themselves the National Right to Food Network (NRFN, formed in 2003), joined forces after recognising the legislative gap in the country's food and nutrition policy and legal framework. The movement began lobbying the government to adopt the food security bill which, although it had been drafted in 2002, had not been enacted into law. Through the collective action of these civil society groups and NGOs the government was forced to engage with them, and eventually it set up a joint drafting committee – consisting of members of the NRFN, the Ministry of Agriculture, the Malawi Human Rights Commission, and the Department of Nutrition – to draft a new Food Security Bill (de Schutter 2012: 9). Members of NRFN envisioned that enacting the Food Security Bill would provide avenues through which the right to food might be given effect. Although the Malawian Constitution recognises the right to food under the directive principles for state policy in Article 13 (b), as well as in the justiciable part of the Constitution under Article 30 (2), the state had up to this point not taken measures to give effect to the right. In fact, the Food Security Bill had been lying idle for seven years without any action being taken to enact it. NRFN members saw its adoption as the basis for engaging with the state more effectively on matters concerning the right to food – by engaging the state on this issue the NRFN envisioned that the Bill would empower citizens to demand government accountability; provide guidance on the practicalities of the right to food (including the minimum entitlement to eligible persons); and facilitate the establishment of institutions that would promote and coordinate measures aimed at giving effect to the right to food (NRFN 2011).

By lobbying and taking an active role in the drafting of the Food Security Bill, the NRFN not only created the foundation on which the struggle could be mounted, but through its protracted campaign – using national and international media – has been able to draw attention to issues of hunger and starvation in the country.

As far as giving effect to the right to food for those who have inadequate and unpredictable access to food is concerned, the biggest achievement in this case does not lie in the fact that the state was pushed into revisiting and redrafting the food security framework law that protected the right to food; but rather in bringing the right to food issue into the public domain – i.e. bringing the issue of access to food into the arena of democratic politics. Although many poor people who suffer from hunger and starvation may not even be aware of these processes, sustained lobbying on this topic has managed to raise access to food as a national concern that requires not just a judicial or legislative response, but also concrete social, economic and administrative responses. The mere fact that 25 different civil society and NGO groups came together to raise concerns around hunger and undernourishment is an indication of the strong public interest surrounding the issue. This strong interest was used to galvanise the critical mass to the point where it was capable of generating sufficient incentive for politicians to tackle the issue rather than ignore it. In this way the NRFN is not acting simply as a pressure group, but rather as a movement with a broader agenda that is ultimately focused on changing power relations and the way that power is distributed and exercised. Although the framework law on the right to food in Malawi is yet to be enacted, momentum has been created and this has helped to sustain public action and support around issues related to the right to food.

Campaign on the Right to Food and Social Security: Bangladesh

The Campaign on the Right to Food and Social Security (CRFSS) in Bangladesh offers similar experience of civil society groups creatively finding strategies to give effect to human rights. Like the NRFN in Malawi, the CRFSS is a network of civil society organisations and individuals. It was formally launched on World Food Day (16 October) in 2011, to promote the realisation of ESCRs – including the right to food. The organisation is combing legal and non-legal strategies to secure basic entitlements for the people. This has so far been achieved through the use of public interest litigation (PIL) tools, as well as through the monitoring of government food and social security programmes – including land reform programmes (Hossain 2012). Apart from the campaign to fully recognise the right to food in the Bangladeshi Constitution, the CRFSS also monitors (through its national network) the implementation of social safety net programmes, as well as lobbying for the formulation and implementation of programmes to mitigate the impact of disasters when they occur. Different strategies range from public rallies in cities and villages, hosting seminars, and establishing monitoring teams and networks at district and village levels, to litigation (ibid.). Although this is a fairly recent initiative, the broader approach adopted can help more effective engagement at different levels.

Additionally, linking the right to food with the issue of food security provides a more integrated approach to hunger, poverty, landlessness and vulnerability. As noted earlier, the right to food is often linked to a complex set of factors including access to land, social security, and exclusion from political and economic decision-making process, etc. Huguette Akplogan-Dossa[2] notes that

> it is almost impossible to find one person among the powerful in society and politics worldwide, who does not have enough to eat. The tendency is for exclusion from economic and political decision-making to go hand in hand with incidents of hunger and malnutrition.
>
> RFN 2012, PRESS RELEASE

The right to food is never fulfilled merely by ensuring access to a specified number of calories: it includes processes that allow people to provide food for themselves with dignity (*General Comment 12*: para. 6). As some analysts have argued, food security and the right to food "can never be achieved without addressing issues of production" (Patnaik 2011b: 37). Thus, giving effect to the right to food requires broader and more flexible strategies which take into account the multifaceted nature of the entitlements and obligations that the right encompasses.

The Right to Food Campaign: India

An internationally renowned example of the struggle to give effect to the right to food is the Right to Food Campaign (RFC) in India. This campaign, which

2 Akplogan-Dossa is currently the west Africa regional director of the African Network on the Right to Food (ANORF). The body was founded in 2008 in Cotonou, Benin, with representatives from 40 civil society groups from 18 African countries. Akplogan-Dossa is also director of the NGO, United Sisters at Work.

has inspired various right to food struggles globally, is an informal network of over 2,500 community-based organisations (CBOs), NGOs, trade union movements, social movements, analysts, academics, legal and human rights activists. The network originated from the famous case, *People's Union for Civil Liberties* (*PUCL*) *v. Union of India & Others* (henceforth, PUCL) in 2001 (Patnaik 2011b). As an informal network of diverse civil society groups, the RFC did not have a formal beginning; it started as a meeting to share concerns around hunger and starvation in the Indian state of Rajasthan in 2000. During this period, when Rajasthan was experiencing food shortages, the country as whole was producing cereal far in excess of the amount needed to meet national demand.[3] Reports indicate that the initial meeting at which hunger and starvation in the midst of plenty was discussed was attended by more than 300 civil society groups from across Rajasthan (RFC 2005). When the food crisis worsened as a result of the state's lack of an effective response, the campaign intensified. As it gained momentum, one of the civil society group members (the PUCL) decided to approach the court to force the state to respond, resulting in the famous PUCL case.

Although the campaign started in a single state, it spread to all parts of India and now has a national network with members in most districts in the country. And while the campaign started by focusing on petitioning the state to provide food relief to drought-stricken families in some parts of Rajasthan, it has since expanded its scope to included school meals, the Public Distribution System (PDS), employment guarantee programmes for poor families, as well as homes for the homeless in both urban and rural areas. Although not all these programmes have been implemented effectively in all states, analysts note that, overall, these struggles have made a noticeable difference in poor people's lives and that there is still potential for an even greater impact (Srivinasan and Narayanana 2007).

An important lesson that this struggle reveals is that gains are never won in a single court battle; rather, they occur as part of a continuous struggle. It has taken several court orders to give effect to the meaning of the right to food, such that since the 2001 court ruling

> the Supreme court has passed over a hundred judgements in this case which have, *inter alia*, universalized school feeding and child care programs, created the conditions for the passage of the universal rural

3 It has been reported that in 2001 India had a surplus stock of 61.7 million metric tons of rice and wheat, far more than the required buffer stock of 24.1 million metric tons (see Srinivasan and Narayanan 2007: footnote 2).

> employment guarantee program, guaranteeing every rural household a hundred days of work at centrally determined minimum wages; created legal entitlements for social security; and now, helped create a series of legally justiciable rights for the urban homeless.
>
> PATNAIK 2011B: 37

The relative success of this campaign has been attributed to a number of factors, including a massive mobilisation through national networks.

> Critical to this mobilisation of support for the RFC was Rajasthan's long tradition of partnerships among civil society actors in fighting for a common cause. The network comprised many organisations with very different profiles, sources of funding, sizes, and ideologies. They were also well distributed geographically, covering most districts.
>
> SRIVINASAN AND NARAYANANA 2007: 3

The campaign's strength also came from its strong and broad base – including from among people suffering from hunger and undernourishment. The network was built upon a solid base that represented all of those interested in fighting for an improved food situation in the country, thereby creating strong and widespread foundations for building of sustained pressure. This pressure took the form of monitoring at the community level, as well as a continuous rounds of courtroom battles and lobbying in support of enabling legislation. The role of a progressive judiciary, which has been willing to hear petitions on ESCRs, has been instrumental in these struggles (Ahluwalia 2004). The judiciary's willingness to take a purposive and integrated approach to the interpretation of constitutional rights – thereby making it possible to use justiciable parts of the constitution to protect non-justiciable rights – has been widely acknowledged by many analysts as one of the contributing factors to the success of this struggle in India (Ahluwalia 2004; Courtis 2007; FAO 2011a; Knuth and Vidar 2011).

The combination of a more progressive judiciary, together with active civil society groups, has not only brought issues around food and other basic necessities into the limelight, it has ensured that these issues continue to be prioritised by the state at the national and district levels. As a result of constant pressure from the RFC network, and in the context of state failure to implement court orders, a Supreme Court Commission was set up specifically to monitor their implementation.

From this experience it is very clear that the campaign combines a number strategies, including: court action; protests; monitoring and documenting cases of non-compliance or intimidation; promoting community awareness of the right to food; promoting the right to information as a tool for effective monitoring; lobbying for appropriate legislation and policies; and media publicity and the uncovering of corrupt practices among those involved in running food programmes. The campaign can be said to have taken the fight for the right to food to various levels, which can be grouped into two broad categories: policy change and policy implementation. At the level of policy change, the campaign has involved engaging – and sometimes strategically working with – policy-makers, to ensure that the right policies and legislation are in place. But that is not sufficient to make the right to food a reality for many people; this requires going a step further to ensure that the policies and legislation adopted are implemented *effectively* and in accordance with the broader values that they embody. This has entailed involvement in another aspect of struggle to ensure that issues of hunger and poverty are not merely on the political agenda, but that they are given the priority and attention they deserve. This struggle for the right to food has involved constant battles on the streets, to parliament, via the courts, and back again (Patnaik 2011b).

Experience from the struggle in India suggests that a legal strategy alone is not sufficient to give effect to the right to food. The RFC case demonstrates that giving effect to the right to food is, broadly speaking, a political undertaking; little can be achieved without engaging in *realpolitik*. In a fundamental way the "battle for the right to food is a political battle that has to be fought on all fronts" (Patnaik 2011a: 31). In practice, this means that campaigning for human rights should not be limited to exerting pressure on the state to give attention to these rights; it fundamentally demands working to a broader vision of changing society with the aim of overcoming barriers that prevent people from living a life of dignity.

SERAC: Nigeria

While the Indian campaign relied on mobilisation of civil society groups as well as a progressive judiciary, other battles for human rights in general and the right to food in particular have relied on the legal route using regional bodies. The best example in this category is the Social and Economic Action Rights Centre (SERAC[4] – or the Ogoni case as it is widely known) in Nigeria. In this case a human rights NGO (SERAC) – after gathering sufficient evidence of the violation of human rights of the local community of Ogoni land by the multinational oil company (Shell Petroleum Development Corporation, or Shell for

4 SERAC brought the case to the ACHPR jointly with an American human rights NGO, the Centre for Economic and Social Rights (CESR), and relied on the Public Interest Litigation (*actio popularis*) principle.

short) – approached the African Commission on Human and People's Rights (ACHPR, henceforth the African Commission) to seek an urgent injunction to stop the Nigerian government and its partners from colluding to bring such a violation about. One of the most interesting effects of this case is that SERAC relied entirely on the *regional* human rights instruments – the *African Charter* – and not the Nigerian Constitution or the Nigerian courts.

Acknowledging a lack of domestic court action on the matter, the African Commission argued that since several communications concerning the alleged violations had been sent to the Nigerian government, but ignored, then "in the absence of a substantive response from the Respondent State [the African Commission] must decide on the facts provided by the Complainants and treat them as given" (SERAC 2001: para. 40). Here we see the African Commission demonstrating its willingness to hear cases even in situations where internal or local remedies had not been exhausted. However, addressing the requirement to exhaust local remedies, the African Commission argued that the

> purpose of the exhaustion of local remedies requirements is to give the domestic courts an opportunity to decide upon cases before they are brought to an international forum, thus avoiding contradictory judgements... Where a right is not well provided for in domestic law such that no case is likely to be heard, potential conflict does not arise. Similarly, if the right is not well provided for, there cannot be effective remedies, or any remedies at all. Another rationale for the exhaustion requirement is that a government should have notice of a human rights violation in order to have the opportunity to remedy such violations, before being called to account by an international court.
>
> SERAC: para. 37–8

So while, ultimately, the African Commission proved itself toothless in this case – and many victims of human rights abuses were frustrated by the fact that the Nigerian state ignored its decisions and remedies[5] (Hansungule 2009) – the creation of a forum, other than the national courts, in which violations of human rights could be heard and discussed has certainly been an unprecedented

5 The ACHPR was replaced by two courts: The African Court on Human and Peoples' Rights, which came into effect in 2004, and the Court of Justice of the African Union, established in 2003. In 2008 the two courts were merged to form the African Court of Justice and Human Rights, which has not yet come into force because although more than 15 countries have signed the protocol that establishes the court, very few have actually ratified the protocol – which is a requirement for the court to become operational.

achievement in Africa's human rights history. However, the problem of a lack of teeth is, as noted earlier, a general problem with international law.

In its communication to the African Commission, SERAC alleged that the Nigerian government "destroyed and threatened Ogoni food sources through a variety of means". It was further alleged that the government

> participated in irresponsible oil development that ... poisoned much of the soil and water upon which the Ogoni farming and fishing depended. In their raid on villages, Nigerian security forces...destroyed crops and killed farm animals. The security forces ... created a state of terror and insecurity that has made it impossible for many Ogoni villagers to return to their fields and animals. The destruction of farmlands, rivers, crops and animals ... created malnutrition and starvation among certain Ogoni Communities.
>
> SERAC: para. 9

SERAC argued that by engaging in such activities, the Nigerian government was in violation of Articles 2, 4, 14, 16, 18(1), 21 and 24 of the *African Charter*. The specific rights alleged to have been violated included the right to health, the right to a clean environment, the right to housing, and the right to adequate food. The African Commission ruled that by destroying fields, raiding communities, and polluting the soil by reckless oil drilling, the government of Nigeria had failed to fulfil its obligation to respect, promote, protect and fulfil these rights. In this case even the minimum obligation to respect the rights of the Ogoni people had not been met. Meeting the obligation to respect the right to adequate food in this case required that the Nigerian government refrain from activities which could lead to the Ogoni people failing to provide adequate food for themselves and their families.

The Nigerian government was adjudged to have failed in its responsibility to protect – via the actions of the Nigerian National Petroleum Company (NNPC, a major shareholder in Shell) – and to have participated in acts that led to the violation of the right to food for the Ogoni people. The obligation to protect in this instance required the Nigerian government to ensure that the activities of its agencies (or third parties) did not threaten access to food for local people. Thus, failure to regulate the actions of Shell and the NNPC – which resulted in the Ogoni people being unable to acquire adequate food for themselves – was a *prima facie* case of failure to comply with the obligation to protect.

However, although the African Commission found the Nigerian government in breach of the rights cited by the complainant, and although it appealed to the Nigerian government to ensure that the violation of these rights was halted, this appeal was ignored. But despite the fact that little concrete relief was provided in this particular case, the major achievement was that through this court action SERAC managed to bring human rights violations into the public domain not just in Nigeria, but globally. Furthermore, the ruling of the African Commission provided the moral force for future and further collective action to push the Nigerian government into paying greater attention to the rights in question.

Like the PUCL case in India, the court process and rulings served only to provide grounds and a basis for *further* action aimed at ensuring the state gives future attention to the right to food. In the PUCL case, this has involved relentless pressure being brought to bear in the matter of rights, and a constant merry-go-round of action and protest from the community filtering up via the courts to parliament, and then back again as the contest is played out. This supports the view that human rights are not given on a silver platter, but are the result of a long and protracted contest. Furthermore, evidence from the Indian and Nigerian cases confirms the view that reliance on court litigation alone is insufficient when it comes to giving effect to human rights, especially ESCRs. Constant vigilance and sustained pressure is a critical part of monitoring compliance with court orders.

Citizens Against Hunger and Poverty: Brazil

While some campaigns have combined court action with popular protests and agitation, there are other strategies that have relied largely on mobilising the support of the wider civil society to bring issues of hunger and the right to food into the public domain. One example of this is the Brazilian network of social movements under the umbrella of Citizens Action Against Hunger and Poverty and For Life, which started in 1993 and gained moment in 1999 when hunger became widespread in Brazil. Through the activities of this network of NGOs and social movements, issues of hunger were forced onto the political agenda, such that the 2002 election campaign adopted the campaign against hunger as the top priority of government. A wide network of civil society groups – including faith-based organisations, research institutions, social movements, trade unions and student unions – managed to influence the thinking and work of the state around hunger, leading to the ambitious Zero Hunger programme (*Fome Zero* in Portuguese).

The struggle was spearheaded by civil society groups way before the Inacio Lula da Silva government started to pay attention to issues of hunger and food security. The campaign gained momentum when Lula da Silva's was elected as president of Brazil in October 2002. During the election campaign Lula picked up the issue of hunger as one of his campaign pillars, promising the nation that if elected he would dedicate a great deal of effort towards overcoming hunger. In his subsequent victory speech Lula returned to the issue of eradicating hunger in Brazil, stating "If at the end of my mandate every Brazilian can eat three times a day, I will have fulfilled my life's mission" (cited in Takagi 2011: 55). In 2003, and working alongside various civil society groups, the government managed to re-establish the National Food and Nutrition Security Council (CONSEA) to oversee and coordinate the implementation of the Zero Hunger programme. Though the state often did not use the language of rights, it did acknowledge that access to food was a human right guaranteed under the Brazilian Constitution, and that the state held primary responsibility for ensuring that this right was realised for everyone.

The strong political will and commitment to end hunger in Brazil, together with strong civil society participation, ensured that priority was given to a wide array of programmes and policies that could make it possible for many people to realise the right to food (da Silva *et al.* 2011). As a result of widespread campaigns to raise awareness about hunger and poverty – spearheaded by civil society groups – broad public support was generated, built largely upon the strong realisation that eradicating hunger was a national issue and that this was not the responsibility of individuals or the state alone, but of everyone (Aranha 2011: 88). A massive campaign was launched to solicit the support and participation of all members of society. Not only did citizens participate in the rallies and workshops, they also participated in discussions surrounding public allocation of resources to the various programmes; and it has been reported that in the first year of its existence, recommendations from public meetings on the topic resulted in the allocation of US$1.8 billion to the Zero Hunger programme. In addition to these civil society groups, private corporations were asked to participate by contributing either money or in-kind assistance to the Fund for Combating and Eradicating Hunger (which was established in 2003). Private sector groups, together with individual citizens, donated food, money and other resources which were used in the fight against hunger (Takagi, 2011).

The dynamics of the Zero Hunger programme neatly illustrate the power that can be derived from securing a broad support base for a campaign to realise human rights, including the right to food. It is also evident from the Zero Hunger programme example that collective action need not be necessarily against the state; in certain situations the state can be a strategic ally in giving effect to human rights. In the case of the rights to water and food, the state has an enormous responsibility – as well as the means – to realise such rights, as long the commitment to them is sufficiently secured. The process of securing that commitment can be initiated and sustained via the sort of collective action that the state will find it difficult to ignore. As noted earlier, sufficiently cohesive collective action is a necessary requirement for driving the issues of access to water and food into the public discourse, as well as creating a situation which politicians will find difficult to ignore. Once there are clear indications of strong state commitment to a particular right, civil society groups can work strategically with it – at various levels, and in ways that improve capacity-building, training, and programme evaluation.

However, working with the state to give effect to the right to water or food should not lead to complacency; vigilance is always needed to keep the vision of genuine social change in focus. This means having the state as a strategic ally, while at the same time maintaining a safe distance from which it is still possible to criticise it when its actions or policies deviate from a course that makes genuine change possible. Experience from the Zero Hunger programme demonstrates that even if civil society groups are working together with the state in the fight against hunger, they can still remain alert to actions that run counter to this vision. For instance, many civil society groups have been able to remain critical of the Brazilian government's attempts to exclude some people from being beneficiaries of the Zero Hunger and other social security programmes (da Silva *et al.* 2011). Furthermore, a number of civil society groups have been alert to the possible bureaucratisation of the CONSEA as a result of its close association and cooperation with government structures (Aranha 2011). Nonetheless, the Zero Hunger programme is an example of a successful partnership between civil society and the state in the fight against a common cause: hunger. While the danger of civil society groups being co-opted by strong state actors remains, the partnership has recorded significant successes using methods that are being adapted in other countries and in other contexts (FAO 2006).

Serikat Petani Indonesia (SPI): Indonesia

Other than campaigns that have focused on specific rights, there are others which address a wide range of issues that have direct and indirect influence on the right to food. For instance, the Serikat Petani Indonesia (SPI) has sought to address the right to food by lobbying for the rights of peasants to land and water. The SPI's work, in this regard, has involved campaigns against land-grabbing which results in peasants losing their land and with it their ability to produce their own food. In one particular case, a multinational company which secured the lease of 2,386 hectares for sugar cane production is reported to be denying access to local villages to land inside the plantation boundaries. Local people who have resisted the land grab are reported to have been intimidated and victimised by the local police (Mann 2011). The SPI campaign, in this regard, is aimed at persuading the "authorities to respect the rights of peasants and indigenous Indonesians [so that they can] access the forest for the resources they need to sustain decent livelihoods" (ibid.: 19). In its struggle, the SPI has adopted a two-stage campaign which first of all involves lobbying the local state to enact laws that protect the rights of vulnerable groups living on the fringes of plantation forests. At this stage of the campaign, the SPI focuses on lobbying for changes to policies which do not respect or pay attention to the rights of peasants. The SPI has also taken its campaign to the United Nations level, where it has lobbied for the UN system to put pressure on the local state to ensure that it respects the rights of peasants and indigenous populations. Lobbying at the UN level is targeted at sympathetic UN agencies, the CESCR, and UN Committee members, as well as other international civil society or NGO groups which exert influence at the UN and national levels.

The Right to Water Strategies

Like the right to food, the struggles aimed at giving effect to the right to water have been adopted by different human rights advocates, activists and practitioners in various parts of the world. However, unlike the right to food, there have been fewer courtroom battles involving the right to water. Some analysts attribute this to the fact that the right to water was recognised at the international level only in 2002, but as there is only a three-year difference between the formal recognition of the right to food (1999) and the right to water (2002) it seems unlikely that this can account for the higher number of legal cases involving the right to food. A more convincing explanation is that there are fewer countries that recognise the right to water, directly, in their constitutions or framework laws. While more than 100 countries have, in some way, recognised the right to food in their constitutions (and many more in their national framework laws, see Chapter 6), fewer countries have directly mentioned water as a human right (see Chapter 5). The few that have *explicitly* mentioned water have done so in their directive principles of state policy, or of social and economic objectives[6] (see Scanlon *et al.* 2004: 42–6; Chitonge 2007: 156). In most cases the right to water is only *implied*, and as such it is derived from other rights such as the right to health, to a clean environment, to life, to housing,

6 For instance, Articles 14 (b) and 21 of the Ugandan Constitution provide for "clean and safe water" under its social and economic objectives section. Similarly, Article 90 (1) of the Ethiopian Constitution provides that "all Ethiopians [have] access to public health and education, clean water, housing, food and social security". Water is explicitly recognised in the Bill of Rights in the new Kenyan Constitution (2010, Article 43 (d)), the South African Constitution (1996, Section 27 (b)), and the Zambian draft Constitution (2012, Article 62 (1d)).

to a reasonable standard of living, or to food, etc. This is not only the case for domestic legal and statutory instruments – as noted in Chapter 5 the right to water in most international human rights instruments is only *implicitly* recognised. Thus, for human rights activists relying on the legal route to give effect to the right to water, the situation presents huge barriers. The fact that water is not explicitly recognised makes it difficult even to initiate public debates and campaigns, let alone mobilise support. As is the case with the right to food, in contexts where the right is not explicitly recognised, many human rights practitioners – including lawyers and judges – are reluctant to take up the baton – not because they do not want to, but because they have little experience of contesting outside the courtroom.

However, despite the low levels of recognition of water as a human right in domestic situations (both constitutionally and in domestic framework law), there have been an increasing number of civil society groups around the globe which are involved in various advocacy, lobbying and campaign activities, including the push for an explicit recognition of the right to water (WaterAid 2011). In many countries lobbying and advocacy work has been affected by this lack of recognition of the right to water – to the point that discourse around access to water is rarely formulated in the language of rights. This situation has affected both the procedural as well as the substantive elements of the right, making it difficult for civil society groups to actively participate and influence processes and decisions around how water is produced, distributed and accessed. Unlike the right to food, case law specifically generated to cover the right to water has been rare; cases that have involved access to water have largely come about in relation to the broader ESCRs. An exception is the *Mazibuko & Others v. City of Johannesburg*[7] case in South Africa where the right to water was specifically decided in the courts.

This was a case involving five[8] residents of the Phiri township (in Soweto), which falls under the Johannesburg Metro jurisdictional area. In an affidavit, the applicant stated that they were acting on their own behalf,

> as well as on behalf of our children and those aged members of our households who cannot bring this application themselves. We also bring this application on behalf of other residents of Phiri who are in the same position as we are, as well as in the public interest.
>
> FOUNDING AFFADAVIT 2006

7 *Mazibuko and Others v. City of Johannesburg* [2009] ZACC 28, (CCT39/09), BCLR.

8 In the Founding Affidavit (2006) there were seven applicants in 2006, but this number dropped to five by the time the case was heard in the Constitutional Court in September 2009 (see the Founding Affidavit, 2006).

Although this was a group of individuals acting on their own, we know that behind the scenes civil society groups and social movements were helping and encouraging them to challenge the City of Johannesburg's (CJ) decision to introduce pre-paid water meters and restrictions on free basic water (FBW) to only 25 litres per person per day (6 kilo-litres per household per month). The Anti-Privatisation Campaign (APC), a social movement based in Johannesburg, supported the applicants; as did another civil society organisation – the Centre on Housing Rights and Evictions – which played a crucial role in getting the case together and later entered the case as *amicus curiae* (friend of the court). Thus, although the formal applicantion was made by just five residents of the Phiri township, civil society groups would play a critical role in gathering the information needed to put the case together.

The applicants argued that the restriction of FBW to just 6 kilo-litres per household per month via Operation Gcin Amanzi (OGA),[9] was in contravention of Section 27 (1b) and Section 27 (2) of the South African Constitution. The applicants further argued that the 2003 installation of pre-paid water meters by Johannesburg Water (JW) in place of the flat rate system was not in line with Section 3 (1 and 2) of the Water Services Act 108 of 1997, which stipulated that "Everyone has the right of access to basic water supply and basic sanitation", and that "Every water services institution must take reasonable measures to realise these rights". The minimum basic service levels for water are specified in the National Water Standards Regulation No. 3, which sets the minimum standard of water services at "25 litres per person per day or 6 kilolitres per household per month". In making these arguments the applicants were asking the court to set aside OGA and instead provide them with an option for a metered connection. They also sought a court order to the effect that the City of Johannesburg should provide 50 litres of water per person per month, rather than the 25 litres per month that it had introduced (see Founding Affadavit 2006: para. 13).

The case started in the Johannesburg High Court which ruled in favour of the applicants. On appeal the Supreme Court of Appeal upheld most of the conclusions and decisions of the High Court. The City of Johannesburg

9 This is a Zulu phrase meaning "conserve water". OGA was linked to the pre-paid water system in that "[t]he prepayment water meters work on the basis that a household will only receive the 6,000 [6 kilo] litres free at the beginning of every month. Thereafter, there will be no water supply unless the consumer buys more water credits". According to a document provided by Johannesburg Water entitled "Special Projects: Prepayment Water Meter", the benefit of such a system would be that consumers could buy water "to suit their pockets" and that the cutting off of water supplies would "[not be] unexpected" (see Founding Affadavit 2006: para. 94).

appealed again and the case went to the Constitutional Court. It is not necessary here to review the arguments except to state that the Constitutional Court ruled that JW's policy did not in fact in conflict with either Section 27(1) or 27 (2) of the Constitution, or Section 3 (1 and 2) of the National Water Services Act, and as such did not violate the applicants' right to water.

Looking at the case, it is clear that without a clear recognition of the right to water provided by the Constitution, and followed up with clear framework laws and regulations, it is difficult to contest the right to water through the legal route. Without a clear stipulation of what constituted "minimum basic water services" it proved difficult to determine whether the service provider was in fact in compliance with regulation or not. However, as noted earlier, the legal route is not the only way to give effect to ESCRs such as the rights to water and food, and many civil society groups have used other means to ensure that the right to water becomes a reality, including by lobbying for the formal recognition of the right in the national constitution.

Water and Sanitation Civil Society Network in Africa

One example of civil society groups deploying a non-legal route in the struggle to give effect to the right to water is the African Civil Society Network on Water and Sanitation (ANEW), which was launched in 2007 in Nairobi during the World Social Forum. This is a continent-wide network of civil society groups and organisations working in the area of water supply and sanitation services, and which aims at supporting and strengthening African CSO capacity, commitment and participation in water governance and services management issues. The initiative to launch a continent-wide forum was motivated by the understanding that

> civil society in many parts of the world has been instrumental in water and sanitation provision, through its direct involvement in policy formulation through advocacy, participation in water resources development and management, campaigns for required national legislation and budgetary resources, public awareness raising, and empowerment of local communities through knowledge-sharing and capacity building. In Africa, a number of national and local initiatives instituted by various CSOs have gone a long way in providing safe water and adequate sanitation, especially in rural and slum areas.
>
> ANEW 2007

Many national civil society groups in Africa are members of ANEW and participate in the sharing of experiences, support and the strengthening of advocacy measures around water supply services and sanitation. A study conducted by ANEW to assess the capacity of national organisations working on issues of water and sanitation in Africa reported that the main concerns among such organisations include limited resources – financial, human and technical, and also challenges around "sustainability and scalability of their efforts" (ANEW 2007). As a result of of limited resources most of the organisations operate on a limited scale, usually confining their efforts to the major cities and towns, and unable to extend their work to other parts of the country.

Since this is a fairly new initiative it is too early to assess its actual impact on the right to water, although there is great potential to strengthen the capacity of civil society groups in Africa to play an active role in various processes including policy formulation, implementation, monitoring, evaluation and the gathering of information on the impact of water service policies and programmes. Sharing of experiences and resources will not only strengthen the capacity of members of ANEW, but may also lead to more coordinated responses to the challenges that these organisations face in their work at both national and continental levels.

Water and Sanitation Alliance: Zambia

An example of a local civil society member of ANEW is the Zambia Water and Sanitation Alliance (ZWASA), which was officially established in December 2007 with the aim of promoting the provision of safe and clean water and acceptable sanitation for all – especially the poor (ZWASA 2010). In its operations ZWASA has adopted a number of strategies, including lobbying for a formal recognition of the right to water in Zambia's draft Constitution,[10] promoting public debate on access to water in communities and schools, strategic engagements with decision-makers, promoting community participation in decision-making processes, and dissemination of information regarding the right to water. Although the current Zambian Constitution and framework law does not fully recognise the right to water, ZWASA has been using the language of rights to talk about water in communities, and in its advocacy and lobby work.

One of the lessons learned from working in the area of water and sanitation is that the right to water will be of no effect if people are not participating in the processes aimed at realising it, and that realising the right to water requires the existence of a solid institutional framework which can respond to the challenges of giving effect to the right. A study conducted in 2006–07 reported little or no

10 Zambia's new draft Constitution includes the right to water in its Bill of Rights. Article 62 (1d) states that "[a] person has a right to...clean and safe water in adequate quantity and quality and to a reasonable standard of sanitation".

civil society activity being conducted around the right to water, noting the conspicuous absence of public and media debate on the same issue (see Chitonge 2007). But it seems that the launching of a network of civil society groups and organisations (ZWASA) working on water- and sanitation-related issues has brought the debate into the public domain, especially in the case of the public submissions that were made during the drafting of the new Constitution. According to ZWASA, "more people are now debating water and sanitation rights in communities and schools which previously could only be perhaps heard in the corridors of parliament" (2010: 2). While it is too early to say what the impact of civil society initiatives will be in realising the right to water, the very fact that the public is now using the language of rights to talk about its provision creates a fertile ground for more advanced collective action in the future.

Dialogue Day: Mali

In Mali, civil society groups working in water- and sanitation-related areas have come together to initiate a Dialogue Day at which various governance issues, including water supply services, are heard and discussed in every local community. These public hearings are open to all people including local government authorities and provide space where citizens can express their views and sentiments on water services – spaces that were non-existent a few years earlier. Kolleen Bouchane, the Freshwater Action Network action and learning officer, explains how the Dialogue Day is organised:

> First, programme partners involve communities using two or three animators who visit villages to share information about the event and ask them to prepare questions or comments on WASH [water, sanitation and hygiene] services. A week later the animators [facilitators] return to collect the questions. The questions and comments are then sent to the local council and they are given two weeks to prepare their answers. [On the dialogue day] in front of the audience, the local council answers questions – the only day in the year when they have to do this. This is followed by a general discussion during which participants develop recommendations.
>
> BOUCHANE 2011: 27

While Dialogue Days provide the space for the community to engage with those responsible for delivering water services, including the mayor and other council officials, there are still many challenges that such initiatives have to address in terms of fulfilling the right to water. Participation rates are low, for various reasons, but chiefly because getting to the meetings can involve having to travel long distances. People also also take a lot of persuading to go in the first place, as Ould Dah of the WaterAid Policy Office, explains: "We need to persuade them [members of local communities] of the benefits of regular engagement with local government, to do more to, focus their attention. We are considering having dialogues on the local government quarterly report" (cited in Bouchane 2011: 27).

Also, although the Dialogue Days are chaired by a local civil society member, local government officials can often turn these spaces into talk shops – they come, they listen and then they go back to business as usual. Unless there is active and sustained collective pressure to make local government officials act with the awareness that there is someone watching what they are doing, such initiatives can become routine and a place where local officials merely fulfil their job description and an apparent duty of being being socially responsive. In order to "ensure that recommendations are implemented throughout the year, rather than just in the two months preceding the public hearing [i.e. the Dialogue Day], programme partners have pressed for the creation of multi-stakeholder Local Development Platforms [LDPs]" (ibid.: 28).

As is the case with ZWASA in Zambia, the impact of these initiatives in Mali are difficult to access given their short life span. But there are reports of regular engagements between the communities and local government officials resulting in improved trust and confidence between the two parties, with communities now feeling more confident about approaching local authorities about the problems they face. LDPs have created a means through which allocation, use and effectiveness of local resources can be monitored (ibid.). An important lesson from this experience points to the critical role of public involvement in the processes around the production, distribution and delivery of water services. It is through this involvement that spaces for contesting and claiming the right to water can be created, and public support for the right to water can be sustained. Multi-stakeholder platforms such as LDPs – where local authorities, communities, private service providers, civil society groups and social movements and marginalised people meet and engage – "can contribute to building political will and the appropriate design of reforms in water management, taking into account the various needs and rights of various groups" (SDC 2008: 7).

Budget Tracking: Tanzania

One common strategy that is used by many civil society organisations and groups to promote the right to water is engagement around the various national budgetary processes, including: lobbying for increased allocation of water services; tracking the use of allocated resources; dissemination of information to user networks on how resources are allocated at local level; and the holding of public hearings at which community members can express their views about the budget. One good example of this strategy in action is the Tanzania Civil Society Network on Water and Sanitation (TAWASANET). TAWASANET has, since 2006, combined budget analysis and tracking of the water and sanitation budget allocation to investigate whether equity principles are followed in the implementation of water services programmes. Budget analysis and tracking have also been used to investigate how the allocated resources are translated into tangible outcomes in both urban and rural areas (WaterAid 2010). By using central administration budget documents, together with fieldwork data collected through the use of Geographical Information Systems (GIS), TAWASANET has managed to carry out a spatial mapping process that marks the locations of water service facilities. These spatial maps help in the analysis of equitable supply issues by linking the allocation of resources to the actual water facilities in any given area. If more resources are allocated to areas that are already well-served, this raises issues of equity and discrimination which may be in conflict with basic human rights principles. In cases where this is proved, the state should justify that such action was reasonable.

This strategy has proved successful in highlighting water service issues at the national level in many parts of the developing world, and also as a way of lobbying for increased resource allocations to sectors which have often been neglected (see Chitonge 2007). When deployed by an active civil society corpus, this strategy can contribute significantly to creating an environment in which the chances of realising the right to water are improved. Drawing from the Nepalese experience, it has been reported that

> [t]his tactic has contributed to successes for the sector, including securing a separate budget head for sanitation. Supported with evidence from rapid analysis of the new budget, as well as previous analyses, the policy messages (including "One House, One Toilet") were welcomed, while implementation of the policy was challenged.
>
> WATERAID 2010: 37

One main drawback in using this strategy is that budget analysis and tracking requires middle-level skills that many civil society groups and social movements may not have access to. Furthermore, national budgets are complex and politically exclusive processes, with most of the decisions taking place behind closed doors, making it difficult for civil society to actively engage in the process (WaterAid 2011: 26). However, where spaces and capacity for tracking budgets are available, they present an invaluable opportunity.

Anti-Privatisation Strategy: Uruguay, Brazil, Venezuela, Bolivia and Mexico

Another common strategy used by many civil society groups and social movements in their effort to realise the right to water is the campaign against the privatisation of water services. The underlying reason for this strategy is that it is difficult to realise the right to water for many poor people if water is provided just like any other non-essential commodities – like mobile phone units or fuel. Supporters of the anti-privatisation movement argue that the private sector's exaggerated concern about efficiency overlooks issues of equity that should be at the heart of the right to water. Central to the debate is the moral argument that water is not like any other commodity: it is thus too "special or precious" to be treated as if it were (AEFJN 2003; Jolly 1998; Petrella 2001). It is also argued that private operators' preoccupation with profit often serves to exclude the poor from major decisions concerning pricing and investment, This runs contrary to the principles of non-discrimination and equality embraced by international human rights, as noted in Chapter 3. It is further argued that privatisation of water services amounts to dispossession, and often leads to the unequal distribution of water (Bond 2004; Swyngedouw 2005), making it difficult to give effect to the right to it. The anti-privatisation campaigns also point out that the lack of provision of water to poor areas by the private water companies often does not receive the attention it merits, resulting in the right to water not being realised for many. This argument is supported by wide experience that demonstrates private service providers are often not interested in servicing low income areas because of alleged low returns on investment (Njiru 2004; UNDP 2006). This is seen as contrary to the widely accepted notion that water is a human right, and as such should be distributed equitably and without discrimination.

The anti-privatisation strategy has been most commonly used in Latin America, in countries such as Venezuela, Bolivia, Brazil, Uruguay and Mexico. In Uruguay, a network of social movements called the National Commission in Defence of Water and Life (CNDAV) was established in 2002 in response to the Uruguayan government's agreement with the IMF to privatise water and sewerage services. CNDAV began a campaign against the plan and in 2003 collected 283,000 signatures, which were submitted to parliament as evidence of the strength of feeling against privatisation (Santos and Villareal 2006). According to CNDAV, and because of the massive social mobilisation against the plan, the Uruguayan government was forced to cancel most of the contracts that had already been awarded to a number of private companies.

A similar strategy was adopted in the Brazilian city of Porto Alegre, where civil society groups campaigned against a move there to privatise water services. The campaign advocated instead for a public service provider. A public water utility company, DMAE, was established instead, and it is reported that the utility has been financially sustainable, accountable, environmentally responsible, and has extended water services to poorer areas of the city (Maltz 2005). In Caracas, Venezuela, the Water Communal Council, set up in 1999 by the then newly elected president Hugo Chavez, and comprising civil society groups including trade unions, student movements, environmentalists, human rights activists, academics and neighbourhood associations, engineered the creation of the public water utility HYDROCAPOTAL, which is now responsible for providing water services. The council has been maintained as the forum through which the community can participate and exercise control on matters relating to water services. The main task of the council is envisioned as "exert[ing] social control over the public company" (Rodriguez 2005). Such initiatives have been offered as alternative models to privatisation, though some analysts are sceptical about their viability in other parts of the world.

Lessons and Strategies

What the case studies on the rights to water and food demonstrate is that there are various ways of giving effect to these rights. Which particular strategy to adopt depends very much on what is possible in a particular context. It also means that strategies aimed at promoting these rights need not be the same everywhere, and what has worked in one context may not work in another. A more flexible and integrated approach is most likely to be effective. As a number of the above examples show, it is often essential to combine several strategies to realise these rights. The experience of the human rights strategies reviewed above shows that information-sharing and learning lessons from what works and what doesn't can provide guidance and encouragement for the future.

There are, of course, many strategies that human rights activists, civil society groups, social movements and practitioners are using to promote the realisation of human rights and social change; but broadly speaking there are four common ones that are associated with ESCRs such as the rights to water and food (Patnaik 2011a). One strategy that has been used in a number of countries is to combine both international and domestic provisions concerning a particular right to then seek protection for it. In many cases the complainant relies on domestic law, but also cites international human rights instruments to strengthen their case.

Another strategy is to rely entirely on international human rights instruments, particularly regional ones. This approach is mainly used in cases where domestic law does not adequately or directly protect the right in question. An example of this is the Ogoni case in Nigeria, cited above.

A third strategy is to seek the intervention of a quasi-judicial body including the UNCESCR, national human rights commissions, or the ombudsman in countries where these exist. A fourth strategy commonly used by NGOs and other civil society groups is the parallel reporting mechanism provided for by the CESCR, which allows civil society groups to send separate country reports highlighting the plight of human rights in a particular country. Under this mechanism, local and international civil society groups are invited to submit reports on a particular country, and the report can focus on particular rights such as the right to water or the right to food. Parallel reports "by civil society are especially valuable and influential if they contain a comprehensive analysis of the status of ESCR in the country in question" (Patnaik 2011a: 32).

Despite the numerous challenges around giving effect to the right to food, especially in the Global South, there are many activists and practitioners who are using human rights instruments and language as the basis for their actions in the courtrooms, the streets, the boardrooms, the roundtables and the parliamentary caucuses. Indeed

> thousands of victims [and human rights activists] have used at least one of these ways of seeking remedies for violations of the right to food. In many cases, their effort led to small but real improvements. In a few cases – for example in the Ogoni case – the impact was minor or non-existent. [But] one of the most important tasks for the right to food defenders in the years to come will be to share more information about these different cases and try to understand why some succeeded and others failed to improve the effective enjoyment of the right to food.
>
> GOLAY N.D.: 17

In all these strategies, whether they involve courtroom or street battles, or lobbying at roundtable meetings, the basic aim of civil society action is to lift human rights issues into the public domain and use this as a tool for social change. Once the issue is in the public domain, it is then possible to mobilise support to create the critical mass needed to take the struggle to the next level. Crucial in all these strategies is an active civil society (whatever form it might take) which takes the initiative in bringing a particular human right to public attention. Interestingly, in almost all of the cases mentioned in this chapter, the involvement of civil society has been crucial. Whether it is a case of lobbying for enabling framework law on the right to food in Malawi, or submitting a petition to court in India, or whether it be mobilising support for the fight against hunger in Brazil, civil society groups of one form or another initiate the process and sustain it. Empirical evidence from different countries confirms the indispensability of civil society at every stage of the struggle for human rights, especially in the initial ones.

Bibliography

Africa-Europe Faith and Justice Network (AEJN, 2003). "Water a Right for All! Privatisation of Water and Sanitation Services in Africa." *Action Plan*.

African Civil Society Network on Water and Sanitation (ANEW, 2007). "Analysis of Water and Sanitatian Policies and Status of IWRM in Africa: Advocacy Capacity and Assessment of African Civil Society on Water Supply and Sanitation." *Summary Report*. Available at: http://freshwateraction.net/sites/freshwateraction.net/files/ANEW (accessed 25 March 2013).

African Commission on Human and People's Rights (ACHPR, 2001, final decision). *Social and Economic Action Rights Centre (SERAC) v. the Federal Republic of Nigeria*, 27 May 2001, (ACHPR/COMM/A044/1).

African Network for the Promotion of the Right to Food (ANPRF, 2008). *Report on the Workshop Proceedings on the Launching of the African Network for the Promotion of the Right to Food*, held at Palais des Congres, Cotonou Benin. July 9–11, 2008.

Ahluwalia, Pooja (2004). "Implementation of the Right to Food at the National Level: A Critical Examination of the Indian Campaign on the Right to Food as an Effective Operationalization of Article 11 of ICESCR." Centre for Human Rights and Global Justice Working Paper No. 8. New York University School of Law, New York, USA.

Alston, Philip (1979). "The Right to Development at the International Level" in Dupuy, Rene-Jean (ed.) *Workshop on The Right to Development at the International Level*. The Hague: Sijthoff & Noordhoff. 99–114.

Alston, Philip (1984). "International Law and the Human Right to Food" in P. Alston and K. Tomasevski (eds). *The Right to Food*. Leiden: Martinus Nijhoff. 9–68.

Alston, Philip (1988). "International Law and the Right to Food" in A. Eide, W. Barth Eide, S. Goonatilake, J. Gussow and Omawale (eds). *Food as a Human Right* (2nd edition). Kuala Lumpar: United Nations University. 162–174.

Alston, Phillip and Quinn, Gerald (1987). "The Nature and Scope of States Parties' Obligations under the International Covenant on Economic, Social and Cultural Rights." *Human Rights Quarterly*. Vol. 9, No. 2. 156–229.

Alston, Philip and Robinson, Mary (2005). "The Challenges of Ensuring the Mutuality of Human Rights and Development Endeavours" in P. Alston and M. Robinson (eds). *Human Rights and Development: Towards Mutual Reinforcement*. Oxford: Oxford University Press. 1–19.

Andreasson, A. Bard (2003). "Shifting Notions of Development – Implications for the Right to Development?" *The Right to Development: Reflections on the First Four Reports of the Independent Expert on the Right to Development*. Geneva: SIDA.

Annan, Kofi (1997). "Address at the University of Tehran on Human Rights Day." *Electronic Journals of the United States Information Agency*. Vol. 3, No. 3. 22–24.

Aranha, Viega Adriana (2011). "Project Turned into a Government Strategy" in J.G. da Silva, M.E. del Grossi and C.G. de Franca (eds). *The Fome Zero (Zero Hunger Programme): The Brazilian Experience.* Brasilia: Ministry of Agrarian Development. 87–112.

Aristotle (2000). *The Politics of Aristotle* (Translated with Introduction, Notes and Appendices by Ernest Barker). London: Oxford University Press.

Arts, Karin (1996). "Implementing the Right to Development? An Analysis of European Community Development and Human Rights Policies" in Baer P. Sadiwa, L. and Smith, J. (eds). *Human Rights in Developing Countries: Year Book 1996.* The Hague: Kluwer Law International.

Ashworth, Andrew and Steiner, Eva (1990). "Criminal Omissions and Public Duties: the French Experience." *Legal Studies*, 10. 153–164.

Bakker, Karen (2007). "The 'Commons' versus the 'Commodity': Alter-globalisation, Anti-globalisation and the Human Right to Water in the Global South." *Antipode.* Vol. 39, Issue 3. 430–455.

Balanya, Belen, Brennan Brid, Hoedeman, Olivier, Kishimoto, Satoko and Terhorst, Philip (2005). "Reclaiming Public Water: Achievements, Struggles and Visions from Around the World." Published by Transnational Institute (TNI) and Corporate Europe Observatory (CEO). Available at: www.corporateeurope.org (accessed 21 August 2006).

Banik, Dan (2008). " Rights, Legal Empowerment and Poverty: An Overview of the Issues" in Banik (ed.) *Rights and Legal Empowerment in Eradicating Poverty.* Surrey, UK: Ashgate.

Barth, Eide, W. and Kracht, U. (2005). *Food and Human Rights in Development: Legal and Institutional Dimensions and Selected Topics.* Antwerpen: Intersentia.

Baxi, Upendra (2006). "Amartya Sen and Human Rights." *Paper Presented at the Human Rights and Global Conference, 29–31 March 2006.* University of Warwick, UK.

Bedjaoui, Mohammed (1991a). "General Introduction" in Bedjaoui, Mohammed (ed.) *International Law: Achievements and Prospects.* Paris: Martinus Nijhoff. 1–23.

Bedjaoui, Mohammed (1991b). "The Right to Development" in Bedjaoui, Mohammed (ed.) *International Law: Achievements and Prospects.* Paris: Martinus Nijhoff. 1177–1204.

Bentham, Jeremy (1987 [1816]). "Anarchical Fallacies" in Waldron Jeremy (ed.) *Nonsense Upon Stilts: Bentham, Burke and Marx on the Rights of Man.* London/New York: Methuen. 46–76.

Biswas, K. Asit (1997). "Mar del Plata: Twenty Years Later – Concluding Remark." Mar del Plata 20-year Anniversary Seminar, organised by the Stockholm Water Institute, Stockholm, August 1997. Available at: http://www.siwi.org/documents/Resources/Reports/Report1_Mar_del_Plata_1997.pdf (accessed 23 September 2007).

Bond, Patrick (2004). "The Economics of Water Resources Allocation." *Encyclopedia of Water*, New York: Wiley.

Bond, Patrick (2005). "Globalisation/Commodification or Deglobalisation/Decommodification in Urban South Africa." *Policy Studies*. Vol. 26, Nos. 3–4. 337–58.

Bond, Patrick (2006). "Water Commodification: Can Human Rights Trump the Market?" *Asian Exchange*. Vol. 21–22, Nos. 1–2. 39–62.

Booth, Ken (1999). "Three Tyrannies" in Dunne, Tim and Wheeler, Nicholas (eds). *Human Rights in Global Politics*. Cambridge, UK: Cambridge University Press. 31–70.

Booysen, Susan (2004). "The Effect of Privatisation and Commercialisation of Water Services on the Right to Water: Grassroots Experience in Lukhanji and Amahlati." Research Report conducted for the Community Law Centre. Western Cape, South Africa: University of Western Cape. August 2004.

Bouchane, Kolleen (2011). Learning from Experience: Rights and Governance Advocacy in the Water and Sanitation Sector. Freshwater Action Netwrok/WaterAid. Available at: www.freshwateraction.net/governance (accessed 25 March 2013).

Brooks, David (2006). "Modern Views of Water Scarcity: The Theoretical Base for Water Soft Path." *Friends of the Earth*. Available at: www.foecanada.org (accessed 22 June 2006).

Brother, Mona (2008). "Legal Empowerment as a New Concept in Development: Translating Good Ideas into Action" in D. Banik (ed.) *Rights and Legal Empowerment in Eradicating Poverty*. Surrey, UK: Ashgate. 45–65.

Brouwer, Marjolein, Grady, Heather, Traore, Valerie and Wordofa, Dereje (2005). "The Experience of Oxfam International and Its Affiliates in Rights-Based Programming and Campaigning" in Paul Gready and Jonathan Ensor (eds). *Reinventing Development: Translating Rights-Based Approaches From Theory into Practice*. London/New York: Zed Books. 63–78.

Brown, Chris (1999). "Universal Human Rights: A Critique" in Dunne, T. and Wheeler, N. (eds). *Human Rights in Global Politics*. Cambridge, UK: Cambridge University Press. 103–27.

Brown, Michael (2008). "Cultural Relativism 2.0." *Current Anthropology*. Vol. 49, No. 3. 363–73.

Calaguas, Belinda (1999). "The Right to Water, Sanitation and Hygiene and the Rights-Based Approach to Development." WaterAid Briefing Paper.

CARE International (2007). "The Impact of Rights-Based Approaches to Development: Evaluation/Learning Process." Bangladesh, Malawi and Peru.

Chambers, Robert (1983). *Rural Development: Putting the Last First*. Essex: Longman Scientific & Technology.

Chapman, Jennifer, Miller, Valerie, Soares, Adriano and Samuel, John (2005). "Rights-Based Development: The Challenge of Change and Power." Paper presented at the Global Poverty Research Group Conference: "The Winners and Losers from Rights-Based Approach to Development," Institute for Development Management, University of Manchester, Manchester, UK. 21–22 February 2005.

Cheng, Bin (1991). "Introduction to Subjects of International Law" in Bedjaoui, Mohammed (ed.) *International Law: Achievements and Prospects*. Paris: Martinus Nijhoff. 23–40.

Chileshe, Paxina, Trottier, Julie and Wilson, Lean (2005). "Translation of Water Rights and Water Management in Zambia." Paper presented at the International Workshop on African Water Laws: "Plural Legislative Framework for Rural Water Management in Africa." 26–28 January 2005, Johannesburg, South Africa.

Chitonge, Horman (2005): "The Right to Development Discourse in the Context of Global Inequality." Unpublished MA thesis, University of KwaZulu-Natal.

Chitonge, Horman (2006). "The Role of Civil Society in New Development Approaches." Available at: http://ccs.ukzn.ac.za/files/Chitonge%20development%20rights.pdf (accessed 12 March 2014).

Chitonge, Horman (2007). "Exploring the Challenges of Implementing a Rights-Based Approach to Development: The Case of the Right to Water in Peri-Urban Zambia." Unpublished PhD thesis, University of KwaZulu-Natal.

Chitonge, Horman (2007). *Focus Group Discussions*, Lusaka (on CD-ROM).

Chitonge, Horman (2007). Interviews with Policy Makers in the Water Sector in Zambia (on CD-ROM).

Chitonge, Horman (2011). "A Decade of Implementing Water Services Reforms in Zambia: Review of Outcomes, Challenges and Opportunities." Water Alternatives. Vol. 4, No. 3. Available at www.water-alternatives.org (accessed 23 October 2011).

Cohen, Marc and Brown, A. Mary (2008). "Legal Empowerment and the Right to Food" in D. Banik (ed.) *Rights and Legal Empowerment in Eradicating Poverty*. Surrey: Ashgate. 131–54.

Collier, Paul (2008). "The Politics of Hunger: How Illusion and Greed Fan the Food Crisis." *Foreign Affairs*. Vol. 87, No. 6. 67–79.

Committee on Economic Social and Cultural Rights (CESCR, 1990). *General Comment 3: The Nature of States Parties Obligations*.

Committee on Economic Social and Cultural Rights (CESCR, 1998). *General Comment 9: Domestic Application of the Covenant*. Committee on Economic, Social and Cultural Rights.

Committee on Economic Social and Cultural Rights (CESCR, 1999). *General Comment 12: The Right to Adequate Food*. Committee on Economic, Social and Cultural Rights 20th Session.

Committee on Economic Social and Cultural Rights (CESCR, 2000). *General Comment 14: The Right to the Highest Attainable Standard of Health*. Committee on Economic, Social and Cultural Rights, 22nd Session.

Committee on Economic Social and Cultural Rights (CESCR, 2002). *General Comment 15: The Right to Water*. E/C.12/2002/11.

Conway, Tim, Caroline Moser, Andy Norton and John Farrington (2002). "Rights and Livelihood Approaches: Exploring Policy." *Natural Resources Perspectives* (ODI). No. 78, May: 1–6.

Coomans, Fons (2007). "Application of the International Covenant on Economic, Social and Cultural Rights in the Framework of International Organisation" in A. von Bogdandy and R. Wolfrum (eds.) *Max Planck Yearbook of United Nations Law.* Vol. II. Amsterdam: Brill. 359–390.

Corbin, Arthur (2005). "Foreword" in Hohfeld, N. Wesley (ed.) (1919) *Fundamental Legal Conceptions as Applied in Judicial Reasoning* (edited by Walter Cook). New Jersey: Lawbook Exchange.

Corder, Hugh (2002). "Reviewing Review: Much Achieved, Much More to Do" in Hugh Corder and L. Vijver (eds). *Realising Administrative Justice.* Cape Town: Siber Ink: 1–18.

Courtis, Christian (2007). "The Right to Food as a Justiciable Right: Challenges and Strategies." *Max Planck Year Book of United Nations Law.* Vol. 11. 317–337.

Craig, David and Porter, Dough (2003). "Poverty Reduction Strategy Papers: A New Convergence." *World Development.* Vol. 31, No. 1. 53–69.

Cranston, Maurice (1973). *What are Human Rights?* London: The Bodley Head.

Cruz, Luisa (2011). *Report of the Special Rapporteur on the Right to Food on his Mission to South Africa (7–15 July, 2012).* A/HRC/19/59/Add.3.

da Silva, Jose Graziano, Mauro Eduardo del Grossi and Cia Galvao de Franca (2011). "The Zero Hunger Project: A Proposal for a Food Security Policy for Brazil" in J.G. da Silva, M.E. del Grossi and C.G. de Franca (eds). *The Fome Zero (Zero Hunger Programme): The Brazilian Experience.* Brasilia: Ministry of Agrarian Development. 13–40.

Danino, Robert (2005). "The Legal Aspects of the World Bank's Work on Human Rihgts" in P. Alston and M. Robinson (eds.) *Human Rights and Development: Towards Mutual Reinforcement.* Oxford: Oxford University Press. 509–524.

de Albuquerque, Catarina (2012). "Statement by the Special Raporteur on the Right to Safe Drinking Water and Sanitation at the 67th Session of the General Assembly of the UN." Available at: www.ohchr.org (accessed 14 March 2013).

de Schutter, Oliver (2012a). "Countries Tackling Hunger with a Right to Food Approach." United Nations Special Rapporteur on the Right to Food, Briefing Note 1. May 2010.

de Schutter, Oliver (2012b). *Report of the Special Rapporteur on the Right to Food on His Mission to South Africa (7–15 July, 2011).* A/HRC/19/59/add.3

De Waal, Johan, Iain Currie and Gerhaed Erasmus (2001). *The Bills of Rights Hand Book* (4th editon). Cape Town: Juta.

Delvin, Patrick (1983). "Moral Enforcement" in Beauchamp, T. and Pinkard, T. (eds). *Ethics and Public Policy.* New Jersey: Prentice-Hall. 51–61.

Dennis, Michael and Stewart, David (2004). "Justiciability of Economic, Social and Cultural Rights: Should there be an International Complaints Mechanism to Adjudicate the Rights to Food, Water, Housing and Health?" *American Journal of International Law.* Vol. 98, No. 3. 462–515.

Dias, Clarence (2002). "No Development Without Human Rights." *United Nations Chronicles.* Vol. 30, No. 3.

Dinar, Ariel, Rosegrant, Mark and Meinzen-Dick, Ruth (n.d.). "Water Allocation Mechanism – Principles and Examples." Policy Research Working Paper, No. 1779.

Diokno, Maria Socono (1999). "A Rights-Based Approach Towards Budget Analysis available at http://www.crin.org/docs/resources/publications/hrbap/RBABudgetAnalysis.pdf accessed 19.07.06." Paper commissioned by the International Human Rights Internship Programme.

Donald, Alice and Mottershaw, Elizabeth (2009). "Poverty Inequality and Human Rights: Do Human Rights Make a Difference?" Joseph Rowntree Foundation. Available at: www.jrf.org.uk (accessed 27 February 2012).

Donnelly, Jack (1984). "The 'Right to Development': How Not to Link Human Rights and Development" in Welch, C. and Meltzer, R. (eds). *Human Rights and Development in Africa*. New York: State University of New York Press. 261–84.

Donnelly, Jack (1989). *Universal Human Rights in Theory and Practice*. New York/London: Cornell University Press.

Donnelly, Jack (2006). "Cultural Relativism and Universal Human Rights" in C. Heyns and K. Stefiszyn (eds). *Human Rights, Peace and Justice in Africa: A Reader*. Pretoria: PULP. 96–106.

Drèze, Jean (2005). "Democracy and the Right to Food" in P. Alston and M. Robinson (eds). *Human Rihgts and Development: Towards Mutual Reinforcement*. Oxford: Oxford University Press. 45–64.

Dubreuil, Celine (2006). "Synthesis on the Right to Water – 4th World Water Forum, Mexico." World Water Council. Available at: www.worldwaterconcil.org (accessed 2 April 2007).

Dugard, John (2000). *International Law: A South African Perspective*, 2nd edition. Cape Town: Justa.

Dworkin, Ronald (1977). *Taking Rights Seriously*. London: Duckworth.

Elman, R. Service (1966). *The Hunters*. Englewood Cliffs: Prentice-Hall.

Eyben, Rosalind (2005). "Donors, rights-based approaches and implications for global citizenship: a case study from Peru" in Kabeer, N. (ed.). *Inclusive Citizenship*. London: Zed Books. 251–68.

Falkenmark, Malin (1999). "Forward to the Future: A Conceptual Framework for Water Dependence" (Volvo Environmental Prize Lecture 1998). *Ambio*. Vol. 28, No. 4. 356–61.

Feinburg, Joe (1973). *Social Philosophy*. Englewood Cliffs, NJ: Prentice-Hall.

Finnis, John (1980). *Natural Law and Natural Rights*. Oxford: Clarendon Press.

Fletcher, A. William (1981). "The Discretionary Constitutional Institutional Remedies and Judicial Legitimacy." *Yale Law Journal*. Vol. 91, No. 4: 635–97.

Fletcher, P. George (1996). *Basic Concepts of Legal Thought*. New York, Oxford: Oxford University Press.

Food and Agriculture Organisation (FAO, 2004). *A Report on the Intergovernmental Working Group for the Elaboration of a Set of Voluntary Guidelines to Support the*

Progressive Realisation of the Right to Adequate Food in the Context of National Food Security. Rome: FAO. Available at: ftp://ftp.fao.org/docrep/fao/meeting/008/j2475e.pdf (accessed 5 March 2013).

Food and Agriculture Organisation (FAO, 2005). *Voluntary Guidelines to Support the Progressive Realization of the Right to Adequate Food in the Context of National Food Security*. Rome: FAO.

Food and Agriculture Organisation (FAO, 2006). *The Right to Food Guidelines: Information Papers and Case Studies*. Rome: FAO.

Food and Agriculture Organisation (FAO, 2009). *The Right to Food and Access to Justice: Examples at the National, Regional and International Levels*. Rome: FAO.

Food and Agriculture Organisation (2011a). *Right to Food: Making it Happen – Progress and Lessons Learned Through Implementation*. Rome: FAO. Available at: http://www.fao.org/docrep/014/i2250e/i2250e.pdf (accessed 17 April 2013).

Food and Agriculture Organisation (FAO, 2011b). *Crop Prospects and Food Production, No. 1*. Rome: FAO.

Food and Agriculture Organisation (FAO, 2012). *The State of Food and Agriculture: Investing in Agriculture for a Better Future*. Rome: FAO.

Food and Agriculture Organisation (FAO, 2014). *World Cereal Production in 2014 to Surpass the Record in 2013*. Available at: http://www.fao.org/worldfoodsituation/csdb/en/ (accessed 12 November 2014).

Food and Agriculture Organisation and International Fund for Agricultural Development (FAO/IFAD, 2014). *The State of Food Insecurity in the World*. Rome: FAO/IFAD.

Freeden, Michael (1991). *Rights*. Buckingham, UK: Open University Press.

Gathii, T. James (1999). "Good Governance as a Counter Insurgence Agenda to Oppositional and Transformative Social Projects in International Law." *Buffalo Human Rights Law Review*. Vol. 5, 111–51.

Gaventa, John (2002). "Introduction: Exploring Citizenship, Participation and Accountability." *Institute for Development Studies Bulletin*. Vol. 32, No. 2. 1–18.

Gawanas, Bience (2009). "The African Union: Concepts and Implementation Mechanism Relating to Human Rights" in A. Bosl and J. Diescho (eds). *Human Rights in Africa: Legal Perspectives on their Protection and Promotion*. Windhoek, Namibia: Macmillan. 135–62.

Gewirth, Alan (1982). *Reason and Morality*. Chicago: University of Chicago Press.

Gewirth, Alan (1996). *The Community of Rights*. Chicago/London: University of Chicago Press.

Ghai, P.D., Khan, A.R., Lee, H.L.E and Alfthan, T. (1977). *The Basic Needs Approach to Development: Some Issues Regarding Concepts and Methodology*. Geneva: International Labour Organisation.

Ghazi, Baharm (2005). *The IMF, The World Bank Group and the Question of Human Rights*. Leiden: Brill.

Gleick, H. Peter (1998). "The Human Right to Water." *Water Policy*. Vol. 1. 487–503.

Gleick, Peter, Lucy Allen, Michel J. Cohen, Heather Cooley, Jason Christian-Smith, Matthew Heberger, Jason Morrison, Meena Palaniappan and Paul Schulte (2011). *The World's Water*. Vol. 7. Washington DC: Island Press.

Gleick, Peter (1996). "Basic Water Requirements for Human Activities: Meeting Basic Needs." *Water International*. Vol. 21. 83–92.

Golay, Christopher and Ozden, Melik (no date of publication in the cited paper). *The Right to Food: A Fundamental Human Right Affirmed by the United Nations and Recognised in Regional Treaties and Numerous National Constitutions*. Europe-Third World Centre (CETIM) Human Rights Programme Series. Available at: http://www.cetim.ch/en/documents/Br-alim-A4-ang.pdf (accessed 12 February 2013).

Gready, Paul (2008). "Rights-Based Approach to Development: What is the Value Added?" *Development in Practice*. Vol. 18, No. 6. 735–47.

Gready, Paul and Ensor, Jonathan (2005). "Introduction" in P. Gready and J. Ensor (eds). *Reinventing Development: Translating Rights-Based Approaches from Theory into Practice*. London/New York: Zed Books. 1–46.

Gustavsson, Jenny, Christel Cederberg, Ulf Sonesson, Robert van Otterdijk and Alexandre Meybeck (2011). *Global Food Losses and Food Waste: Extent, Causes and Prevention*. Rome: Swedish Institute for Food and Biotechnology (SIK) and FAO.

Hafner-Burton, Emilie and Tsutsui, Kiyoteru (2005). "Human Rights in a Globalising World: The Paradox of Empty Promises." *American Journal of Sociology*. Vol. 110, No. 5: 1373–1411.

Hafner-Burton, Emilie and Ron, James (2007). "Human Rights Institutions: Rhetoric and Efficacy." *Journal of Peace Research*. Vol. 44, No. 4. 379–383.

Hall, David and Lobina, Emmanuel (2006). "Pipe Dream: The Failure of the Private Sector to Invest in Water Services in Developing Countries." PSIRU/PSI/WDM. Available at: www.wdm.org.uk accessed 17 November 2006).

Hansugule, Michelo (2009). "African Courts and the African Commission on Human and People's Rights" in A. Bosl and J. Diescho (eds). *Human Rights in Africa: Legal Perspectives on their Protection and Promotion*. Windhoek: Macmillan. 233–71.

Hansungule, Michelo (2004). "Human Rights and Constitutional Practice: International Human Rights Law." Lecture Notes, Centre for Human Rights. Pretoria, South Africa: University of Pretoria.

Hart, H.L.A. (1963). *Law, Liberty and Morality*. London: Oxford University Press.

Hart, H.L.A (1982). *Essays on Bentham: Jurisprudence and Political Theory*. Oxford, UK: Clarendon Press.

Hart, H.L.A (1983). *Essays in Jurisprudence*. New York: Claredon, UK: Oxford Press.

Hart, H.L.A. (1994 [1961]). *The Concept of Law*. Oxford, UK: Clarendon Press.

Harvey, David (2000). *Spaces of Hope*. Edinburgh, UK: Edinburgh University Press.

Hathaway, Oona (2002). "Do Human Rights Treaties Make a Difference?" *Yale Law Journal*. Vol. III. 1935–2042.

Haugen, M. Hans (2007). *The Right to Food and TRIPS Agreement.* Leiden, Boston: Martinus Nijhoff.

Heyns, Christof (2006). "'Struggle Approach' to Human Rights" in C. Heyns and K. Stefiszyn (eds). *Human Rights, Peace and Justice in Africa: A Reader.* Pretoria: PULP. 15–35.

Hinz, Manfred (2009). "Human Rights between Universalism and Cultural Relativism? The Need for Anthropological Jurisprudence in the Globalising World" in A. Bosl and J. Diescho (eds). *Human Rights in Africa: Legal Perspectives on their Protection and Promotion.* Windhoek, Namibia: Macmillan. 3–32.

Hodgson, Stephen (2004). "Land and Water – the Rights Interface." FAO Legal Papers Online, para. 36. Available at: www.fao.org/legal/publication (accessed 18 September 2005).

Hohfeld, N. Wesley (2005 [1919]). *Fundamental Legal Conceptions as Applied in Judicial Reasoning.* (Edited by Walter Cook). New Jersey: Lawbook Exchange.

Horn, Nico (2009). "Human Rights Education in Africa" in A. Bosl and J. Diescho (eds). *Human Rights in Africa: Legal Perspectives on their Protection and Promotion.* Windhoek, Namibia: Macmillan. 53–78.

Hossain, Zakir (2012). "The Right to Food In Bangladesh: Analysis and Campaign Challenges" in *Right to Food and Nutrition Watch 2012: Who Decides Global Food and Nutrition?* Stuttgart: Bread for Life/FIAN/ICCO. 77–79.

Howard, Roda and Donnelly, Jack (1986). "Human Dignity, Human Rights and Political Regimes." *The American Political Science Review.* Vol. 80, No. 3: 801–817.

Howard, Roda (2006). "The Full-Belly Thesis: Should Economic Rights Take Priority over Civil and Political Rights?" in C. Heyns and K. Stefiszyn (eds). *Human Rights, Peace and Justice in Africa: A Reader.* Pretoria: PULP. 75–82.

Hunt, Paul, Nowak, Manifred and Osmani, Siddiq (2003). "Human Rights and Poverty Reduction Strategies." Discussion Paper for the UN Office of the High Commissioner for Human Rights.

Ife, Jime (2002). *Community Development.* French Forests, NSW: Pearson Education.

Institute for Democracy and Electoral Assistance (IDEA, 2002). "Democracy Assessment: The Basics of the International IDEA Assessment Framework." Available at: www.idea.int/publication/sod/upload/demo_as_inlay_eng_l.pdf (accessed 19 April 2006).

Institute of Development Studies (IDS, 2003). "The Rise of Rights: Rights Based Approach in International Development." IDS Policy Briefing, Issue 17.

Institute for International Economics (2004). "The Patterns of Economic Growth 1950–2000." Available at: www.iie.com/ (accessed 29 March 2007).

Jochnick, Chris (1999). *The Human Rights Challenge to Global Poverty.* New York: Center for Economic and Social Rights. Available at: http://www.cesr.org/publications.htm (accessed 20 February 2012).

John, Wilson (1951). *The Culture of Ancient Egypt.* Chicago: Chicago University Press.

Jolly, Rebbecca (1998). "Water and Human Rights: Challenges for the Twenty-first Century." Address at the Conference of the Belgian Royal Academy of Overseas Sciences, 23 March, Brussels.

Jones, Andrew (2005). "The Case of CARE International in Rwanda" in P. Gready and J. Ensor (eds). *Reinventing Development: Translating Rights-Based Approaches from Theory into Practice*. London/New York: Zed Books. 79–98.

Jones, Peter (1994). *Rights*. New York: Palgrave.

Jonsson, Urban (2005). "A Human Rights-Based Approach to Programming" in P. Gready and J. Ensor (eds). *Reinventing Development: Translating Rights-Based Approaches from Theory into Practice*. London/New York: Zed Books. 47–62.

Jubilee, South (2000). "World Bank and PRSP: Flawed Thinking and Failed Experience." *Memo*. Available at: www.focusweb (accessed February 2006).

Kabudi, J. Palamagamba (1995). "Directive Principles of State Policy versus Duties of the Individual in East African Constitutions." *VRU*. Vol. 28. No. 3: 271–303.

Keetharuth, Sheila (2009). "Major African Legal Instruments" in A. Bosl and J. Diescho (eds). *Human Rights in Africa: Legal Perspectives on their Protection and Promotion*. Windhoek, Namibia: Macmillan. 163–232.

Kennedy, Duncan M (2001). "The Critique of Rights in Critical Legal Studies" in J. Halley and W. Brown (eds). *Left Legalism/Left Critique*. Durham, North Carolina: Duke University Press. 178–228.

Kent, A. Edward (1970). "Legal rights: Introduction" in A. Edward (ed.) *Law and Philosophy: Readings in Legal Philosophy*. New Jersey: Prentice-Hall. 115–18.

Klare, Karl (2001). "The Politics of Duncan Kennedy's Critique." Available at: www.cardozo.yu.edu/cardlrev/pdf/223conaghan.pdf (accessed 12 May 2005).

Knuth, Lidija and Vidar, Margret (2011). *Constitutional and Legal Protection of the Right to Food around the World. Right to Food Studies*. Rome: Food and Agriculture Organisation. Available at: http://www.fao.org/righttofood/publications/publications-detail/en/c/80544/ (accessed 21 January 2013).

Lappe, M. Frances and Collins, Joseph (1986). *World Hunger: 12 Myths*. London: Earthscan Publishers.

Lee, Nancy Swan (1950). *Food and Money in Ancient China*. Princeton: Princeton University Press.

Lefebvre, Henri (1994). *The Production of Space*. London/New York: Blackwell.

Limburg Principles on the Implementation of the International Covenant on Economic Social and Cultural Rights (2006). Available at https://www.escr-net.org/docs/i/425445accessed 27.03 07.

Lorenzi, Maximiliano (2006). "Power: A Radial View By Steven Lukes." *Crossroads*. Vol. 6, No. 2. 87–95.

Lukes, Steven (1974). *Power: A Radical View*. London: Macmillan.

MacIntyre, Alasdair (1985). *After Virtue*, 2nd edition. London: Duckworth.

Maltz, Helio (2005). "Porto Alegre's Water: Public and For All" in B. Balanya, B. Brennan, O. Hoedeman, P. Tehorst and S. Kishimoto (eds). *Reclaiming Public Water: Achievements, Struggles and Vision from around the World*. Amsterdam: TNI/CEO. 29–36.

Mann, Alana (2011). "Lobbying the UN to Advance Peasant Rights" in *Right to Food and Nutrition Watch 2011*. Stuttgart: Bread for Life/FIAN/ICCO. 18–22. Available at: http://www.rtfn-watch.org (accessed 18 March 2013).

Marx, Karl (1823). *On the Jewish Question*. Available at: www.marxist.org/reference/archieve/hegel/index.htm (accessed 26 February 2007).

Mbaye, Keba (1991). "Human Rights and the Rights of Peoples: Introduction" in M. Bedjaoui (ed.) *International Law: Achievements and Prospects*. Paris: Martinus Nijhoff: 1043–60.

McDonald, David and Ruiters, Greg (2005). "Introduction" in D. McDonald and G. Ruiters (eds). *The Age of Commodity: Water Privatisation in Southern Africa*. London: Earthscan. 1–12, 13–42.

Mehta, Lyla and Ntshona, Zolile (2004). "Dancing to Two Tunes? Rights and Market-based Approach in South Africa's Water Domain" in *Sustainable Livelihoods in Southern Africa. IDS, PLAAS and UICN Research Paper No.17*. Available at: www.ids.ac.uk/sha (accessed 27 January 2007).

Mehta, Lyla (2005). "Unpacking Rights and Wrong: Do Human Rights Make a Difference? The Case of Water Rights in India and South Africa." *Institute of Development Studies (IDS) Working Paper No. 260*.

Mehta, Lyla (2006). "Do Human Rights Make a Difference to Poor and Vulnerable People? Accountability for the Right to Water in South Africa," in P. Newell and J. Wheeler (eds). *Rights, Resources and Politics of Accountability*. London: Zed Books. Chapter 3.

Midgley, Mary (1999). "Towards an Ethic of Global Responsibility" in T. Dunne and N. Wheeler (eds). *Human Rights in Global Politics*. Cambridge: Cambridge University Press. 160–74.

Mohan, Giles and Holland, Jeremy(2001). "Human Rights and Development in Africa: Moral Intrusion or Empowering Opportunity?" *Review of African Political Economy*. Vol. 28, No. 88. 177–96.

Mollinga, Peter, Meinzen-Dick, S. Ruth and Merry, J. Douglas (2007). "Politics, Plurality and Problems: A Strategic Approach for Reform of Agriculture Water Resource Management." *Development Policy Review*. Vol. 25, No. 6. 699–719.

Monsalve, Sofia and Seufert, Phillip (2012). "A New Tool for the Fight against Resource Grabbing? New Guidelines on the Responsible Governance of Tenure of Land, Fisheries and Forests." *Right to Food Journal*. Vol. 7, No. 1. 2–3.

Mosdell, Tim and Leatt, Annie (2005). "On Tap: A Review of the Free Basic Water Policy" in A. Leatt and S. Rosa (eds). *Towards the Means to Live: Targeting Poverty Alleviation to Make Children's Rights Real.* Cape Town: Children's Rights Institute, University of Cape Town (CD-ROM).

National Right to Food Network (NRFN, 2011). "Campaign for the Right to Food in Malawi." Available at: http://www.actionaidusa.org/malawi/2011/04/campaign-right-food-malawi (accessed 05 May 2013).

Neier, Aryeh (2006). "Social and Economic Rights: A Critique." *Human Rights Brief.* Vol. 13, No. 6: 1–3.

Neumayer, Eric (2005). "Do International Human Rights Treaties Improve Respect for Human Rights?" *Journal of Conflict Resolution.* Vol. 49, No. 6. 925–53.

Njiru, Leticia (2004). "Privatising Water Services in Developing Countries." *Water Management.* Vol. 157, Issue 3. 123–30.

Nyamu-Musembi, Celestine and Cornwall, Andrea (2004). *What is the 'Rights-based Approach' All About? Perspectives from International Development Agencies.* Institute of Development Studies (IDS) Working Paper 234. Sussex: IDS.

Offenheiser, Raymond and Holcombe, Susan (2003). "Challenges and Opportunities in Implementing a Rights-Based Approach to Development: An American Perspective." *Quarterly.* Vol. 32, No. 2. 268–306.

Office of the High Commissioner for Human Rights (OHCHR, 1966). *International Covenant on Civil and Political Rights.* Available at: http://www.unhchr.ch/menu3/b/a ccpr.htm (accessed 3 May 2005).

Office of the High Commissioner for Human Rights (OHCHR, 1966). *International Covenant on Economic Social and Cultural Rights.* Available at: http://www.unhchr.ch/menu3/b/a escr.htm (accessed 3 May 2005).

Office of the High Commissioner for Human Rights (OHCHR, 2002). *Draft Guidelines: A Human Rights Approach to Poverty Reduction Strategies.* Available at: www.ohchr.org (accessed 4 October 2005).

Office of the High Commission for Human Rights (OHCHR, 2004). *Human Rights and Poverty Reduction: A Conceptual Framework.* Geneva: OHCHR.

Office of the High Commissioner for Human Rights (OHCHR, 1993). *Vienna Declaration and Programme of Action.* Available at: http://www.ohchr.org/EN/ProfessionalInterest/Pages/Vienna.aspx (accessed 10 March 2014).

Office of the High Commission on Human Rights/Food and Agriculture Organisation (OHCHR/FAO, 2010). *The Right to Adequate Food: Fact Sheet No. 34.* Available at: http://www.ohchr.org/Documents/Publications/FactSheet34en.pdf (accessed 14 February 2013).

Olowu, Dejo (2009). *An Integrated Rights-Based Approach to Human Development in Africa.* Pretoria: Pretoria University Law Press.

Onora, Oneil (2000). *Towards Justice and Virtue.* Cambridge: Cambridge University Press.

Onuma, Yasuaki (1981). "Nationality and Territorial Change: In Search of the State of the Law." *The Yale Journal of World Public Order*. Vol. 8, No. 1. 1–35.

Osmani, Siddiq (2003). "Some Thoughts on the Right to Development" in *The Right to Development: Reflections on the First Four Reports of the Independent Expert on the Right to Development*. Geneva: Franciscan International.

Parish, Esther, Evan Kodra, Karsten Steinhauser and Auroop Ganguly (2012). "Estimating Future Global Water Availability Based on Changes in Climate and Population." *Computer Geosciences*. Vol. 42. 79–86.

Patnaik, Biraj (2011a). "Implementation of Judicial Decisions on the Right to Food: A Review" in *Right to Food and Nutrition Watch 2011*. Stuttgart: Bread for Life/FIAN/ICCO. 30–33. Available at: http://www.rtfn-watch.org (accessed 18 March 2013).

Patnaik, Biraj (2011b). "The Right to Food Campaign in India" in *Right to Food and Nutrition Watch 2011*. Stuttgart: Bread for Life/FIAN/ICCO. 37–9. Avalaible at http://www.rtfn-watch.org (accessed 18 March 2013).

Perret, Sylvain (2002). "Water Policies and Smallholdings Irrigation Schemes in South Africa: A Historical and New Institutional Challenge." *Water Policy*. Vol. 4, No. 3. 280–300.

Petrella, Riccardo (2001). *The Water Manifesto: Arguments for a World Water Contract*. London. Zed Books.

Piron, Laure-Helene and O'Neil, Tammie (2005). *Integrating Human Rights into Development: A Synthesis of Donor Approaches and Experiences*. Prepared for the OECD DAC Network on Government (GOVNET).

Polanyi, Karl (1944). *The Great Transformation: The Political and Economic Origins of Our Time*. Boston: Beacon Press.

Pollis, Adamantia and Schwab, Peter (2006). "Human Rights: A Western Construct with Limited Applicability" in C. Heyns and K. Stefiszyn (eds). *Human Rights, Peace and Justice in Africa: A Reader*. Pretoria: PULP. 88–96.

Prasad, Naren (2006). "Privatisation Results: Private Sector Participation in Water Services After 15 Years." *Development Policy Review*. Vol. 24, No. 6. 669–92.

RAPDA (2010). *The Right to Food Study: A Case Study Report on Zambia 2010*. Available at: http://www.rtfn-watch.org/uploads/media/Case_Study_Report_on_Zambia.pdf (accessed 17 November 2012).

Rawls, John (1999/1971). *A Theory of Justice* (revised edition). Oxford: Oxford University Press.

Raz, Joseph (1986). *The Morality of Freedom*. Oxford, UK. Clarendon Press.

Report of the United Nations Conference on Sustainable Development held in Rio De Janeiro, June 20–22, Brazil (Rio +20, 2012). Available at: http://www.uncsd2012.org/content/documents/814UNCSD%20REPORT%20final%20revs.pdf (accessed 18 February 2013).

Ricouer, Paul (1981). *Hermeneutics and the Human Sciences* (translated by John Thompson). London: Cambridge University Press.

Rieff, David (2002). *A Bed for the Night: Humanitarianism in Crisis*. New York: Simon & Schuster.

Right to Food Campaign (RFC, 2005). Foundation Statement. Available at: http://rightofoodinidia.org/foundation.html (accessed 23 February 2013).

Right to Food and Nutrition Watch (2012). "Occupy the Food System! Civil Society Organisations Call for a Turnaround in Global Decision-making on Food and Nutrition." Press Release, 25 September 2012. Available at: http://www.rtfn-watch.org/fileadmin/mediartfn-watch.org (accessed 19 March 2013).

Robinson, Mary (2001). *Bridging the Gap Between Human Rights and Development: From Normative Principles to Operational Relevance*. World Bank Presidential Fellow's Lecture, 3 December 2001. Available at: www.worldbank.org (accessed 18 September 2006).

Robinson, Mary (2005). "What Rights Can Add to Good Development Practice" in P. Alston and M. Robinson (eds.) *Human Rights and Development: Towards Mutual Reinforcement*. Oxford: Oxford University Press. 25–43.

Rodriguez, A. Santiago (2005). "The Venezuela Experience in the Struggle for People-centred Drinking Water and Sanitation Services" in B. Balanya, B. Brennan, P. Hoedeman, P. Tehorst and S. Kishimoto (eds). *Reclaiming Public Water: Achievements, Struggles and Vision from Around the World*. Amsterdam: TNI/CEO. 131–7.

Rogers, Peter (1997). "Preparing for the Future Hydroeconomics: Getting Water into National Economic Planning." *Proceedings of Mar del Plata 20-Year Anniversary Seminar*. 16 August, Stockholm.

Roithmayr, Daria (2001). "Critical Legal Studies (Debut de Siècle: A Symposium on Duncan Kennedy's, *A Critique of Adjudication*) Critical Legal Politics: Left vs MPM." *Cardoso Law Review*. Vol. 22, No 3–4. 1113–35

Roosevelt, F. (1937). "Franklin Roosevelt Second Inaugural Address", Wednesday, 20 January 1937. Available at: http://www.bartleby.com/124/pres50.html (accessed 13 September 2006).

Saleth, Maria (2002). "Introduction" in Maria Saleth (ed.) *Water* Resources *and Economic Development*. Cheltenham, Gloucestershire, UK: Elgar. Ix–xii.

Salomon, E. Margot (2003). "The Nature of the Right: The Right to a Process in the Right to Development" in A. Sengupta (ed.). *The Right to Development: Reflections on the First Four Reports of the Independent Expert on the Right to Development*. Geneva, Switzerland: SIDA.

Santos, Carlos and Villareal, Alberto (2006). "Uruguay: Direct Democracy in Defence of the Right to Water" in B. Balanya, B. Brennan, P. Hoedeman, P. Tehorst and S. Kishimoto (eds). *Reclaiming Public Water: Achievements, Struggles and Vision from Around the World*. Amsterdam: TNI/CEO. 173–80.

Scanlon, John, Cassar, Angela and Nemes, Noemi (2004). "Water as a Human Right?" International Union for the Conservation of Nature and Natural Resources (IUCN), Gland Switzerland and Cambridge UK, ix + 53pp. Available at: www.iucn.org/bookstore.

Sederberg, C. Pater (1984). *The Politics of Meaning*. Tucson: University of Arizona Press.

Sen, Amartya (1981). *Poverty and Famine: An Essay on Entitlement and Deprivation*. London: Oxford University Press.

Sen, Amartya (1992). *Inequality Re-examined*. New York: Clarendon.

Sen Amartya (1994). " The Political Economy of Hunger." Paper presented at a Conference on Actions to Reduce Hunger Worldwide, entitled, "Overcoming Global Hunger" and hosted by the World Bank. Bender Arena. Washington, DC: The American University. 30 November–1 December 1993.

Sen, Amartya (1999). *Development As Freedom*. New York: Alfred Knopf.

Sengupta, Arjun (2000). "Realizing the Right to Development." *Development and Change*. Vol. 31; No. 3. 553–72.

Sen, Amartya (2003). "Hunger in India." Address made at a public hearing on hunger and the right to food. Delhi University, 10 January 2003. Available at: http://www.righttofoodindia.org/data/amartya.pdf (accessed 14 January 2013).

Sengupta, Arjun (2003). "The Fifth Report on the Right to Development" in *The Right to Development: Reflections on the First Four Reports of the Independent Expert on the Right to Development*. Geneva: SIDA.

Sen, Amartya (2004). "Elements of a Theory of Human Rights." *Philosophy and Public Affairs*. Vol. 32, No. 4. 315–56.

Sengupta, Arjun (2004). "The Human Right to Development." *Oxford Development Studies* Vol. 32, No. 2. 179–203.

Sengupta, Arjun (2008). "The Political Economy of Legal Empowerment of the Poor" in D. Banik (ed.) *Rights and Legal Empowerment in Eradicating Poverty*. Surrey: Ashgate. 31–46.

Shivji, Isa (1989). *Concept of Human Rights in Africa*. Dakar: CODESRIA Book Series.

Sieghart, Paul (1983). *The International Law of Human Rights*. Oxford: Oxford University Press.

Skogly, I.S (1999). "The Position of the World Bank and the International Monetary Fund in the Human Rights Field" in R. Hanshi and M. Suksi (eds). *An Introduction to the International Protection of Human Rights*. London: Cavendish. 231–50.

Slaymaker, Tom and Newborne, Peter (2004). *Implementing Water and Sanitation Programmes under PRSP – Synthesis of Research Findings from Sub-Saharan Africa*. ODI Water Policy/Water Aid Working Paper No. 17.

Slim, Hugo (2002). "A Response to Peter Univ – Making Moral Low Ground: Rights as the Struggle for Justice and the Abolition of Development." *The Fletcher Journal of Development Studies*. Vol. 17. 1–5.

Smith, Steve (1996). "Positivism and Beyond" in Smith, S., Booth, K. and M. Zalewski (eds). *International Theory: Positivism and Beyond*. New York: Cambridge University Press. 11–46.

Social and Economic Action Rights Centre & Another v. the Federal Republic of Nigeria (SERAC, 2001), ACHPR/Comm/A044/1. 27 May 2002.

South African Human Rights Commission (SAHRC, 2006). *Sixth Economic and Social Rights Report 2003–2006*. Pretoria: SAHRC.

South African Human Rights Commission (SAHRC, 2009). *Seventh Report on Economic and Social Rights: Millennium Development Goals and the Progressive Realisation Economic and Social Rights*. Johannesburg: SAHRC.

South African Human Rights Commission (SAHRC, 2013). *Human Rights Report Card*. Pretoria: SAHRC.

Srinivasan, Vivek and Narayanan, Sudha (2007). *Food Policy and Social Movements: Reflections on the Right to Food Campaign in India*. Food Policy for Developing Countries Programme, Case Study No. 11.1. Cornell University, New York.

Steiner, J. Henry and Alston, Philip (2000). *International Human Rights in Context: Law, Politics and Morals, Texts and Materials* (2nd Edition). Oxford: Oxford University Press.

Stiglitz, Joseph (1998). "Towards a New Paradigm for Development Strategies, Policies, and Processes". Paper presented as a Prebisch Lecture at the UNCTAD, Geneva, 19 October.

Streeten, Paul (1979). "Transnational Corporations and Basic Needs" in Jegen E. Mary and Wilber, Charles K. (eds). *Growth with Equity: Strategies for Meeting Human Needs*. New York: Paulist Press. 163–74.

Streeten, Paul, Burki, Shahid, Haq, ul Mahbub, Hicks, Norman and Stewart, Frances (1981). *First Things First: Meeting Basic Needs in Developing Countries*. New York: World Bank.

Supreme Court of India (2001). *People's Union for Civil Liberties (PUCL, 2001) v Union of India & others*, case No. 196 of 2001.

Supreme Court of India (2003). *People's Union for Civil Liberties (PUCL, 2003) v Union of India & others*, 2 May 2003 (interim order).

Swiss Agency for Development Cooperation (SDC, 2008). *A Human Rights-Based Approach to Water and Sanitation: Briefing Paper*.

Swyngedouw, Erick (2005). "Dispossessing H2O: The Contested Terrain of Water Privatization." *Capitalism Nature Socialism*. Vol. 16, No. 1. 81–98.

Tabbush, Constanza (2005). *Civil Society in United Nations Conferences: A Literature Review*. Geneva: United Nations Research Institute for Social Development.

Takagi, Maya (2011). "Implementation of the Zero Hunger Program in 2003" in J.G. da Silva, M.E. del Grossi and C.G. de Franca (eds). *The Fome Zero (Zero Hunger Programme): The Brazilian Experience*. Brasilia: Ministry of Agrarian Development. 55–86.

Thiis, W. Oyvind (1996). "Norwegain Development Assistance and the Right to Development" in Baer P., Sadiwa, L. and Smith, J. (eds). *Human Rights in Developing Countries: Year Book 1996*. The Hague: Kluwer Law International. 3–36.

Tostensen, A. (2002). "Are Smart Sanctions Feasible?" *World Politics*, No. 54. 373–407.

Tsikata, Dzodzi (2004). "The Rights-Based Approach to Development: Potential for Change or More of the Same?" *Institute for Development Studies Bulletin*. Vol. 35, No. 4. 130–3.

United Nations (1945). *Charter of the United Nations* (available at www. unhchr.ch/ html).

United Nations Children's Fund (UNICEF, 1978). *UNICEF Annual Report 1978*. Geneva: UNICEF.

United Nations Department of Economic and Social Affairs, Population Division (DESA, 2011). *World Population Prospects: The 2010 Revision, Volume I: Comprehensive Tables* (ST/ESA/SER.A/313). New York: DESA.

United Nations Department of Economic and Social Affairs, Population Division (DESA, 2014). *Concise Report on the World Population Situation in 2014*. New York: United Nations (DESA).

United Nations Development Programme (UNDP, 2000). *Human Development Report 2000*. New York: Oxford University Press for UNDP.

United Nations Development Programme (UNDP, 2003). *Human Development Report 2003*. New York: Oxford University Press for UNDP.

United Nations Development Programme (UNDP, 2006). *The Human Development Report 2006: Beyond Scarcity, Power and Poverty in Global Water Crisis*. Available at: www.undp.org/hdr2007.

United Nations Development Programme (UNDP, 2010). *Human Development Report 2010. The Real Wealth of Nations: Pathways to Human Development*. New York: Palgrave Macmillan for UNDP.

United Nations Development Programme (UNDP, 2014). *The Human Development Report 2014. Sustaining Human Progress, Reducing Vulnerabilities and Building Resilience*. New York: UNDP.

United Nations Economic and Social Council for Asia and the Pacific (ESCAP). Online Database. Available at: http://www.unescap.org/stat/data/statdb/DataExplorer .aspx (accessed 22 February 2013).

United Nations Economic Commission for Africa (UNECA, 2009). *Africa Governance Report*. New York: Oxford University Press.

United Nations Education, Science and Cultural Organisation (UNESCO, 2006). *World Water Development Report 200 – Water: a Shared Responsibility*. Available at: www .unesco.org/water/wwap (accessed 17 November 2006).

United Nations General Assembly (UDHR, 1948). *Universal Declaration of Human Rights*.

United Nations Population Fund (UNFPA, 2004). *A Human Rights-Based Approach to Programming: Practical Implementation Manual and Training Materials*. Available at: http://www.unfpa.org/sites/default/files/resource-pdf/hrba_manual_in%20full. pdf (accessed 22 July 2012).

Univ, Peter (2002). "On the High Moral Ground: The Incorporation of Human Rights by the Development Enterprise." *Fletcher Journal of Development Studies*, Vol. XVII. 1–11.

Univ, Peter (2004). *Human Rights and Development*. Sterling, Virginia: Kumarian Press.

Vaneklasen, L., Miller, V., Clark C. and Reilly, M. (2004). *Rights-Based Approach and Beyond: Challenges of Linking Rights and Participation*. IDS Working Paper No. 235. Available at: www.ids.ac.uk/ids/bookshop/wp.wp235pdf (accessed 23 October 2007).

Vasak, Karel (1975). *Third Generation of Human Rights: The Rights of Solidarity*. Inaugural Lecture at the 10th Study Session. International Institute of Human Rights (English Version) July 1979.

Veltmeyer, Henry (2004). *Civil Society and Social Movement: The Dynamics of Intersectoral Alliances and Urban–rural Linkages in Latin America*. Geneva: United Nations Research Institute for Social Development.

Vincent, R. John (1986). *Human Rights and International Relations*. Cambridge: Cambridge University Press.

Waldron, Jeremy (1987). "Natural Rights in the Seventeenth and Eighteenth Centuries" in Waldron, Jeremy (ed.) *Nonsense Upon Stilts: Bentham, Burke and Marx on the Rights of Man*. London/New York: Methuen. 7–21.

WaterAid (2007). *The Advocacy Source Book*. London: WaterAid.

WaterAid (2010). *Budget Advocacy for Water and Sanitation Sector in Nepal: A Primer for Civil Society Organisations*. Available at: www.wateraid.org/nepal (accessed 25 March 2013).

WaterAid (2011). *Rights-based Approaches to Increasing Access to Water and Sanitation*. WaterAid Discussion Paper. Available at: www.wateraid.org (accessed 23 March 2013).

Webb, Patrick and Iskandarani, Maria (1998). *Water Insecurity and the Poor: Issues and Research Needs*. Discussion Paper on Development Policy, No. 2, Bonn, October 1998.

WHO/UNICEF (2012). *Progress on Sanitation and Drinking Water: Update 2012*. Available at: http://www.unicef.org/media/files/JMPreport2012.pdf (accessed 25 February 2013).

William, Glyn (2004). "Evaluating Participatory Development: Tyranny, Power and Re-politicisation." *Third World Quarterly*, Vol. 25, No. 3. 557–78.

Wolfenson, James (2005). "Some Reflections on Human Rights and Development" in P. Alston and M. Robinson (eds). *Human Rights and Development: Towards Mutual Reinforcement*. Oxford: Oxford University Press. 19–24.

World Bank (1986). *Poverty and Hunger: Issues and Options for Food Security in Developing Countries*. Washington DC: The World Bank.

World Bank (2010). *World Development Indicators 2010*. Washington DC: The World Bank.

World Food Programme/Food and Agriculture Organisation (WFP/FAO, 2010). *The State of Food Insecurity in the World: Addressing Food Insecurity in Protracted Crisis*. Available at: http://www.fao.org/3/a-i1683e/ (accessed 12 March 2013).

World Health Organisation (WHO, 2003). *The Right to Water*. Health and Human Rights Publications, Series No. 3. Available at: www.who.org.

Wronka, Joseph (1998). *Human Rights and Social Policy in the 21st Century*, 2nd edition. Lanham: University Press of America.

Zambia Water and Sanitation Alliance (ZAWASA, 2010). *The Right to Water and Sanitation for All – The Case of Zambia*. Available at: http://www.freshwateraction.net/sites/freshwateraction.net/files/Case%20Study%20-%20Zambia%20Water%20and%20Sanitation%20Alliance.pdf (accessed 25 November 2013).

Zeleza, T. Paul (2006). "The Struggle for Human Rights in Africa" in C. Heyns and K. Stefiszyn (eds). *Human Rights, Peace and Justice in Africa: A Reader*. Pretoria: PULP. 42–8.

Ziegler, Jean (2001). *Right to Food: Report Submitted by the Special Rapporteur on the Right to Food to the Commission on Human Rights*. Economic and Social Council. E/CN.4/2001/53.

Ziegler, Jean (2002). *Report by the Special Rapporteur on the Right to Food*. Submitted to the 58th Session of United Nations Commission on Human Rights. E/CN.4/2002/58.

Ziegler, Jean (2003). *Right to Food: Report Submitted by the Special Rapporteur on the Right to Food to the Commission on Human Rights*. Economic and Social Council. E/CN.4/2003/54.

Ziegler, Jean (2006). *Report of the Special Rapporteur on the Right to Food*. Submitted to the 62nd Session of the Commission on Human Rights. E/CN.4/2006/44.

Index

Access to water and food
  bedrock on which other rights rests 4
  as social matters of justice 1
Action for Nutrition and Human Rights (Brazil) 210
African Charter of Human and Peoples' Rights 36, 227
African Commission on Human and Peoples Rights 226–227
American Anthropological Association on human rights 13, 21
American declaration of independence ix, 31n2, 36
Ancient Egypt 153
Annan, Kofi 64, 126n, 127
Anti-privatisation campaign 233
Anti-privatisation strategy (Uruguay, Brazil, Venezuela, Bolivia and Mexico) 239–240
Austin, John 22

Babylonian food rations 153
Basic human need 2
Bentham, Jeremy 22
Beyond parliament xi, xii, 53
Budget tracking (Tanzania) 237–238
Burke, Edmond 22

Campaign on the Right to Food and Social Security (Bangladesh) 221–222
Carter, Jimmy 10b
Citizens against Hunger and Poverty (Brazil) 228–231
Civil and political rights
  impose negative duty 25
  as only genuine rights 25
Civil law tradition 194. *See also* footnotes 9 and 10
Civil society
  definition, 70n7
  deploy democratic politics to realise rights 185
  involvement is crucial 242
  key to demoing state responsibility towards rights 185
Collective struggle
  for basic necessities 27
  as effective means of giving effect to rights 16
  integrated approach 215
  role of public pressure 218
  thrives on collective values 87
Commission on World Hunger 10
Common law traditions 139, 188. *See also* n25
Convention on the elimination of all forms of discrimination against women: explicitly provides for the right to water 8
Correlation
  between lack of basic needs and violation of human rights 4
  resource availability and socioeconomic rights 176
  rights and duties 35
Covenant on the rights of a child
  explicitly provides for the right to water 8
Cranstonian Paradigm 81. *See also* Second generation rights, and Cranstonian critique
Cranstonian three test criterion
  paramount importance test 25–26
  practicability test 25
  universality test 24
Cranston, Maurice 81
Cultural
  cross-fertilisation 51
  imperialism 51
  neither static nor impervious 50
  relativism as a discourse 14
  relativists 50

Debates on state parties obligations 173–176. *See also* Obligations under ICESR
Defeatism xi, 213–214
Democratic politics
  built on local solidarities 87
  challenge existing power relations 84
  contest existing structures 85
  at core of human rights 6, 84

create spaces 141 (*see also* Human rights)
creates opportunity for radical change 142
create opportunity to transform power structures 84
definition of 141
emphasise the primacy of political engagement 85
help bring issues of hunger into political spaces 182
importance of participation 72
lead to creation of spaces (*see also* Human rights)
radical xi
rooted in people's daily struggles 87
rooted in the struggle over meaning 96
Democratic politics as a game of numbers 216–217
Depolitised approach 5
Dialogue Day (Mali) 236–237
Direct democracy 98
Directive principle of state policy
countries with 203
non-justiciability of 204
origins of 203
position of the Nigerian Constitution Drafting Committee on 203
purpose of 203
right to food recognised under 160
in Zambian constitution 190
Duty to respect, protect and fulfil 36

Economic social and cultural rights
challenges of 15
critics of 15
Employment guarantee programme 223
Empowerment of the poor 5. *See also* Principle-of empowerment

First generation rights, as legal rights 32
Food
global consumption trends 147–149
in global context 142
global food supply 144
global situation of 141
linked to human dignity 4
wasted xi, 145, 147–48
Formal recognition of rights important 185
Fox, Vicente 127
Free Basic Water Policy 139, 233–234
French Declaration of the rights of man and citizen 20, 31n2, 36
French law of criminal omission 35
Fundamental legal concepts 38

General Comment 3
duties of states parties to the Covenant 73
obligation to fulfil 138, 172
obligation to fulfil (facilitate) 176
obligation to fulfil (provide) 176
obligations to protect 138
obligation to respect, protect and fulfil 175–176
obligation to take steps/measures 137
General comment 12
for a broader definition of the right to food 158
elaborate on the right to food 8
focus on the primary norm of the right to food 165
on meaning of the right to food 157
General Comment 15
elaborates on the right to water 8
obligation to ensure equitable distribution of water 111
on non-derogable obligation 11
Giving effect to human rights 16
Global north 3
Global social justice 2
Global South (definition) 1
Global water availability per capita 103

Hart, L.A 46–47, 53
Hohfeldian categories of right
claim-right 38–40
classification of 38
correlative and opposites in 38
immunities 41–43
Jural relationship 38
limitations of the Hohfeldian scheme 43–44, 47
power 40–42
power as absence of liability 40
power as ultimate sovereignty 41
privileges 40
Homo sapiens ix, 18, 31, 75

Hugo Shavez 240
Human
  dignity ix, 53
  nature 53
Human beings
  endowed with equal worth and dignity x
  endowed with unalienable rights x
  with incontrovertible worth ix
  have inherent dignity 75
  have unalienable entitlements 31
Human rights
  anti-colonial struggles drew inspiration from 13
  appealing, but contentious 13
  based on western experience 13
  as basic politics 84
  challenge unequal power relations 186
  as cherished values society gives to itself 101
  common understanding and standards of 31
  counter-critiques 49–57
  create spaces of hope 52
  different from aspirational goals 184–185
  discourse 13, 18–28, 31–36
  evolving with changing society 122
  flourish on collective political engagement 187
  fragmented approach to 214–215
  generational approach to 25, 54
  hard and practical question about 15
  history 11–15
  as a language of possibilities 206
  legalistic approach to 15
  normative approach to 165
  not given by a benevolent state 101
  not given on a silver platter 228
  primary focus of 58
  principles adopted by UN 62
  product of collective struggle 183
  product of contest 87
  as product of protracted struggle 170
  a product of struggle for ordinary people 16
  promote individualism 26, 47
  as radical politics 85
  as a reformist strategy 52
  as simple nonsense 19
  split between civil and political, and economic, social and cultural 54
  as tools for social change xii, 49, 208, 211–213
  as tools for creating democratic politics 206
  tramped by markets 182
  unify diverse constituencies 186
  widely invoked 33
Human rights and development:
  a common ground of 58
  an integrated approach 29
  economic growth not an end in itself 58
  merging of rights and development approaches 58
  ultimate goal of economic growth 58
Human rights critiques:
  Cranstonian critique still influential 56
  elaborate on what human rights are 27
  generational critique 23
  Marxist critique 26
  ontological critique 22
  positivist critique 22
  as a product of Cold War Politics 55, 56
  relativist critique 20
  types of 19–28
Human rights struggles framed narrowly 182

IMF 65–66 68n, 78, 200, 239
Indirect democracy 98
International Covenant on Economic, Social and Cultural Rights
  absence of individual complaint mechanism 55
  critics of 73
  hybrid interpretation of article 2(1) of ICESRC 173
  immediate obligations 179 (*see also* Obligation to take steps/measures)
  nature of obligations of state parties to 173–176
  obligations under 8 (*see also* General Comment 3)
  optional protocol of 198n (*see also* Individual complaint mechanism)
  ratification only the starting point 192
  reason d'etre of 174
  and the role of international cooperation 177

International financial institution and human rights 200–202
International Human rights
 assessing efficacy of international human rights law 192
 impact on realisation of rights 191.
 individual complaint mechanism 198n (*see also* ICESCRS)
 its role in social change 181
 weak foundation for building human rights struggles 191
International law
 and legal positivism 205
 and smart sanctions 198
 and the doctrine of consent 198
 debates on legal standing of individual 197–198
 nature of 197–200
 use of sanctions 198

Johannesburg Water 233

Kennedy, Duncan 20

Language of rights
 deployed by the rights based approach 78
 force of 126–127
 gained popularity 13
 key to the politics of change 96
 as means of changing the world 36
 moral force of 152
 policies shied away from using the 207
 has the potential to reconfigure power 95
Lefebvre, Henry 87
Legal positivism
 framework 47
 tradition 19
Legal rules 32
Legal strategies not sufficient 225
Lessons from past and current human rights struggles 209–211
Levels of commitment indicators
 acknowledgment 82
 giving effect 83
 measurable targets 83
 proclamation 82
 taking measures 82
Limburg Principles
 on resource availability and Covenant obligations 55
 on scarcity of resources 74
Local remedies 226
Lula da Silva, Ignacio 127

Maastricht Guidelines on the Violations of Economic Social and Cultural rights 128 n17. on obligation of conduct and obligation of result 135–138
Mar de Plata 111–113
Maurice, Cranston 23
McIntyre, Alasdair 21
Measures taken should be deliberate, targeted 73. *See also* Taking measures, and also nature of obligations of state parties
Morality and law
 global moral community 34
 no clear separation between morality and law 33
 separation of the legal from the moral 32
Multi-stakeholder Platforms 237

National Right to Food Network (Malawi) 210, 220–221
Natural rights as rhetorical nonsense 19
Negative duty 35
Negative rights 8, 25
Nigerian National Petroleum Company 227

Ogoni Case 225–228, 241. *See also* SERAC
Ogoni People 227
Operation Gcin Amanzi 233
Orders of water scarcity 112n7

Parallel reporting mechanism 241
People's Union for Civil Liberties 210, 223
Per capita water withdraw 103
Porto Alegre 240
Position 89
Positive duty 35
Positive right 35
Power
 as a delicate concept 91
 exercise of 95

Power (cont.)
as manifesting in different forms 91
-over 92
as a property of a collective 95
relational nature of 95
as a relational property 95
as a resource 91
three dimensions of 92–93
through shared meaning 93–95
types and dimensions 9
types and meaning of 92–96
-with 92
Primary norm 164
Primary rules 32
Principle of
deprivation focus 49, 75, 134
difference principle 75, 134
empowerment 76 (*see also* Principles of the rights the based approach)
equality and non-discrimination 74–75
judicial deference 204
participation and citizenship 96 (*see also* Principles of the rights the based approach)
progressive realisation 72–74, 174, 178 (*see also* Principles of the rights the based approach)
redistribution 153
separation of powers 204
Principles of rights based approach
accountability 68–71
bias towards the poor 75
discussion of 67–76
empowerment 76
equality and non-discrimination 74–76
equality of opportunity 75
few governments adopt it 81
mechanism of accountability 69
participation 71–72
progressive realisation 72–74
Production of space
actual production of space 89–91
concept of 17, 89–88
processes leading to the 90
Progressive judiciary 224
Promoting community awareness 225
Public distribution system 223
Public interest litigation 221
Raz, Joseph 45
Rights
in the broad sense 38
community of 48
concept of 34
as creatures of history 54
effectuation of 48
independent of duties 47
in the narrow sense 38
use of the term 34
versatility of the term 37
Rights based approach
vs. basic needs approach 77–79
challenges of implementing 81–83
common understanding document 61
complaint procedure 70n6
complementary perspective of 63
creates political and social spaces 78
critics of 67, 78–81
definition and meaning 59–62
to development 29
different views on 29n20
emphasises national as well as international responsibility 79
integrates human rights and development 5
low awareness of 58
no single framework 59
origins of 64
predominantly NGO-driven 66
reasons for its rise 62–63, 65–67
as repackaging of old wine 81
as rhetoric without responsibility 80
within the UN system 61
use 2
valued added 77–79, 163
weaknesses and challenges of 5
Right to development
declaration of 54
on equality and non-discrimination 74
inspired the emergence of RBA 66
promotes development with the people 98
and rights based approach 60
as solidarity rights 26
as third generation right 26
Right to food
African countries with explicit provision for the right to food 188n1. *see also* 160n5

beneficiaries of 171–172
basic minimum of 165
current status of 160–163
explicitly recognised 10, 160. *see also* 160n5
vs. food security 159
and food sovereignty 159
and freedom from hunger 19, 164
in international human rights law 161–164
legal basis of 6
meaning of 156
normative content of 164–169
normative definition 156
not a right to a number of calories 158
origins 141, 152–156
as a political battle 225
as a right to adequate food 164–67
scope of 171–172
special Rapporteur's definition of 156
two articles on the 164–165
under a purposive approach 158

Right to food campaign 180, 222–225

Right to water x
and African Charter on Human and Peoples' Rights 121
in the African Charter on the Rights and welfare of the Child 124
African countries that provide for water in their constitutions 188n2
and anti-privatisation movements 115, 238
basis for asserting the 6
in CEDAW 123
as collective human aspiration 101–102
and commondification of water 115–116
content 129–133
content should not be narrowed 133
controversial nature of 100
in the Convention on the Rights of the Child 124
and the Declaration on the Right to Development 120
derived from other rights 121–22
difference it makes 127–128
explicitly provision 122–124
and the Geneva Conventions 122
and human dignity 131
and ICCPR 119
and the ICESCR 117
implicitly recognised 10, 116–122
in international human rights law 116–121
its substantive elements 129
linked to the right to food 131
nature of obligations generated by 6
scope of 133–135
substantive elements of 129
and the UN Charter 117
from the Universal declaration of Human Rights 117
violations of 135–137
vs. water rights 116n10

The Rights to water and food
challenges of giving effect to 210–215
importance of formal recognition of 185
merits for recognising the 184–187
as most basic of human needs 7
multidimensional nature of 9
not explicitly recognised in many countries 188–190
often depoliticised to maintain status quo 183
practical implication of 6
strangled by defeatism 213–215 (*see also* Defeatism)
as young rights 7, 170
why focus on 7

Robinson, Mary 67

Saudi Arabia, opposition to freedom of religion 14
Second generation rights 19
Second generation rights, as moral aspirations 32
Sen, Amartya xi
SERAC (Nigeria) 210, 225–228
Serikat Petani (Indonesia) 230–231
Similane, Manzi 43
Social change
broader vision of 218
citizenship as vehicle for social change dynamics of 87
human rights contribution 208 (*see also* Human rights)
politics of 208
possible through power contest 96
Social Development Summit of 1995 65

Social mobilisation 206, 224
Social space
  definition 88
  not as passive surface 17
  vs. physical space
  produced space 88
  as a product of contestation 17
South Africa 139, 190
South African constitution
  on interpreting international treaties 199–200
  provision for the right to water 233
South African Constitutional Court
  on a society based on human dignity 9
South African Human Rights Commission, on challenges to fulfil rights protected in constitution 189
Special rapporteur, right to food
  affirmation of the right to food 169
  earth produces enough food for everyone 146
  meaning of the right to food 169
  on the right to food 8
  on root causes of hunger 146
State
  alliances with 219
  as an arena of contestation 219
  built on citizens 98
  and citizenship 98–99
  and direct forms of governance 98
  enthusiastically ratify international treaties 187–188
  impose normalcy and homogeneity 94
  not always an enemy 219
  as primary respondent 48, 135
  rationality of 89
  role in giving effect to human rights 218–220
  -space 17, 220
  as a strategic ally 230
  why they ratify treaties 193
Streeten, Paul 77
Sub-norm 164
Sub-Saharan Africa
  faces greatest challenge 3
  population with access to clean water 106–111
  prevalence of undernourishment 150
  see also 3n5
  renewable freshwater resources 106
  urban and rural access to water 106–111
  undernourishment highest in 149
Supreme court commission 224

Tanzania Civil Society Network on Water and Sanitation 238
Theories of Rights
  choice/will theory 45, 47–48
  interest/benefit theory 45–46
Treaties in domestic law:
  dualist approach 195–96
  harmonisation (Hybridisation) approach 195–197
  hybridisation common 196
  monist approach 195–96
  non-self-executing norms 199
Two stage campaign 231

Unequal power relations 2
UNICEF, on adjustment with a human face 65
United Kingdom 23
United Nations Charter
  implicit provision for the right to food 162
  implicit provision for the right to water 117
  on instrumentality of human rights ix–X
  preamble of 12
United Nations Committee on Economic, Social and Cultural Right (CESCRs)
  elaborates on the right to food 166 (*see also* General Comment 12)
  mandate to elaborate on ESCRs 8
  purpose and work 166
  on the right to food 166 (*see also* General comment 12)
  right to food key to enjoying other rights 172
  on the right to water 129 (*see also* General comment 15)
  on the scope of the right to food 171
  three levels of obligations for state parties 175
United States of America 20, 23
Universal application of rights 123 (*see also* Scope of the right to water)
Universal Declaration of Human Rights
  ix, 31n2, 36, 74, 117, 161

Universalism
  as a discourse 14
  vs. relativism 49–51
  no universal culture 51
Universal suffrage for women 11

Vienna Convention on the law of Treaties 194
Vienna Convention on Human Rights
  on interdependence and indivisibility of human rights 10–11
Vienna Declaration and Plan of Action
  dismissed notion of classes or generations of rights 54, 136–138
  on interdependence and indivisibility of rights 54, 124–126

Water and Sanitation Alliance (Zambia) 235–236
Water and Sanitation Civil Society Network in Africa 234–235
Water crisis 102, 105, 111
Water resources
  attracting political attention 112
  demand for fresh- 102–103
  demographic pressure on 102–03
  for food production 131
  global and regional profile of 102–105
  pressure from growing economy 104–106
  unequally shared 102–105
Water taken for granted 126
Water wars 114, 116n9
World Bank 65–66, 68n, 71, 78, 200
World Bank's Article iv of articles of agreement 201–202
World Conferences on food 153–155
World Food Day 221

Zambia 137, 190
Zambian draft constitution 235
Zero Hunger Programme 180, 217, 228

www.ingramcontent.com/pod-product-compliance
Lightning Source LLC
Chambersburg PA
CBHW031321230926
51848CB00001B/46
9789004226203